Rethinking Peace and Conflict Studies

Series Editor
Oliver P. Richmond
University of Manchester
Manchester, UK

This agenda-setting series of research monographs, now more than a decade old, provides an interdisciplinary forum aimed at advancing innovative new agendas for approaches to, and understandings of, peace and conflict studies and International Relations. Many of the critical volumes the series has so far hosted have contributed to new avenues of analysis directly or indirectly related to the search for positive, emancipatory, and hybrid forms of peace. New perspectives on peacemaking in practice and in theory, their implications for the international peace architecture, and different conflict-affected regions around the world, remain crucial. This series' contributions offers both theoretical and empirical insights into many of the world's most intractable conflicts and any subsequent attempts to build a new and more sustainable peace, responsive to the needs and norms of those who are its subjects.

More information about this series at
http://www.palgrave.com/gp/series/14500

D. B. Subedi

Combatants to Civilians

Rehabilitation and Reintegration of Maoist Fighters in Nepal's Peace Process

D. B. Subedi
University of New England
Armidale, NSW, Australia

Rethinking Peace and Conflict Studies
ISBN 978-1-137-58671-1   ISBN 978-1-137-58672-8   (eBook)
https://doi.org/10.1057/978-1-137-58672-8

Library of Congress Control Number: 2018934638

© The Editor(s) (if applicable) and The Author(s) 2018
The author(s) has/have asserted their right(s) to be identified as the author(s) of this work in accordance with the Copyright, Designs and Patents Act 1988.
This work is subject to copyright. All rights are solely and exclusively licensed by the Publisher, whether the whole or part of the material is concerned, specifically the rights of translation, reprinting, reuse of illustrations, recitation, broadcasting, reproduction on microfilms or in any other physical way, and transmission or information storage and retrieval, electronic adaptation, computer software, or by similar or dissimilar methodology now known or hereafter developed.
The use of general descriptive names, registered names, trademarks, service marks, etc. in this publication does not imply, even in the absence of a specific statement, that such names are exempt from the relevant protective laws and regulations and therefore free for general use.
The publisher, the authors and the editors are safe to assume that the advice and information in this book are believed to be true and accurate at the date of publication. Neither the publisher nor the authors or the editors give a warranty, express or implied, with respect to the material contained herein or for any errors or omissions that may have been made. The publisher remains neutral with regard to jurisdictional claims in published maps and institutional affiliations.

Cover credit: Ruby/Alamy Stock Photo

Printed on acid-free paper

This Palgrave Macmillan imprint is published by the registered company Macmillan Publishers Ltd. part of Springer Nature
The registered company address is: The Campus, 4 Crinan Street, London, N1 9XW, United Kingdom

Acknowledgements

Writing this book has been a long and exciting journey, which would not have been possible without generous cooperation, support and help from different people. I would, therefore, like to acknowledge their valuable contribution to my research journey.

First and foremost, I am indebted to my Ph.D. principal supervisor and my mentor into the academic world, Dr. Bertram Jenkins, who has been an invaluable source of knowledge, inspiration and motivation to help me carry out this research. I express my humble gratitude to Dr. Jenkins for his constant mentoring, coaching and encouragement, which proved to be a key to producing this thesis. Similarly, I am also highly thankful to Prof. Helen Ware, my co-supervisor. Her feedback and comments on my Ph.D. thesis on which this volume is based, were very helpful.

I owe sincere thanks to all the respondents of my study on which this volume is based. They offered their valuable time and provided me with their insights, views and experience by participating in interviews and focus group discussions. Without their invaluable cooperation, this book would not have been simply possible.

I am also greatly thankful to Prof. Alpaslaz Özerdem, Dr. Bishnu Raj Upreti and Irma Specht. Their invaluable feedback and encouraging comments were inspirational and instrumental to improve my work.

I cannot remain without expressing sincere gratitude to my mother, Bal Kumari Subedi. She is my first teacher, affectionate counsellor and a never-ending source of inspiration in my life.

Last, but certainly not least, my loving wife Deena and son Ashwin deserve special thanks. Deena, you have been an endless source of courage. Thank you for supporting me during the ups and downs of the research journey. Both of you never complained even though you lost your weekends and holidays in the last few years when I was working on this project; rather you always filled me with fun and joy whenever I was down. You both proved to be incredible supporters in my research endeavour, and especially during the write up of this volume.

Armidale, NSW, Australia   D. B. Subedi
November 2017

Contents

1	Reintegrating Combatants in War to Peace Transition	1
2	Why People Choose to Become a Combatant?	43
3	The Peace Process and Management of Maoist Arms and Armies	71
4	The Dilemma of DDR	93
5	Process and Outcomes of DDR	107
6	Rehabilitation of Verified Minors and Late Recruits	129
7	Economic Reintegration	163
8	Social Reintegration	199
9	DDR and Peacebuilding: Implications for Peace and Security	223
10	Conclusions: What We Learn from Nepal?	263
Index		275

Abbreviations

AMMAA	Agreement on Monitoring of the Management of Arms and Armies
ANM	Auxiliary Nurse Midwife
APF	Armed Police Force
AISC	Army Integration Special Committee
AYON	Association of Youth Organisation Nepal
CA	Constitution Assembly
CAFAG	Children Associated with Armed Forces and Groups
CAR	Central African Republic
CBS	Central Bureau of Statistics
CDO	Chief District Officer
CFUG	Community Forest User Group
CIDDR	Cartagena Contribution to Disarmament, Demobilisation and Reintegration
CMA	Community Medical Assistant
CPA	Comprehensive Peace Agreement
CPN-M	Communist Party of Nepal—Maoist
CPNUML	Communist Party of Nepal United Marxist and Leninist
CRC	Convention on the Rights of the Child
CRP	The Communist Revolutionary Party
CTEVT	Centre for Technical Education and Vocational Training
DDC	District Development Committee
DDR	Disarmament, Demobilisation and Reintegration
DFID	Department for International Development
DRC	Democratic Republic of Congo
FGD	Focus Group Discussion
FNCCI	Federation of Nepalese the Chamber of Commerce and Industries

GDP	Gross Domestic Product
GIZ	Deutsche Gesellschaft für Internationale Zusammenarbeit
GoN	Government of Nepal
GT	Grounded Theory
HLPM	High Level Political Mechanism
ICG	International Crisis Group
ICRC	International Committee of Red Cross
IDDRS	Integrated DDR Standard
IDP	Internally Displaced Person
ILO	International Labour Organisation
IMF	International Monitory Fund
INGO	International Non-Governmental Organisation
INSEC	Informal Sector Service Centre
IRIN	Integrated Regional Information Network
JMCC	Joint Monitoring and Coordination Committee
LPC	Local Peace Committee
LV	Limbuwan Volunteer
MDGs	Millennium Development Goals
MDRP	Multi-Donor Reintegration Programme
ME	Micro Enterprises
MJF(D)	Madhesi Janadhikar Forum (Democratic)
MJF	Madhesi Janadhikar Forum
MoF	Ministry of Finance
MoHA	Ministry of Home Affairs
MoHP	Ministry of Health and Population
MoLD	Ministry of Local Development
MoPR	Ministry of Peace and Reconstruction
MoYS	Ministry of Youth and Sports
NA	Nepal Army
NC	Nepali Congress
NGO	Non-Governmental Organisation
NPTF	Nepal Peace Trust Fund
NRCS	Nepal Red Cross Society
NRs	Nepalese Rupees
NSP	Nepal Sadbhawana Party
NSTB	National Skill Testing Board
NVB	National Volunteer Bureau
OCHA	Office for the Coordination of Humanitarian Affairs
PB	Production Brigade
PGW	Protracted Guerrilla War
PLA	People's Liberation Army
PND	People's New Democracy

PR	Permanent Revolution
PS	The Private Sector
SALW	Small Arms and Light Weapons
SC	Special Committee
SIDDR	Stockholm Initiative for Disarmament, Demobilisation and Reintegration
SLA	Sustainable Livelihood Approach
SLC	School Leaving Certificate
SLF	Sustainable Livelihood Framework
SMEs	Small and Medium Enterprises
SPA	Seven Party Alliance
SSR	Security Sector Reform
TRC	Truth and Reconciliation Commission
UCPNM	United Communist Party of Nepal Maoist
UK	The United Kingdom
UMDF	United Madhesi Democratic Front
UN	United Nations
UNDP	United Nations Development Programme
UNFPA	United Nations Population Fund
UNICEF	United Nations Children's Fund
UNIRP	United Nations Interagency Rehabilitation Programme
UNMIN	United Nations Mission in Nepal
UNSCR	United Nations Security Council Resolution
USA	Unites States of America
USAID	United States Agency for International Development
USD	United States Dollar
VDC	Village Development Committee
VMLR	Verified Minor and Late Recruit
VOIP	Voice Over Internet Protocol
VST	Vocational and Skill Training
WB	World Bank
WFP	World Food Programme
WSMG	Watershed Management Group
WT	Whole Timer
YCL	Young Communist League
YF	Youth Force

List of Figures

Fig. 1.1	Map of fieldwork districts	6
Fig. 3.1	Map of Nepal with locations of main and satellite cantonments (*Source* Designed by the author, 2013)	82
Fig. 7.1	Districts with high concentration of ex-combatants (*Source* Fieldwork, 2013)	171
Fig. 9.1	Analytical framework for ex-combatant-led violence (*Source* Designed by the author 2013)	230

List of Tables

Table 3.1	Facts and figures of the Maoist ex-combatants (*Source* Fieldwork, 2012 and 2013)	83
Table 7.1	Areas and items of cash spending by combatants (*Source* Fieldwork, 2013)	174
Table 9.1	The groups splintered from the CPNM (*Source* Compiled by the author)	250

CHAPTER 1

Reintegrating Combatants in War to Peace Transition

When an armed conflict ends, a major issue that often emerges in a peace process is how to detach combatants from their armed mobilisers and reintegrate them back into communities. Actors of armed conflicts often mobilise narratives of political violence to justify destructive function of a conflict as an instrument deemed necessary to induce social and political change. Reintegration of ex-combatants at the end of an armed conflict, therefore, becomes a complex process which not only aims to transform narratives of violence into narratives of peace but also transform destructive function of war into constructive social and political change. This change is often characterised by a process of creating enabling social, economic and political conditions in which ex-combatants are able to transform their identity into a new identity of civilians (Bowd, 2006; Kilroy, 2015; Özerdem, 2009, 2012; Porto, Alden, & Parsons, 2007). The process of transforming combatants into civilians is, however, not an easy job, perhaps one of the most challenging issues that any post-conflict peacebuilding process is likely to encounter. Difficulties and dilemmas of reintegrating ex-combatants at the end of an armed conflict and how that concerns with politics of peacebuilding constitute the central theme of this volume.

The examples and case study included in this volume are from Nepal where management of Maoist arms and armies was a key peacebuilding priority, stipulated in the Comprehensive Peace Agreement (CPA) reached between the Government of Nepal and the Communist Party

© The Author(s) 2018
D. B. Subedi, *Combatants to Civilians*, Rethinking Peace and Conflict Studies, https://doi.org/10.1057/978-1-137-58672-8_1

of Nepal Maoists (CPNM)[1] on 21 November 2006. Despite a broad political consensus that reintegration of Maoists ex-combatants would be essential for lasting peace and security in the country, the CPA document remained vague about the process and mechanisms that would be involved in reintegrating Maoist ex-combatants back into communities. Consequently, management of Maoist ex-combatants became a deeply contentious political issue as well as an impasse in the peace process. The impasse led to having the ex-combatants confined in cantonments for five years, between 2007 and 2011.

Much has been already written about disarmament, demobilization and reintegration (DDR) and peacebuilding in a variety of contexts around the world (Alusala, 2008; Barakat & Özerdem, 2005; CICS, 2006; Jennings, 2008; Kilroy, 2015; Kingma & Muggah, 2009; Muggah & O'Donnell, 2015; Özerdem, 2009; Porto et al., 2007). The abundance of the literature on DDR, nonetheless, begs a simple question: Why another book on DDR and peacebuilding? In response, I choose to provide two simple and straightforward justifications.

First, most of the existing studies examine reintegration of ex-combatants in the contexts of traditional DDR programmes. Internationally, DDR of ex-combatants has become a major part of a peacebuilding programme in countries emerging from an armed conflict. Unlike elsewhere, as this volume will show, management of Maoist ex-combatants in Nepal involved some elements of traditional or conventional DDR programmes such as disarmament and demobilisation of combatants in cantonments. Yet, the process did not follow standard DDR practices as recommended by international guidelines, for instance, the United Nations Integrated DDR Standards (UNIDDRS). Rather, a mix model of DDR was adopted, combining disarmament and demobilisation with a cash-based package or the cash-based approach taken to reintegrate ex-combatants. The nuances and anomalies of a cash-based approach, adopted to reintegrate ex-combatants, made the entire process what is called in this volume a "unconventional DDR". This volume is the first in-depth study of the mechanisms, processes and outcomes of a unconventional DDR programme, which was heavily politicised and deeply centralised in Nepal's peace process.

---

[1] The CPNM split off into several groups after the 2006 peace process. This volume, however, mentions CPNM to refer to the original organisation as the mobiliser of the Maoist armed conflict in Nepal.

Second, DDR of ex-combatants is as much a political process as is social and economic one (Özerdem, 2009; Pouligny, 2004). Therefore, processes and outcomes of a DDR programmes are circumstantial, often defined and determined by political economy of the peace process in question, as well as the friction of power relations between key actors involved. Broadly focusing on the political economy of post-conflict peace process as well as social, political and cultural conditions in which the unconventional DDR programme emerged, this volume critically analyses and interrogates theory and practice of reintegration in the light of cash-based approach taken to reintegrate the Maoists ex-combatants. Examining relevance and effectiveness of the cash-based scheme, the volume endeavors to analyse what mechanisms and processes ex-combatants adopt to reintegrate when a formal reintegration support is lacking.

This volume maintains that ex-combatants do not constitute a homogeneous social category. Rather, they form heterogeneous social entities, with individual ex-combatants having different needs, interests and aspirations in the peace process. Most of these ex-combatants operate in highly politicised, securitised and stigmatised environments. It argues that in such a complex environment of war to peace transition, not all ex-combatants reintegrate into society in the same manner. Their capacities to integrate back into society, both socially and economically, largely depend on their ability to forge social networks and social capital—defined as existing networks and trust between individuals and groups (Putnam, 2000)—with their families, kinship network and social networks. However, the role of "war family", a war-driven social network that functions as a moral, emotional and psychological support system and 'safety net' for ex-combatants during an armed conflict, cannot be necessarily overlooked because many ex-combatants also continue to rely on formal and informal networks of the war family in addition to receiving support from their own families and relatives in their reintegration process.

Because social network and social capital of ex-combatants becomes a facilitator to transform combatants into civilian, this volume argues, reintegration of ex-combatants constitutes transformative elements—transformation of their identity, transformation of their livelihood, transformation of destructive function of war system and finally transformation of their relationships with communities where they originally belong to. The transformative aspects of reintegration, therefore, suggest that successful and effective reintegration of ex-combatants must aim at fostering social capital, recognising (a) diverse needs of ex-combatants as a heterogeneous social category, and (b) achieve this aim by recognising the roles of ex-combatants, their families and relatives as well as members of the "war family".

A cash-based scheme adopted to reintegrate ex-combatants not only ignores various socio-economic needs, including gender-specific needs, of ex-combatants but it also fails to bring transformation in the lives and more importantly the identity of ex-combatants. This volume shows, although a cash-based approach to reintegration may pacify ex-combatants and depoliticise DDR, cash alone cannot reintegrate ex-combatants in war to peace transition.

Management of Maoist arms and armies in Nepal was so complex and politically sensitive process that it might be hardly possible to include a detailed account of its entire elements aspects in a single volume. Therefore, at the outset, I prefer to acknowledge the limitations of this volume. One such limitation concerns with the controversy of combatant army-integration (commonly referred to as 'integration' in the peace documents), which dominated the debates and deliberations of the peace process between 2007 and 2011. The contentions and controversy surrounding army integration primarily drew on different theoretical and ideological premises of security sector reform (SSR) in which DDR can be an element. While this volume acknowledges salience of combatant-army integration, and the question of SSR in the peace process, I have deliberately and purposefully excluded the dynamics and analysis of SSR. I am motivated to do so mainly because of the aim of this volume: to critically engage with the theme of community-based reintegration of ex-combatants, which demands analysis of ex-combatants' experience and perceptions of their reintegration at the community level rather than the political debate of SSR at the national level. Perhaps, the ideological, conceptual and practical facets of SSR and peacebuilding in Nepal deserve a separate volume.

The analysis presented in this book is grounded in the narratives and perceptions of ex-combatants as well as other stakeholders such as community people, government officials, political party leaders, family members and relatives of ex-combatants. The field of peacebuilding is an area of reflective practice (Lederach, Neufeldt, & Culbertson, 2007) in which meaning of peace and the formation of peace or building peace from below is derived from people's perceptions, narratives, experiences, local cultural and social realities, and the history that are related to how individuals and groups (people) interact in the construction of social phenomena. Drawing on the idea of peace from below, I maintain Social Constructivist position in collecting and interpreting narratives from the field in order to understand the transformative nature of reintegration process. The idea of social constructivism posits that "there is neither objective reality nor objective truth...reality is constructed" (Sarantakos, 2005, p. 37); it involves a process of understanding a social reality through an interaction between the knower and the knowledge (Gergen, 1994). Therefore, my position is that Social Constructivism as a philosophy is suitable to carry out research on peacebuilding-related activities such as the reintegration of ex-combatants; an areas of inquiry in which truth can only be constructed socially by comparing and constricting views, narratives and opinions of many actors, including ex-combatants, their families, the people from community, government officers, business people and other agents of social change.

The setting of the research on which this volume is base included villages and communities in Nepal, where the Maoist ex-combatants have returned and resettled. The resettlement of the ex-combatants is dispersed; therefore, initially it was difficult to determine the communities and districts where the fieldwork would be conducted. To mitigate this challenge, I started the fieldwork in more central and populated Kathmandu and Lalitpur districts first. With the initial round of interviews, it was possible to locate the districts where there were large concentrations of ex-combatants. Consequently, the first round of fieldwork began between September and December 2011. In this round, fieldwork was conducted in Jhapa, Morang and Sunsari districts in the eastern region, Kathamndu and Lalitpur in the central region, and Banke and Kailali districts in the far western region. However, a second round of fieldwork was conducted between December 2012 and March 2013. In this round, the fieldwork was conducted in Morang district (eastern region), Kathmandu, Lalitpur and Chitwan districts (central region) and Banke and Dang districts (mid-western regions). Figure 1.1 shows the map of the fieldwork districts.

Fieldwork was carried out in two rounds, between September 2011 and January 2012 and December 2012 and February 2013. In the first round of the fieldwork, I conducted interviews with 45 ex-combatants;

Fig. 1.1 Map of fieldwork districts

most of them were Verified Minors and Late Recruits (VMLRs)[2] and some of them were verified ex-combatants who had been living in cantonments. In the second round of the fieldwork, I conducted 50 interviews with ex-combatants who had resettled in communities in different districts. A majority of the interviews for the study were conducted with ex-combatants because a plausible analysis of peace and conflict dynamics can be better accomplished by listening to what the war participants themselves have to say (Graham, 2007).

It is, however, equally essential to compare and contrast the testimonies of ex-combatants with additional information collected from witnesses, victims, leaders and even opposing groups (Barrett, 2011). To this

---

[2] The PLA fighters born after May 25, 1988 (minors) and the combatants recruited after the ceasefire agreement on May 25, 2006 (late recruits) are termed as VMLRs. This category was considered "unverified" combatants, meaning that they were not entitled to the benefits as par the verified combatants. As a result, VMLRs were discharged from the cantonments in late 2010, providing them with a rehabilitation package supported and implemented by the United Nations agencies working in the country.

effect, further in-depth interviews were conducted with non-combatant respondents. As also noted above, this category was diverse and included civil society leaders, business people, youth, leaders of major political parties, including the Nepali Congress (NC), the Communist Party of Nepal-United Marxist and Leninist (CPNUML) and the CPNM, staff of the United Nations (UN) agencies, people working in peacebuilding non-government organisations, and ex-combatants' family members and relatives.

In addition to in-depth interviews, I also visited several locations to observe ex-combatants' everyday life and livelihoods-related activities. In the first round of fieldwork, I visited the training centre in Itahari, Sunsari to observe ex-combatants' vocational training. It was during this visit that an opportunity to interview ex-combatants and their training instructors arose. Furthermore, I visited the VMLR ex-combatants' group-living locations in Dhangadi, Kailali district. Similarly, there was a visit to a tailoring centre run by three female ex-combatants in Jalthal Village Development Committee (VDC) and a poultry farm of VMLR ex-combatants in Kerkha Bazar, Jhapa district. In the second round of fieldwork, visits were made to vegetable and poultry farms, and a dairy farm run by ex-combatants in Dang and Banke districts respectively. Other farm and non-farm micro-enterprises run by ex-combatants in Chitwan district were also visited. The field observations were useful for collecting further information and verifying this against the concepts and themes that were extrapolated from in-depth interviews. It was indeed an opportunity to explore ex-combatants' economic and social reintegration from their real-life settings. Additionally, reports and news covered in various newspapers and news magazines published in Kathmandu have been used. Such sources are referenced or included in footnotes as or where relevant.

I also used the data from the secondary sources to substantiate and strengthen the analysis and arguments. The data collected from secondary sources mostly included published and unpublished reports and agreements by the government and various political parties and UN agencies. Most notable have been the use of the CPA, the Agreement on Monitoring of the Management of Arms and Armies (AMMAA), the Seven Point Agreement (SPA) that was reached between the major political parties on 1 November 2011, and reports and bulletins produced by the United Nations Interagency Rehabilitation Programme (UNIRP).

Defining Ex-combatants

Definition of the tram "ex-combatant" is vague and contested in the literature. When used in the context of DDR, the UN officially considers fighters to become ex-combatants after they are registered as disarmed (UN, 1999). This definition, however, only recognises registered and disarmed fighters who go through a formal DDR programme, but does not sufficiently define who is a fighter. In an inter-state conflict, members of national armed forces who have organised military structures are considered as combatants, but this criteria does not apply in intra-state conflict as some guerrilla groups and paramilitary forces may not have an organised military structure (Nilsson, 2005).

The international community defines ex-combatants based on individual's direct participation in hostilities, violence and atrocities, and the degree to which he/she commits harm to the enemy (Lindsey, 2001). Nilsson (2005) states that an individual, who is directly involved in intra-state armed conflict and hostility, has caused violence and damages to physical materials, and has been registered as "disarmed", can be considered as an ex-combatant. While this broad definition is certainly useful, it should, however, be recognised that some individuals who directly participated in armed conflict and insurgencies might not be officially disarmed, or may not be officially registered as a combatant. Drawing on these different criteria, for the purpose of this volume, the Maoist fighters who were involved in the Maoist armed conflict and who attended the combatant verification process, have been considered as ex-combatants. The term combatant and ex-combatant are used interchangeably.

Conceptualising Peace

Before going any further to contextualise reintegration of ex-combatants within the field of peacebuilding, it is useful to discuss the idea of "peace" that this volume has adopted. Although the word "peace" has become one of the most frequently used terms, especially by philosophers, religious thinkers, politicians, social scientists, and donors and public policy experts, a common definition of peace is difficult to find. This is perhaps because the meaning and quality of peace is attached to different frameworks and theoretical traditions. For instance, the way Christians,

Buddhists or Hindus see peace within their corresponding religious philosophies will be different from how social scientists and political philosophers define peace (Rummel, 1981). Interpretation of peace may also vary across cultures. In some societies, the term peace might even cause tensions and resentments "due to experiences of oppression inflicted in the name of peace" (Berghof Foundation, 2012, p. 60).

According to Webel (2007), peace has both internal and external dimensions. In its internal dimension, peace is often equated to love and happiness, but in the external dimension, "peace is a lynchpin of social harmony, economic equity and political justice...[it] is also constantly ruptured by wars and other forms of violent conflict" (Webel, 2007, pp. 5–6). In Webel's view (2007, p. 7), peace is not and should not be the mere absence of war. Using the concept of violence, Johan Galtung (1969, 1990) distinguishes between the idea of positive and negative peace. He proposes that to understand how peace is defined in a given social and political context, we first need to gain clarity on the concept of violence.

Based on how violence is manifested, he has developed the concept of personal/direct violence, structural violence, and cultural violence. While personal/direct violence is manifested at a personal level and there is a definite actor who carries out violence, structural violence is understood as a form of indirect "systemic" violence which is induced by exclusionary, exploitative and coercive political and economic systems and structures (Galtung, 1969). Rather than an individual or a group, existing systems that promulgate violent structures, are the primary actors in structural violence, although an individual or identifiable group may be the authors, organisers or power brokers behind the specific violent system. Cultural violence, on the other hand, is embedded in cultural norms and belief systems, and these are often used as a tool to legitimise or normalise structural violence (Galtung, 1990). Using the concepts of violence, Galtung (1964) defines negative peace as an absence of direct violence, while positive peace is a condition where all forms of violence are absent. The notion of positive peace also includes increases in social justice and the promotion of culture of peace.

Although Galtung has made an historical contribution to peace research, his work is not critique-free. Since the concept of violence has broadened the concept of peace, it is contended that "peace in its positive form is more difficult to articulate, and possibly more difficult to achieve than its negative version" (Barash & Webel, 2013, p. 8).

The Berghof Foundation (2012, p. 59) notes that a frequent criticism of positive peace is that "it lacks conceptual clarity". Kenneth Boulding (1977) contends that by introducing the idea of structural violence, Galtung has downgraded international peace to the level of negative peace and that the dichotomies such as that of personal and structural violence are unnecessarily complicated. Boulding (1977, p. 78) also contends that positive peace is "not opposite of negative peace".

Positive peace is not a real state that exists, but it is an ongoing goal towards which peacebuilding initiatives should aspire to evolve, irrespective of how inconvenient or challenging it might be. We must recognise that although there might not be a situation, which is completely free from any form of violence (direct/personal, structural or cultural), the idea of positive peace provides a recipe to the peacebuilding community to think of and act on a goal towards social change, equity and social justice. While it might be difficult to specifically point out particular ways of achieving positive peace, Jenkins and Branagan (2014) argue that social justice could be an element as well as an entry point to work towards positive peace. Social justice in the context of DDR can be a useful idea, because provisions of social justice provided to victims of conflict including ex-combatants may lessen their grievances, which can further contribute toward a more peaceful and cohesive society.

Despite critiques, Galtung has made a remarkable contribution to the field of peace research. His view is that peace cannot be achieved through "securitisation"; it can only be achieved by addressing root causes of conflict and also by transforming structural inequalities and relationships. This idea has substantially provided a basis for practices in the field of post-conflict peacebuilding. In a similar vein, John Paul Lederach (1997) has also stressed that peace can be achieved through transformations at different levels: personal, relational, structural and cultural.

Change in one's attitude and behaviour determines personal/individual changes, while relational changes refer to rebuilding relationships between people, and with their families and communities, as well as between adversaries (Lederach, 1995, 1997, 2003). Structural level transformations are required to bring about changes in systems and institutions that can help people to manage conflict non-violently. Culture is fundamentally about people and how they construct the meaning of the social reality they experience. Conflict affects people and community deeper than the structural level, and at the level of culture, though such effects may not even be visible and we are less conscious of the effects. Therefore, for sustainable peace, there is a need to transform how conflict-affected people and society construct the meaning of peace and peaceful culture (Lederach et al., 2007). The ideas propounded by Galtung and Lederach provide a reference for conceptualising peace in this volume.

PEACEBUILDING

According to Galtung (1996), peacebuilding is a way of empowering people to reduce violence in a non-violent way and bringing about peace by peaceful means. Peacebuilding originally evolved out of an institutional adjustment surrounding peacekeeping and humanitarian interventions to respond to increasing intra-state conflict situations in post-conflict periods (Jeong, 2005, p. 1).[3]

Peacebuilding received enormous theoretical and policy attention when it was first incorporated in the report "Agendas for Peace", by the then UN Secretary General Boutros Boutros Ghali. He defined peacebuilding as an "action to identify and support structures which will tend to strengthen and solidify peace in order to avoid a relapse into conflict" (Boutros-Ghali, 1992, p. 11). Since then, the term peacebuilding has been used interchangeably to refer to a wider range of concepts and practices, including conflict prevention and resolution, conflict transformation, post-conflict recovery and development (Call, 2004).

As the field of peacebuilding has broadened, it has involved complex activities often geared towards multiple directions: promoting security, democratisation, reconciliation and development. Hanggi (2005) states that peacebuilding encompasses three-dimensional processes associated with security, political and socio-economic. The security dimension entail DDR of ex-combatants, mine action, control of weapons, particularly small arms and light weapons (SALW), and SSR. The political dimension may involve activities such as support for political and administrative authorities and structures, good governance, democracy and human rights, and reconciliation and transitional justice. Similarly, the socio-economic dimension may entail activities including reparation and

---

[3]With the end of the Cold War in the early 1990s, the patterns of interstate conflict shifted to intra-state armed conflict and civil war. Of 111 armed conflicts that occurred between 1989 and 2000, 95 were intrastate, taking place within the boarder of a state (Wallensteen & Sollenberg, 2001).

reintegration of refugees and internally displaced persons (IDPs), reconstruction of infrastructure, development of education and health, private sector development, employment creation, and trade and investment. With diversification of activities, post-conflict peacebuilding has tended to be a complex and all-encompassing social engineering process, which reflects so many different ideas at any one time. It is also equally important to clarify that the idea of peacebuilding is different from mere implementation of a peace agreement. Successful implementation of a peace agreement might create a favourable political condition to carry out activities for post-conflict peacebuilding. Yet, peace cannot be achieved by only implementing the agreement.

Critiques of peacebuilding contend that peacebuilding has shifted to the domain of the neo-liberal paradigm in which building peace is accomplished through institutionalising free market economy and democratisation from "above" (Newman, Paris, & Richmond, 2009; Paris, 1997, 2004). Peacebuilding is neither neutral in their normative orientation nor can be framed with a universalistic model; therefore, there are limitations in what international peacebuilding actors can achieve in post-conflict societies (Newman et al., 2009). Despite the fact that the goal of liberal peacebuilding may be desirable to address cycles of violence, it creates institutions that are top-down and exclusionary; undertakes market reforms that sometimes widens socio-economic inequalities; and fail to garner local ownership of peace process, taking into account of local social, political and cultural realities of peace and conflict dynamics (Cooper, 2007; Jarstad & Sisk, 2008; Mac Ginty, 2011; Paris, 2010; Richmond, 2009, 2014; Visoka, 2016).

The critique of liberal peacebuilding has been divided into two camps. At one end, there is a group of scholars who have less contention with the ultimate goal of liberal peace, but they see fundamental problems with whether peacebuilding intervention can be accomplished in complex emergencies and fragile political environments (see Newman, 2009; Paris, 1997; Paris & Sisk, 2009). The problem here is not so much about the goal but in the process or even the viability of peacebuilding. According to Roland Paris (2004, p. 7), an alternative solution to this problem could be that creating strong institutions before peacebuilding accelerates liberalisation, or "institutionalization before liberalization". Others, however, think that the goal of liberal peacebuilding is problematic because it is a hegemonic project associated with neo-liberalism and imperialism (Cooper, 2007; Pugh, 2005; Richmond, 2009). Richmond

(2009) argues that although post-conflict peacebuilding aims to build liberal democracy by strengthening corresponding formal and political institutions, in reality, there is always local resistance to these processes; as a result of resistance and local power dynamics, a new form of hybrid liberal peace emerges.

Although liberal thinking has shaped the mainstream approach to building peace in countries emerging from armed conflicts and civil wars, it is argued that the univesalisation of peacebuilding models and frameworks have done more harm to the local social, cultural and economic conditions than good (Newman et al., 2009, p. 11).

Alternatively, the idea of transformatory peacebuilding has emerged as a new domain of thinking with regard to localising peace building as an emancipatory process. Transformative peacebuilding challenges the universalistic character of liberal peacebuilding and its attendant policies and programmatic templates (Newman, 2009). As such, it intends to offer an alternative thinking to liberal peace by exploring context-specific and culturally sensitive practices of peace that suit to address underlying causes of conflict. According to Newman (2009), this approach is based on the assumption that durable peace and stability necessitates achievement of positive peace and allowing opportunity for the expression to local voices, desires and forms of politics that suits the local contexts.

The literature suggests that trasnformatory peacebuilding has several virtues that deserve a brief discussion here. First, it has a universal appeal to peace but it rejects a universalising vision of peacebuilding which is a dominant feature in liberal peacebuilding practice (Newman, 2009). Second, its goal is transformatory, aiming to bring about changes at individual, societal or relational, structural and cultural levels in post conflict society (Lederach, 2003). Third, transformatory peacebuilding is community oriented, context-specific and aims to foster local institutions, vision, norms and agency of peace. Fourth, it aims to foster social justice, accountability of the past and human security needs based of those who have suffered conflicts; therefore, it not only represents powers but also take into account the effects of power at local level (Campbell, Chandler, & Sabaratnam, 2011). Thus transformatory peacebuilding has an emancipatory goal seeking to foster social change by engaging peace actors from below.

It must be recognised that transformatory peacebuiding involves slow and time-consuming process that requires a lot of resources and specialised capacities that might not be available in countries affected by armed conflicts. Therefore, there may be a tendency to "romanticise the locals" while there is limited capacity to determine which local practices are constructive and (un)acceptable (Newman, 2009, p. 47). A peace process is also a political process; peacebuilding cannot take place in isolation from broader local, national and international politics and power dynamics (Cousens, Kumar, & Wermester, 2001). Thus while the transformatory approach may be attractive, it tends to downplay the role that power and politics can play in transforming conflicts (Newman, 2009).

While this volume sufficiently recognises limitation of transformatory peacebuilding, it is useful to clarify that by using the term peacebuilding, this study partly follows the ideas of transformatory peacebuilding. Accordingly, in methodological term, the focus is on the analysis of how people, including people at the community level and the actors in a conflict, such as the Maoist ex-combatants themselves, interact and collaborate and how their experiences are crucial to the meaning of peace, rather than relying on the standard formula that focuses on incorporating marketisation, democratisation and institutionalisation at the national level. Nevertheless, this study partly refers to the idea of liberal peacebuilding because, macro institutions and mechanisms employed to deal with ex-combatants have indispensable effects on ex-combatants' lives, including the changes that occur or do not occur in social and economic lives of ex-combatants who struggle to reintegrate into the mainstream following on from their experiences during the war.

DDR AS AN ELEMENT OF POST-CONFLICT PEACEBUILDING

DDR as an element peacebuilding takes place in a variety of post-conflict contexts. As Colletta, Kostner, and Wiederhofer (1996a) assert, there are generally two types of DDR found in practice: those programmes taking place after a decisive military victory, focusing on demilitarisation, and those taking place in war to peace transitions. The former takes root in a context where a war ended in a military victory, and the focus of DDR remains on demilitarisation, including reducing the number of military personnel as well as military expenditure, and eliminating the culture of militancy; examples include countries such as Nigeria and Sri Lanka. The latter form of DDR takes place in a situation where there is no clear victory, and DDR evolves out of an agreement, often clearly stipulated in the documents of a negotiated peace process. Examples of this category can be drawn from Zimbabwe, Mozambique, Liberia, Sierra Leone, Timor Leste, and Nepal.

Different components of DDR can be explained as follows:

> Disarmament is the collection, documentation, control and disposal of small arms, ammunition, explosives and light and heavy weapons used by combatants and often also the civilian population. Disarmament also includes the development of responsible arms management programmes.
>
> Demobilisation is the formal and controlled discharge of active combatants from armed forces or other armed groups. The first stage of demobilization may extend from the processing of individual combatants in temporary centres to the massing of troops in camps designated for this purpose (cantonment sites, encampments, assembly areas or barracks). The second stage of demobilization encompasses the support package provided to the demobilised, which is called reinsertion.
>
> Reintegration is the process by which ex-combatants acquire civilian status and gain sustainable employment and income. Reintegration is essentially a social and economic process with an open timeframe, primarily taking place in communities at the local level. It is part of the general development of a country and a national responsibility, and often necessitates long-term external assistance. (UN, 2006a, p. 8)

A provision of DDR is often stipulated in an agreement in situations where the peace process emerges from a political negotiation (Verkoren, Willems, Kleingeld, & Rouw, 2010). As an element of the agreement, DDR is not only a politically sensitive processes (Ball & van de Goor, 2006) but it also poses a risk that DDR could be politicised in the course of implementing the agreement (Pouligny, 2004). In such a situation, policy makers can use DDR either as a means of bargaining for power or a yardstick to map out and measure the success of implementation of the peace agreement, rather than considering DDR as an element of peacebuilding. When DDR programmes emerge from political negotiation between parties to a conflict, DDR becomes a political process rather than what it should be ideally a social an economic process aimed at transforming identity of ex-combatants (Berdal & Ucko, 2009).

Depending on the context of the peace process and the preceding armed conflict, the nature and character of DDR varies from context to context. Yet, there is a growing consensus that DDR and peacebuilding have a reciprocal relationship (Knight & Özerdem, 2004). This means DDR is almost inconceivable without a peacebuilding process, which provides an institutional framework, and operational and bureaucratic structures to implement a DDR programme. Further, by transforming structures of armed conflict such as military organisation of armed groups, DDR contributes to structural transformation as well as a reduction in direct and structural violence.

Since the first UN Security Council sanctioned the DDR programme in Namibia in 1989, sixty documented programmes have been launched by 2010 (Muggah, 2009, p. 7). The lessons learned from different contexts, both successful and unsuccessful, have generated a number of insights. For instance, disarmament as an element of DDR requires military input and technical expertise, whereas reintegration, which is perhaps a decisive element of a DDR programme, necessitates contributions from non-military development experts (UN, 2010b). Thus, DDR, in practice, is a post-conflict social engineering process requiring a rigorous coordination of military and development expertise. Perhaps partly due to this complexity, there is a proliferation of several new and non-traditional actors in the DDR landscape. According to Porto et al. (2007), such new actors include bi-lateral donor governments, non-government organisations (NGOs), civil society organisations and the private sector, all of whom had a relatively limited role to play in earlier DDR programmes in the 1980s and 1990s. Similarly, there have been some remarkable institutional initiatives at the international level, such as the Stockholm Initiatives in DDR (see SIDDR, 2006), the UN Integrated DDR Standards (IDDRS) (see UN, 2006b) and the Multi-Donor Reintegration Programme (see MDRP, 2003).[4] The literature suggests that these initiatives have contributed to deepening the understanding particularly in relation to enhancing the "supply side" of DDR by suggesting recommendations including the selection of appropriate target groups for reintegration, better and effective coordination, and implementation mechanisms among actors leading or supporting the processes (Porto et al., 2007; SIDDR, 2006). Success of a DDR programme depends on how its process recognises the roles of different actors at different programmatic levels. However, it may be argued that how certain non-state actors, such as civil society and the private sector, receive any role in the management of ex-combatants may depend on which political and institutional framework of DDR is adopted and compatible to their roles and involvement.

[4] For more on innovation in DDR research and policy, see Muggah (2010).

Similarly, in what is called "second generation DDR", it is sought to ensure that the national government take front line responsibilities in DDR programmes (UN, 2010b). Such responsibilities include, but are not limited to, deciding the time-frame and scope of DDR, as well as setting selection criteria and implementation modalities for combatants (Harpviken, 2008). This innovation comes as a response to the suggestion that lack of national and local ownership in a DDR process makes it a "supply driven" initiative. When it comes to ownership, there are two dimensions: local and national. Pouligny (2004, p. 11) argues that at the local level, community consultation is essential, not only to become acquainted with the local contexts, but also to increase local ownership. Analysing local and national ownership from countries like El Salvador, Sierra Leone, Kosovo and Afghanistan, Özerdem (2009, p. 214) contends that we must make a clear distinction between "local ownership" and "local participation"; the former is a broader concept than the latter. However, in practice, ownership in DDR programme is limited to the national government and some rebel leaders, while other key stakeholders often remain excluded (CICS, 2006).

In addition to DDR, post-conflict peacebuilding has broader agendas, including SSR, the rule of law and translational justice. In this context, studies have pointed out that DDR and SSR are closely interlinked (Bryden, 2007; Lamb & Dye, 2009; McFate, 2010). DDR can actually become a part of a wider SSR process if the peace negotiation in question has included SSR as an agenda in the peace process. Integration of rebels into the national security force, as was the case in the Philippines (see Hall, 2009), Timor Leste (see ICG, 2008), Burundi (see Samii, 2010), and Nepal (see Nayak, 2009), are some examples of how SSR is linked to management of ex-combatants in the post-conflict period. In the case of Nepal, it was SSR rather than DDR that received more attention in the deliberations surrounding the management of the PLA ex-combatants (Gautam, 2009; Pandey, 2009; Upreti & Vanhoutte, 2009).

Finally, lessons learned from several African countries indicate that there is a need to plan and effectively reorient programmatic focus towards reintegration (Colletta, Kostner, & Wiederhofer, 1996b). Disarmament gets much attention both internally and externally and when it comes to extend support to actually reintegrate ex-combatants, the resources are either scant or there is limited long-term commitment by governments as well as external actors who support the peace process (Kilroy, 2012; Muggah, 2010). After collecting weapons, the mission is often considered "accomplished" (Özerdem, 2009, p. 208). Therefore, when the real time to reintegrate ex-combatants emerges, the resources and commitments become scarce or unavailable. Also, despite several commendable achievements in the field of DDR, the outcomes are mixed and the practicality of a successful reintegration suffers from the latent tensions between policy prescriptions assigned from above and the expected outcomes from below (Muggah, Berdal, & Torjesen, 2009).

REINTEGRATION AND REHABILITATION: INNOVATIONS AND CRITIQUE

The ultimate objective of reintegration should be to create enabling environment to transform ex-combatants into civilians (Ginifer, 2003; Hazan, 2007; Kingma, 1997). A transformation of this nature, however, is a long-term process, with changes occurring not only in the life of individual ex-combatants, but also at the relational level between them and people in their community. Like peacebuilding, reintegration aims to bring about positive change and transformation in the relationships between ex-combatants and people in the community (Kilroy, 2012). However, in practice, reintegration programmes are securitised, meaning that ex-combatants are viewed merely as spoilers of peace processes. As a result, there is limited emphasis on creating citizenry and in shaping the citizen-state interaction in a democratic framework for dealing with ex-combatants in post-conflict periods (Muggah, 2010). In other words, liberal peacebuilding tends to institutionalise reintegration at the centre rather than making it a trasformatory process on the ground.

Effectiveness of reintegration hinges on a host of critical issues, including challenges of setting realistic and achievable objectives, selecting appropriate beneficiaries (Annan & Cutter, 2009; UNDP, 2005), and averting reintegration from becoming a hostage of political manipulation (Ojeleye, 2010). In the meantime, hasty plans and context-insensitive policy responses, marred by inadequate funding continuity and obstruction by the political environment, continue to produce frustrating results in the field.

Over the time, reintegration processes in DDR programmes have experienced a gradual transformation from a narrow security-focused "minimalist" agenda to a "maximalist" one that incorporates socio-economic development agendas into the reintegration phase of DDR (Bryden, 2007; Buxton, 2008; Jennings, 2008; Muggah, 2010). Accordingly, reintegration in the second generation DDR programmes has tended to merge both security and development agendas by incorporating community development agendas (Baare, 2005). This maximalist shift is remarkable in the sense that it locates reintegration of ex-combatants within the discourse of post-conflict recovery and development (SIDDR, 2006).[5] Post-conflict recovery refers to the idea of rebuilding and restoring the capacity of national institutions and communities after a crisis (UNDP, 2007). This idea is often considered in parallel with the concept of transition from war to peace and is being developed as a way of integrating relief and development in post-conflict peacebuilding (Bocco, Harrisson, & Oesch, 2009).

Locating DDR programme in the discourse of post-conflict recovery, reintegration of ex-combatants is thought to be an instrument to promote human development as well as socio-economic development. This shift is also very much influenced by the way human security is thought to have a strong development dimension. In the aftermath of the Cold War, rethinking in human security has shifted its focus from a "state-centric" approach to a "community-centred" approach, in which human security is seen as a dynamic outcome through a balance between "freedom from want" and "freedom from fear" (MacLean, Black, & Shaw, 2006; UNDP, 1994). It is expected that by addressing both security and development, DDR can contribute to post-conflict economic recovery as well as human security. We should recognise a limitation here in that reintegration can only add up to some extent that contributes to both post-conflict recovery and development but it cannot and should not replace development (Ball & van de Goor, 2006).

Another critical issue associated with reintegration is the controversy around identifying appropriate target group(s). The literature demonstrates that currently there are at least two approaches: individual ex-combatant focused, and individual and community focused. Firstly,

---

[5] There is also a line of thinking that in 1980s, the reintegration programme was maximalist, for instance the case of Mozambique, Gwatemala and Liberia (first DDR mission). However, the dominant literature suggests that the reintegration programme has evolved from minimalist trend to more maximalist one.

individual ex-combatant focused reintegration, which is minimalist in nature, provides economic opportunities exclusively to ex-combatants. Some form of individual combatant-focused support includes, but is not limited to, promoting employment in existing enterprises, promoting micro and small business start-ups, the provision of micro-grants or credit, the use of training as a reintegration tool, provision of technical advice, monitoring and supervision, public sector job creation, and education and scholarships (UNDP, 2005). A major critique of the ex-combatant focused approach contends that if ex-combatants are provided with preferential treatment and material incentives while other conflict victims such as unemployed youth, IDPs, war-widows, and war-victims (the families of those who were killed especially if they were innocents) receive markedly less attention, it can generate tensions between ex-combatants and host communities (Annan & Cutter, 2009, p. 10). However, Last (1999) argues that preferential treatment is essential for averting ex-combatants from banditry. He also argues that a preferential system can have political objectives and meaning as agreed to during a peace process. By contrast, Kingma and Muggah (2009, p. 13) opine that in the immediate stabilisation phase, targeted and directed support to ex-combatants and their families is useful; however, over time, reintegration must be organised as part of a post-conflict recovery programme to address grievances of the wider community.

Secondly, a maximalist approach to reintegration is marked by broadening the focus of reintegration programmes from concentrating only on ex-combatants to both ex-combatants and communities. At the heart of the community-focused approach lies the assumption that balancing the support between ex-combatants' specific needs and the needs of the wider community will help to prevent community resentment (UN, 2010b; UNDP, 2005). It is also aimed at providing communities with the capacity to support reintegration of ex-combatants by considering reintegration as part of larger recovery programmes, including the reintegration of refugees and IDPs (Gleichmann, Odenwald, Steenken, & Wilkinson, 2004; Porto et al., 2007). Balancing reintegration support between ex-combatants and the community alike can promote social cohesion in post-conflict societies (Fearon, Humphreys, & Weinstein, 2009).

There are, however, other challenges. Merging reintegration with community development needs a greater deal of coordination between DDR implementers, development actors and national and local governments. It requires merging reintegration into post-conflict development initiatives, which may not always be possible, either due to lack of continuity of funding and resources in the long term, or due to limited political will and a suitable environment in which to embark on such long-term ambitious programmes. Here the key issue is not whether the programme should target a specific social group, but when, to what extent and how to balance resources between specific and general needs of populations (CIDDR, 2009, p. 26). Caution, however, should be taken in that resources invested in reintegrating ex-combatants should not become incentives to spoilers and rebel leaders, nor should the programme be hijacked by the local elites and warlords in order to manipulate the resources in ways that might jeopardise the future of the peace process.

Economic Reintegration

Reintegrating ex-combatants has a strong economic dimension. In the short-run, economic reintegration aims at creating jobs or sustainable livelihoods for ex-combatants while in the long-run, it is aimed at linking reintegration with broader post-conflict socio-economic recovery and development (Bragg, 2006; ILO, 2009; SIDDR, 2006; UN, 2000, 2010b). Creating jobs or providing sustainable livelihood opportunities for ex-combatants often entails vocational and/or skills development training, formal education, life skills training and support to enhance entrepreneurship skills (ILO, 2009; UN, 2010b).

One of the difficult challenges with respect to reintegration programmes is how to find/create jobs or livelihood opportunities for ex-combatants in war-affected communities after they have received additional education, training and vocational skills. An armed conflict leads to job scarcity and a high rate of unemployment accompanied by tough competition, and, above all, a fragile economic growth rate in post-war conditions. On top of these issues, the reality is that much of the physical infrastructures are also destroyed or damaged. It is a well-known fact that poor performance of a post-conflict economy is a hindrance to creation of alternative livelihoods and/or jobs for ex-combatants (UN, 2010a). On the other hand, examples from Nepal show that post-conflict recovery and development programmes themselves become marginalised as a consequence of the politics of peacebuilding (Subedi, 2012).

A healthy civilian identity can be encouraged through vocational training and constructive work that contributes to individual and community well-being (ILO, 1997, p. 14). However, there is often a risk that the ex-combatants might end up frustrated, as the skills gained through training and development initiatives offered by various agencies cannot be guaranteed to lead to employment. If ex-combatants select vocational training based on skill level, entrepreneurial ability, age, needs and aspirations, reintegration support can remain largely supply driven (Body, 2006). Hence, there is often a mismatch between demand and supply in terms of training and employment, which can exacerbate the grievances of the ex-combatants who may have expected more positive outcomes from their efforts, which in return, may trigger resentment and frustration, and is likely to lead to social unrest.

Experience indicates that many ex-combatants may end up opting for self-employment or self-entrepreneurship after receiving relevant technical education or vocational training (Body, 2006; ILO, 1997). Thus, supporting micro-enterprises is a common element in economic reintegration. Micro-enterprises provide an opportunity for: (a) those who cannot find jobs in the local market but are willing to start via self-employment; (b) individual combatants who have the potential to run their own business through which to harness their skills and abilities in order to earn money to sustain a living via self-employment; and (c) micro-enterprises that can contribute to private sector development by linking to various funded initiatives (Body, 2006). It is thus anticipated that self-entrepreneurship can help in the process of reintegrating ex-combatants by also strengthening and enabling post-conflict economic recovery and growth via private enterprise.

The private sector is an actor in peacebuilding who can play an important role in reintegration by providing job opportunities to ex-combatants (International Alert, 2006). There are some examples to suggest that business sometimes benefits from the war economy (such as manipulating legal provisions and doing illicit business under the shadow of conflict), and, in other cases, it can also exacerbate conflict dynamics (Crozier, Gunduz, & Subedi, 2010). A large segment of the business community will, nonetheless, have a vital interest in peacebuilding, because a peaceful environment without war offers conducive environment for doing business. Case studies explored by International Alert (2006) show that the private sector has played an important role in creating jobs and economic opportunities for ex-combatants in

Colombia, Afghanistan and Indonesia. One of the key SIDDR recommendations also highlights that reintegration programmes may benefit from efforts to stimulate the local private business sector and civil society, by such means as the reduction of barriers to doing business, access to credit, technology and technical support (SIDDR, 2006, p. 29).

However, in the aftermath of an armed conflict, the private sector might be sceptical about providing jobs for ex-combatants who have an atrocious past. Lack of trust between the private sector as employer and the ex-combatants as employees may not only lead to perceived insecurity on the part of the employers but it may also cause friction in their working relationship. In this regard, Specht (2010) wisely suggests that policy initiatives might be geared toward promoting a reliable business environment and engaging the private sector in design and implementation of reintegration, in order to build ownership and enhance confidence in the process.

Economic reintegration of ex-combatants further depends on several non-economic factors and conditions at the level of individual combatants as well as the societal level. Therefore, it is important to discuss non-economic social factors from a social reintegration point of view.

SOCIAL REINTEGRATION

In many conflict-ridden societies, the most common devastating effects of violence include disrupted family life, and weakened societal, communal and family level structures and their decision-making systems (Lewis, 1999). Therefore, reintegration programmes in such situations have tended to insist on finding ex-combatants' family or social roots in order to rebuild ties between them (Knight & Özerdem, 2004). Social reintegration, therefore, generally involves an interactive and constructive role of social entities such as family, community, kinship and social network. Although traditionally social reintegration has not been the focus of DDR programmes, more recently, scholars and policymakers have recognised the value of social reintegration in DDR and peacebuilding (see Leff, 2008; Özerdem, 2012). Consequently, as social reintegration is getting currency, its concept has been broadened to such an extent that it includes components as broad as "community sensitization, justice and reconciliation processes, psychological support, life skills, and general involvement in community activities, all of which are needed to build social support, promote community participation and re-knit the social fabric of divided societies" (Annan & Cutter, 2009, p. 2).

Indeed, a broad consensus is lacking about how social reintegration can be achieved in a complex social and political environment after war. Such complexities can be even deeper because social reintegration is all about relationships that hold both formal and informal processes, which are often difficult to observe. Nonetheless, in the literature, social reintegration is conceptualised with key entities as explained below.

Family

Family is a primary constituency in social reintegration. In El Salvador, for example, a vast majority of reintegrated combatants stated that being reunified with their family was the most significant factor in transitioning to civilian life (Verhey, 2001). Although the role of family cannot be denied for a successful reintegration (Özerdem, 2012), there are a number of issues that must be considered. First, there is always a difficulty in tracing the family link for someone who had joined armed militias for a significant part of their life, particularly if this began during childhood. In addition, in some cases, those who were separated from family at an early age can be reluctant to return to their family (Dolan & Schafer, 1997). The extra economic burden caused by returnees can also make some families reluctant to welcome the member who may have been away for a decade or more. The idea of inserting support (insertion) as an economic "safety net" for ex-combatants and their families to cover additional expenses such as buying utensils, clothing and food, which are generally incurred at the time of receiving the ex-combatant back into the family, is a useful means of assisting social reintegration (Kostner, 2001). Similarly, family acceptance can also be largely constrained by a degree of stigma emanating from how an ex-combatant is perceived by society at large. This is particularly the case with female ex-combatants (Sideris, 2003, p. 722). Women who used to carry out traditional roles in the household economy and society may acquire new roles during the war, but they are usually expected to return to their traditional roles after the war (Knight & Özerdem, 2004). Thus, the mismatch between community expectations and women's changed roles, habits, status, personality and behaviour can be problematic in the process of social reintegration. A noteworthy example comes from Eritrea, where, due to the status quo in women's gender roles in post-conflict society, a positive correlation was found between negative community expectations and high divorce rates (Kingma, 2002).

Marriage is an issue centrally associated with family. In Nepal, cross-cultural and inter-caste marriage was common among ex-combatants, but family rejection of such marriages made social reintegration difficult for several female ex-combatants (Saferworld, 2010). Similarly, Colletta et al.'s (1996b, p. 56) account of the relationship between marriage and family reintegration in Uganda is noteworthy; almost one fifth of marriages were not formalised and over one fifth of the wives did not speak the local language, resulting into marriage being a barrier for successful reintegration of ex-combatants into the family.

In contrast, in some societies, marriage can facilitate social reintegration. For instance, Dolan and Schafer (1997) observe that marriage of ex-soldiers with local women played a more significant and enduring role in facilitating reintegration into an alien community in Mozambique, where marriage was the key to setting up a household and gaining access to land.

The extent to which ex-combatants are accepted in or are willing to join a family can also be determined by how ex-combatants are accepted in the community. For instance, in Ethiopia, the more the ex-combatants participated in community activities, the better was the acceptance of the spouse and family (Colletta et al., 1996b). This means that the role of family in social reintegration is partly contingent upon the role of community which is another key constituency of social reintegration.

Community

Community acceptance plays a major role in social reintegration (Bernard et al., 2003; Stark, 2006). Defining a community can be tricky, as the notion of community embraces both geographical/territorial (see Block, 2009) and non-territorial/spatial or symbolic dimensions (Cohen, 1985). This study recognises that in many communities in post-conflict Nepal, people of various social and political backgrounds cohabitate. On the one hand, there are ordinary people living in villages, and on the other hand, victims and perpetrators of the armed conflict, ex-combatants and ex-soldiers of the government forces live together in villages. While recognising this diversity and heterogeneity, for the purpose of this study, Block (2009) as well as Cohen (1985) will be followed to define community as a geographically-bounded physical and social setting, as well as a symbolically constructed space which facilitates social actions and interactions, and also includes formal and informal social organisations and institutions. Furthermore, the term "combatants' community" refers to the members of the Maoist People's Liberation Army (PLA), including both verified and unverified ex-combatants who may be either living in a fixed geographical locus or are symbolically connected across various localities due to their shared past and identity. Similarly, the term "community" in general refers to villagers or city dwellers that do not belong to any group of ex-combatants. Included in this general definition of "community" are conflict victims, security personnel retired from the government, business people, civil society, and non-combatant members of the general public.

Community acceptance can be shaped by a host of factors. Armed conflict disintegrates social structures, dividing people into an "us" versus "them" polarisation (Özerdem, 2012, p. 63). Such polarisation has negative implications for ex-combatants' acceptance in the community, as was the case in Liberia and Sierra Leone (Özerdem, 2012). Verkoren (2005) provides an account of how a degree of mistrust and hostility between Khmer Rouge ex-combatants and people in the community had a negative impact on the acceptance of ex-combatants in the Khmer society in Cambodia.

Similarly, how the communities perceive, celebrate or demonise ex-combatants' identity has further implications. According to Özerdem (2012), if ex-combatants return home as "heroes" of war then social acceptance can be much easier than in a post-conflict environment where they are viewed as troublemakers. The overall political environment of war to peace transition and the extent to which fear, revenge and hatred are entrenched in post-conflict society further determines social reintegration (Duthie, 2005).

The literature has highlighted social reintegration as a collective process at the community level, but ex-combatants' agency in their reintegration and the roles such agency can play in their personal experience with social acceptance has not been explored adequately.

Social Reintegration and Social Capital

While there is no singular definition of social capital, it is widely accepted that social ties, relationships, and networks are the critical building blocks of social capital (Granovetter, 1973; Narayan & Cassidy, 2001; Portes, 1998).

Robert Putnam (1995, pp. 664–665) defines social capital as "features of social life – network, norms, and trust – that enable participants to act together more effectively to pursue shared objectives". Baker (1990, p. 619) defines it as "a resource that actors derive from specific social structures and then use them to pursue their interests; it is created by changes in the relationship among actors". For Fukuyama (1995), trust is a key measuring element of "social capital" which is accumulated through norms of reciprocity and cooperation in networks of civic engagement. While the different elements of social capital discussed here have their own strengths and weaknesses, this study follows Putnam and Fukuyama to conceptualise social capital. Accordingly, in this volume, social capital refers to the networks, relationships and trust between ex-combatants and people in their community.

Social capital has, however, both positive and negative functions. Its positive function provides the members of a group with information and access to resources, and facilitates collective actions for their common good (Portes, 1998). Its negative function can exclude "others" and non-members of a group from access to resources, and alienate and divide people who are excluded from group membership (Gilbert, 2009; Micolta, 2009). Robert Putnam (2000) who popularised the concept of social capital in modern social sciences, recognised the negative function of social capital by making a distinction between "bonding" (exclusive) and "bridging" (inclusive) social capital. He defines bonding social capital as "inward looking [networks that] tend to reinforce exclusive identities and homogeneous groups" whereas, bridging social capital consists of "outward looking networks [inclusive] that encompass people across diverse social cleavages" (Putnam, 2000, p. 22). In other words, bonding social capital reinforces social division while bridging social capital facilitates social integration. As a society with a high degree of social capital is more cohesive, peacebuilding aims to promote social capital in fragmented and divided post-conflict societies (Colletta & Cullen, 2000; Cox, 2009; Paffenholz & Spurk, 2006; Varshney, 2003).

The acceptance of ex-combatants into a community and the degree of trust, reciprocal relationships and networks that exist between them and community people relate to social capital (Annan & Cutter, 2009; Leff, 2008). War induced networks of ex-combatants, what Hazan (2007, p. 1) calls a "war family", can reinforce bonded social capital between ex-combatants, which, in turn, can perpetuate war-time networks and structures in one way or another. There is also an evidence to suggest that bonded social capital can generate violence because actors of violence and crime tend to form close bonded relationships within their formal or informal networks (Gilbert, 2009). As an element of post-conflict peacebuilding, reintegration of ex-combatants should bridge the relationships that exist between ex-combatants, their families and communities so as to promote bridging social capital for the enhancement of social harmony.

The extent to which ex-combatants are able to earn their livelihoods and build social capital depends on their psychosocial health and the manner in which they are assisted to recover from war-related mental and physical health problems. As Kohrt et al. (2010, p. 117) have shown in Nepal, children associated with armed conflict in the armed forces and in armed groups (CAFAG), including child soldiers and ex-combatants who were recruited by the Maoists, suffered from depression, anxiety, post-traumatic stress disorder (PTSD), and general psychological difficulties. As a consequence, the CAFAG have faced many difficulties in reconnecting and rebuilding relationships with communities.

REINTEGRATION AND RECONCILIATION

Reconciliation is not about forgetting the past, but it is about finding new ways to live in a harmonious environment by recognising the past and building collective action to overcome devastating effects induced by violence in the past (Laderach, 1997). Reconciliation ideally prevents, once and for all, the use of the past as the seed of renewed conflict. It consolidates peace, breaks the cycle of violence and strengthens relationships between victims and perpetrators of preceding conflict (Bloomfield, Barnes, & Huyse, 2003, p. 19). Reintegration of ex-combatants, on the other hand, is one of many means of preventing states and societies from slipping back into instability and violent conflict (Ngoma, 2004). As such, reconciliation and reintegration have a shared objective, as both initiatives are generally geared towards the prevention of renewed violent conflict and instead fostering and rebuilding of new relationships.

In many peacebuilding processes, DDR and reconciliation are mentioned as being integral parts of the peace process that is underway. For example, in the Democratic Republic of Congo (DRC) (Lusaka Ceasefire Agreements 1999) and the Central African Republic (CAR) (Bangui Agreements 2003), reconciliation and DDR were clearly mentioned in peace agreement documents, and efforts were made to draw connecting lines between them (ecp, 2008). Similarly, reconciliation was cross-fertilised with reintegration in the peace processes in both South Africa and Cambodia.

Reconciliation and reintegration can have a greater reciprocal relationship if they are carried out simultaneously. The idea here is that many ex-combatants might be seeking ways and options to return to their villages; however, their past and the way the community where they will return to perceives the identity of ex-combatants, can prevent the ex-combatants in finding harmonious and welcoming environment. Therefore, to facilitate ex-combatants to be better accepted in communities, some scholars argue that post-conflict reconciliation and transitional justice activities must be dealt with alongside DDR (Annan & Cutter, 2009; Kingma & Muggah, 2009; Porto et al., 2007). That is to say, if reconciliation is organised in tandem with reintegration, effects of reconciliation may perhaps make it easy for ex-combatants to be accepted in communities. Yet in practice, this is hardly the case. Indeed, reintegration is often starkly isolated or disconnected from much needed reconciliation processes (Kingma & Muggah, 2009).

Referring to the range of mechanism used to assist the transformation of a state from violence or a form of repressive and undemocratic state to the democratic one, the idea of transitional justice has been increasingly discussed in the field of peace and conflict since the beginning of the early twenty-first century. Transitional justice refers to the short-term and often temporary judicial and non-judicial mechanisms and processes that address the legacy of human rights abuses and violence during a society's transition away from conflict or authoritarian rule. The goal of transitional justice often includes: addressing, and attempting to heal, divisions in society that arise as a result of human rights violations; bringing closure and healing the wounds of individuals and society, particularly through "truth telling"; providing justice to victims and accountability for perpetrators; creating an accurate historical record for society; and restoring the rule of law.

Post-conflict societies are apparently fragile in terms of their social, economic and political capacities to manage and accommodate reconciliation processes. In some cases, attempts to reconcile in haste and pressing for transitional justice may push the parties with atrocious pasts away from the peace process. Similarly, in the immediate aftermath of conflict, communities can be divided, and, hence, several conflict-affected individuals and groups may have contradicting expectations from the outcomes of a peace process. Such differences may obviously limit an individual's and a community's capacity to bear with someone who has a brutal history. To reach the transformative levels of bridging differences and restoring trust between hostile groups requires a capacity to transform relationships (Ramsbotham, Woodhouse, & Miall, 2005, p. 233). However, in the immediate aftermath of heinous violence, many post-conflict societies may lack such capacity to accommodate reconciliation in order to move toward a shared future between the erstwhile victim(s) and perpetrator(s). It may take some considerable time before they can engage with this idea under these difficult circumstances.

Structure of the Book

This volume is divided into ten chapters. Chapter 1 introduces background and key argument followed by an overview of the book chapters. Chapter 2 uncovers the dynamics of the Maoist armed conflict and provides an explanation to why people decided join the conflict as a combatant. It analyses both voluntary and involuntary modes of combatant recruitment by the Maoists, and this has been analysed in the light of structural factors, as well as non-structural factors such as the Maoist ideology, coercion and state repression. The assumption is that understanding process and patterns of combatant recruitment could be the first entry point to think how a DDR programme can be geared towards addressing causes of armed conflicts.

Chapter 3 provides a detail account of war to peace transition, with a particular focus on how the trajectories of peace negotiations, albeit failed, culminated into the CPA. Providing an historical account of how DDR emerged as an integral element of the peace agreement, this chapter also describes the mechanisms and processes involved for managing ex-combatants, and the complex environment of post-conflict transitional politics, which shaped the process of DDR.

In Chapter 4, the volume critically engages in a discussion on the dilemma of DDR with particular reference to how transitional politics shaped this dilemma. The impacts of transitional politics on DDR of the Maoist ex-combatants is discussed in Chapter 5. It deals with nuances and anomalies of DDR, uncovering the key outcomes of DDR in a highly politicised environment of war to peace transition.

Chapter 6 exclusively focuses on rehabilitation of VMLR ex-combatants. In particular, how micro and macro-level factors facilitated as well as constrained rehabilitation of the VMLRs is discussed. It has been shown that while some VMLRs have experienced satisfactory rehabilitation, due to the micro and macro factors discussed, a majority of them still have difficulties in earning a living and being accepted in their communities. A major weakness of the liberal peacebuilding approach taken to rehabilitate VMLR ex-combatants was to bring combatants back to work rather than bringing them back to their families, communities and social network; therefore, the entire process lacked social elements of reintegration.

In Chapter 7, economic reintegration of the verified ex-combatants, who have returned to their communities after receiving a cash package as part of their retirement benefit, is studied. First, the patterns of use and misuse of cash are explored, then it is investigated whether the cash package was helpful for ex-combatants in enabling them to reintegrate economically. Forms of livelihood capital (human capital, physical capital, social capital and financial capital) have been used as an analytical tool to uncover ex-combatants' livelihood constraints and immediate outcomes. Furthermore, taking the political economy of peace and conflict into account, economic reintegration and its potential contributions to peacebuilding are discussed.

Social reintegration of ex-combatants is investigated in Chapter 8. In particular, this chapter studies social reintegration as an individual as well as a collective societal process. At an individual level, the agency of the individual ex-combatant in their social reintegration is studied. At the societal level, macro conditions that impact on the process and outcomes of social reintegration are explored. Finally, the present situation and outcomes of social reintegration of ex-combatants using social capital and peacebuilding theory are discussed.

Chapter 9 examines ex-combatants' remobilisation and violence as an immediate consequence of their economic and social reintegration. Discussing different conditions of vulnerability whereby ex-combatants are likely to be remobilised and engage in violence, and further exploring the position and interests of potential remobilisers of ex-combatants, it is shown that weak management of ex-combatants has already produced a considerable amount of ex-combatant-led violence at the micro level. Macro-level security threats emerging as a consequence of the unsatisfactory economic and social reintegration of ex-combatants is also discussed. A synthesis and discussion of the key findings of this study and conclusions are presented in the final chapter.

References

Alusala, N. (2008). *Disarmament, demobilization, rehabilitation and reintegration (DDRR) in Liberia* (Vol. Case study). Centre for International Cooperation and Security, University of Bradford.

Annan, J., & Cutter, A. (2009). *Critical issues and lessons in social reintegration: Balancing justice, psychological wellbeing and community reconciliation.* Retrieved from http://cartagenaddr.org/literature_press/ART_21.pdf.

Baare, A. (2005). *An analysis of transitional economic reintegration.* Stockholm: Swedish Initiative for Disarmament, Demobilization and Reintegration (SIDDR). http://www.ud.se/content/1/c6/06/54/02/05d5985b.pdf.

Baker, W. E. (1990). Market networks and corporate behavior. *American Journal of Sociology, 96*(3), 589–625.

Ball, N., & van de Goor, L. (2006). *Disarmament, demobilization and reintegration: Mappping issues, dilemmas and guiding principles.* Netherland Institute of International Relations, Conflict Reseach Unit, 'Clingendael'. Retrieved from http://www.clingendael.nl/sites/default/files/20060800_cru_paper_ddr.pdf.

Barakat, S., & Özerdem, A. (2005). Reintegration of former combatants: With specific reference to Kosovo. In S. Barakat (Ed.), *After the conflict: Reconstruction and development in the aftermath of war* (pp. 229–247). London and New York: I. B. Tauris.

Barash, D. P., & Webel, C. P. (2013). *Peace and conflict studies* (3rd ed.). Thousand Oaks, CA: Sage.

Barrett, R. S. (2011). Interviews with killers: Six types of combatants and their motivations for joining deadly groups. *Studies in Conflict & Terrorism, 34*(10), 749–764. https://doi.org/10.1080/1057610X.2011.604830.

Berdal, M., & Ucko, D. H. (Eds.). (2009). *Reintegrating armed groups after conflict: Politics, violence and transition.* London and New York: Routledge.

Berghof Foundation. (2012). *Berghof glossary on conflict transformation: 20 notions for theory and practice.* Berlin: Berghof Foundation.

Bernard, B., Brewer, B., Dharmapuri, S., Dobor, E., Hansen, A., & Nelson, S. (2003). *Assessment of the situation of women and children combatants in the Liberian post-conflict period and recommendations for successful integration.* MD. Retrieved from http://pdf.usaid.gov/pdf_docs/Pnacy688.pdf.

Block, P. (2009). *Community: The structure of belonging.* San Francisco: Berrett-Koehler.

Bloomfield, D., Barnes, T., & Huyse, L. (Eds.). (2003). *Reconciliation after violent conflict: A handbook*. Stockholm: International IDEA.

Bocco, R., Harrisson, P., & Oesch, L. (2009). Recovery. In V. Chetail (Ed.), *Post-conflict peacebuilding: A lexicon* (pp. 268–278). Oxford and New York: Oxford University.

Body, T. (2006). *Reintegration of ex-combatants through micro-enterprise: An operational framework*. Retrieved from http://peacebuildingcentre.com/pbc_documents/ReintEx-ComMicroEnt.pdf.

Boulding, K. E. (1977). Twelve friendly quarrels with Johan Galtung. *Journal of Peace Research, 14*(1), 75–86.

Boutros-Ghali, B. (1992). *An agenda for peace: Preventative diplomacy, peacemaking and peace-keeping* (Report of the Secretary General. A/47/277–S/24111). New York. Retrieved from http://www.un-documents.net/a47-277.htm.

Bowd, R. (2006, September 7–9). *The (non)transformation of identity of ex-Kosovo Liberation Army (KLA) combatants through the disarmament, demobilisation and reintegration (DDR) programme*. Paper presented at the ECPR Graduate Conference, University of Essex.

Bragg, C. (2006). *Challenges to policy and practice in the disarmament, demobilisation, reintegration and rehabilitation of youth combatants in Liberia* (Working Paper No. 29, pp. 1–23). Sussex Center for Migration Studies. Retrieved from https://www.sussex.ac.uk/webteam/gateway/file.php?name=mwp29.pdf&site=252.

Bryden, A. (2007, June 12–14). *Understanding the DDR-SSR Nexus: Building sustainable peace in Africa*. Paper presented at the Second International Conference on DDR and Stability in Africa, Democratic Republic of Congo, Kinshasa.

Buxton, J. (2008). *Reintegration and long-term development: Linkages and challenges* (Thematic Working Paper 5). Center for International Cooperation and Security, University of Bradford. Retrieved from http://www.ssddrc.org/uploads/DDRWorkingPaper5.pdf.

Call, C. T. (2004, August 27). *The problem of peacebuilding: How UN thinking has evolved in recent years*. Draft paper prepared for DPA.

Campbell, S., Chandler, D., & Sabaratnam, M. (Eds.). (2011). *A liberal peace? The problems and practices of peacebuilding*. London and New York: Zed Books.

CICS. (2006). *DDR framed from a human security and pro-poor perspective: Literature review and some key lessons and challenges*. Background paper. Bradford: Bradford University.

CIDDR. (2009). *The Cartagena contribution to disarmament, demobilization and reintegration*. Cartagena, Colombia: International Disarmament, Demobilization and Reintegration Congress (CIDDR). Retrieved from http://www-wds.worldbank.org/external/default/WDSContentServer/

WDSP/IB/2012/06/07/000427087_20120607101419/Rendered/ PDF/695120ESW0P0940artagenacontribution.pdf.
Cohen, A. P. (1985). *The symbolic construction of community*. London and New York: Tavistock Publications.
Colletta, N. J., & Cullen, M. L. (2000). *Violent conflict and the transformation of social capital: Lessons from Cambodia, Rwanda, Guatemala, and Somalia.* Washington, DC: The World Bank.
Colletta, N. J., Kostner, M., & Wiederhofer, I. (1996a). *Case studies in war-to-peace transition: The demobilization and reintegration of ex-combatants in Ethiopia, Namibia, and Uganda.* Washington, DC: World Bank.
Colletta, N. J., Kostner, M., & Wiederhofer, I. (Eds.). (1996b). *The transition from war to peace in sub-Sahara Africa.* Washington, DC: World Bank.
Cooper, N. (2007). Review article: On the crisis of liberal peace. *Conflict, Security & Development*, 7(4), 605–616. https://doi.org/10.1080/14678800701693025.
Cousens, E. M., Kumar, C., & Wermester, K. (Eds.). (2001). *Peacebuilding as politics: Cultivating peace in fragile societies.* Boulder and London: Lynne Rienner.
Cox, M. (Ed.). (2009). *Social capital and peace-building: Creating and resolving conflict with trust and social networks.* London and New York: Routledge.
Crozier, R., Gunduz, C., & Subedi, D. B. (2010). *Private sector and public security: Perceptions and responses.* Kathmandu: National Business Initiative (NBI) and International Alert.
Dolan, C., & Schafer, J. (1997). *The reintegration of ex-combatants in Mozambique: Manica and Zambezia provinces* (Final Report to USAID). Retrieved from http://lekiworld.com/AU/docs/201.pdf.
Duthie, R. (2005). *Transitional justice and social reintegration.* Stockholm: Stockholm Initiative on Disarmament, Demobilisation and Reintegration (SIDDR), Ministry of Foreign Affairs, Sweden. Available from http://www.regeringen.se/content/1/c6/06/54/02/7545e870.pdf.
ecp. (2008). *DDR 2008: Analysis of DDR programs in the world during 2007.* Retrieved from http://escolapau.uab.cat/img/programas/desarme/ddr005i.pdf.
Fearon, J. D., Humphreys, M., & Weinstein, J. M. (2009). Can development aid contribute to social cohesion after war? Evidence from a field experiment in post-conflict Liberia. *American Economic Review: Papers and Proceedings*, 99(2), 287–291. http://www.aeaweb.org/articles.php?doi=10.1257/aer.99.2.287.
Fukuyama, F. (1995). *Trust: The social value and the creation of prosperity.* New York: Free Press.
Galtung, J. (1964). An editorial. *Journal of Peace Research*, 1(1), 1–4. https://doi.org/10.1177/002234336400100101.
Galtung, J. (1969). Violence, peace and peace research. *Journal of Peace Research*, 6(3), 167–191.
Galtung, J. (1990). Cultural violence. *Journal of Peace Research*, 27(3), 291–305.

Galtung, J. (1996). *Peace by peaceful means: Peace, conflict, development and civilisation.* Oslo and London: International Peace Research, Sage.

Gautam, K. C. (2009). The rehabilitation and integration of Maoists combatants as part of Nepal's security sector reform. In R. Bhattarai & R. Cave (Eds.), *Changing security dynamics in Nepal.* London: Saferworld.

Gergen, K. J. (1994). *Realities and relationships: Soundings in social construction.* Cambridge, MA: Harvard University Press.

Gilbert, L. (2009). Analysing the dark side of social capital: Organised crime in Russia. In M. Cox (Ed.), *Social capital and peace-building: Creating and resolving conflict with trust and social networks* (pp. 57–74). London and New York: Routledge.

Ginifer, J. (2003). Reintegration of ex-combatants. In S. Meek, T. Thusi, J. Ginifer, & P. Coke (Eds.), *Sierra Leone: Building the road to recovery* (Vol. ISS monograph, no. 80, pp. 39–52). Pretoria, South Africa: Institute for Security Studies (ISS).

Gleichmann, C., Odenwald, M., Steenken, K., & Wilkinson, A. (2004). *Disarmament, demobilization and reintegration: A practical field and classroom guide.* Frankfurt, Germany.

Graham, G. (2007). People's war? Self-interest, coercion and ideology in Nepal's Maoist insurgency. *Small Wars & Insurgencies, 18*(2), 231–248. https://doi.org/10.1080/09592310701400853.

Granovetter, M. S. (1973). The strength of weak ties. *American Journal of Sociology, 78*(6), 1360–1380.

Hall, R. A. (2009). *From rebels to soldiers: An analysis of the Philippine and East Timorese policy integrating former Moro National Liberation Front and Falintil combatants into the armed forces.* Paper presented at the American Political Science Association Meeting Toronto, Canada. http://papers.ssrn.com/sol3/papers.cfm?abstract_id=1460315.

Hanggi, H. (2005). Approaching peacebuilding from a security governance perspective. In A. Bryden & H. Hanggi (Eds.), *Security governance in post-conflict peacebuilding* (pp. 3–19). New Brunswick and London: Transaction Publication.

Harpviken, K. B. (2008). *From 'Refugee Warriors' to 'Returnee Warriors': Militant homecoming in Afghanistan and beyond* (Global Migration and Transitional Politics Working Paper No. 5). Retrieved from https://files.prio.org/publication_files/PRIO/Harpviken%20(2008)%20From%20Refugee%20Warriors%20to%20Returnee%20Warriors.pdf.

Hazan, J. (2007). *Social integration of ex-combatants after civil war.* Retrieved from http://www.un.org/esa/socdev/sib/egm/paper/JenniferHazen.pdf.

ICG. (2008, January 17). *Timor-Leste: Security sector reform* (Asia Report No. 143). Dili/Brussels: International Crisis Group. Retrieved from http://www.ssrnetwork.net/uploaded_files/3886.pdf.

ILO. (1997). *ILO and conflict-affected peoples and countries: Promoting lasting peace through employment promotion.* Geneva: International Labor Office.

ILO. (2009). *Socio-economic reintegration of ex-combatants: Guidelines*. Geneva: International Labor Organization/Crisis Response and Reconstruction Programme (ILO/CRISIS).
International Alert. (2006). *Local business, local peace: The peacebuilding potentials of the domestic private sector*. London: International Alert.
Jarstad, A. K., & Sisk, T. D. (Eds.). (2008). *From war to democracy: Dilemmas of peacebuilding*. New York: Cambridge University Press.
Jenkins, B., & Branagan, M. (2014). Introducting cultivating peace. In H. Ware, B. Jenkins, M. Branagan, & D. B. Subedi (Eds.), *Cultivating peace: Context, approaches and multidimensional models*. Newcastle upon Tyne: Cambridge Scholar Publishing.
Jennings, K. M. (2008). *Seeing DDR from below: Challenges and dilemmas raised by the ex-combatants in Liberia* (FAFO Report No. 3). Oslo: FAFO.
Jeong, H.-W. (2005). *Peacebuilding in postconflict societies: Strategy and process*. Boulder and London: Lynne Rienner.
Kilroy, W. (2012). *From conflict to ownership: Participatory approaches to the reintegration of ex-combatants in Sierra Leone and Liberia* (PhD). Dublin City University, Dublin.
Kilroy, W. (2015). *Reintegration of ex-combatants after conflict: Participatory approaches in Sierra Leone and Liberia*. London and New York: Palgrave.
Kingma, K. (1997). *Post-war demobilization and the reintegration of ex-combatants into civilian life*. Paper presented at the USAID Conference on Promoting Democracy, Human Rights and Reintegration in Post-conflict societies, October 30–31, 1997, Bonn International Center for Conversion (BICC). Retrieved from http://pdf.usaid.gov/pdf_docs/PNACD095.pdf.
Kingma, K. (2002). Demobilization, reintegration and peacebuilding in Africa. In E. Newman & A. Schnabel (Eds.), *Recovering from civil conflict: Reconciliation, peace and development* (pp. 181–201). London: Frank Cass Publishers.
Kingma, K., & Muggah, R. (2009). *Critical issues in DDR: Context, indicators, targeting, and challenges*. Cartagena: Center for International Disarmament Demobilization and Reintegration.
Knight, M., & Özerdem, A. (2004). Guns, camps and cash: Disarmament, demobilization and reinsertion of former combatants in transitions from war to peace. *Journal of Peace Research, 41*(4), 499–516. https://doi.org/10.1177/0022343304044479.
Kohrt, B. A., Perera, E., Jordans, M. J. D., Koirala, S., Karki, R., Karki, R., ... Upadhaya, N. (2010). *Psychosocial support model for children associated with armed forces and armed groups in Nepal*. Kathmandu: Transcultural Psychosocial Organisation-TOP Nepal.
Kostner, M. (2001). *A technical note on the design and provision of transitional safety nets for demobilization and reintegration programs*. Washington, DC: Mimeo, World Bank.

Lamb, G., & Dye, D. (2009). *Security promotion and DDR: Linkages between ISM, DDR, and SSR within a broader peacebuilding framework*. Geneva: Congreso Internacional de Desarme, Desmovilizacion y Reintegracion (CIDDR).

Last, D. (1999). *The human security problem: Disarmament, demobilization and reintegration. A Source Book on the State of the Art in Post-conflict Rehabilitation, PRDU for Regional Socio-economic Development Programme for Southern Lebanon.* York: PRDU, University of York.

Lederach, J. P. (1995). *Preparing for peace: Conflict transformation across cultures*. New York: Syracuse University Press.

Lederach, J. P. (1997). *Building peace: Sustainable reconciliation in divided societies*. Washington, DC: United States Institute of Pecae Press.

Lederach, J. P. (2003). *The little book of conflict transformation*. Intercourse, PA: Good Books.

Lederach, J. P., Neufeldt, R., & Culbertson, H. (2007). *Reflective peacebuilding: A planning, monitoring, and learning toolkit*. Mindanao, the Philippines: University of Notre Dame and Catholic Relief Services.

Leff, J. (2008). The nexus between social capital and reintegration of ex-combatants: A case for Sierra Leone. *African Journal on Conflict Resolution, 8*(1), 9–38. http://dx.doi.org/10.4314%2Fajcr.v8i1.39419.

Lewis, N. (1999). Social recovery from armed conflict. In G. Harris (Ed.), *Recovery from armed conflict in developing countries: An economic and political analysis*. London and New York: Routledge.

Lindsey, C. (2001). *Women facing war: ICRC study on the impact of armed conflict on women*. Geneva: International Committee of the Red Cross (ICRC).

Mac Ginty, R. (2011). Hybrid peace: How does hybrid peace come about? In S. Campbell, D. Chandler, & M. Sabaratnam (Eds.), *A liberal peace? The problems and practices of peacebuilding* (pp. 209–225). London and New York: Zed Books.

MacLean, S. J., Black, D. R., & Shaw, T. M. (Eds.). (2006). *A decade of human security: Global governance and new multilateralisms*. Aldershot and Burlington: Ashgate.

McFate, S. (2010). *The link between DDR and SSR in conflict-affected countries* (Special Report 238). Washington, DC.

MDRP. (2003). *Position paper: Linkages between disarmament, demobilization and reintegration of ex-combatants and security sector reform*.

Micolta, P. H. (2009). Illicit interest groups, social capital and conflict: A study of the FARC. In M. Cox (Ed.), *Social capital and peace-building: Creating and resolving conflict with trust and social networks* (pp. 75–91). London and New York: Routledge.

Muggah, R. (2009). Introduction: The emperor's clothes? In R. Muggah (Ed.), *Security and post conflict reconstruction: Dealing with fighters in the aftermath of war*. London and New York: Routledge.

Muggah, R. (2010). *Innovations in disarmament, demobilization and reintegration policy and research: Reflections on the last decade* (NUPI Working Paper 774). Norwegian Institute of International Affairs. Retrieved from http://english.nupi.no/content/download/13642/128894/version/6/file/WP-774-Muggah.pdf.

Muggah, R., Berdal, M., & Torjesen, S. (2009). Conclusions: Enter an evidence-based security promotion. In R. Muggah (Ed.), *Security and post conflict reconstruction: Dealing with fighters in the aftermath of war* (pp. 268–284). London and New York: Routledge.

Muggah, R., & O'Donnell, C. (2015). Next generation disarmament, demobilization and reintegration. *Stability: International Journal of Security and Development, 4*(1), 1–12.

Narayan, D., & Cassidy, M. F. (2001). A dimensional approach to measuring social capital: Development and validation of a social capital inventory. *Current Sociology, 49*(2), 59–102. https://doi.org/10.1177/0011392101049002006.

Nayak, N. (2009). PLA integration into the Nepal Army: Challenges and prospects. *Strategic Analysis, 33*(5), 730–744. https://doi.org/10.1080/09700160903064547.

Newman, E. (2009). "Liberal" peacebuilding debates. In E. Newman, R. Paris, & O. P. Richmond (Eds.), *New perspectives on liberal peacebuilding* (pp. 26–53). Tokyo, New York and Paris: United Nations University Press.

Newman, E., Paris, R., & Richmond, O. P. (2009). Introduction. In E. Newman, R. Paris, & O. P. Richmond (Eds.), *New perspectives on liberal peacebuilding* (pp. 3–25). Tokyo, New York and Paris: United Nations University Press.

Ngoma, N. (2004). Disarmament, demobilization and reintegration: A conceptual discourse. In G. Chileshe (Ed.), *Civil military relation in Zambia: A review of Zambia's contemporary civil military relation and challenges to DDR* (pp. 79–89). Pretoria: Institute for Security Studies (ISS).

Nilsson, A. (2005). *Reintegrating ex-combatants in post-conflict societies*. SIDA Retrieved from https://www.pcr.uu.se/digitalAssets/67/c_67211-l_1-k_sida4715en_ex_combatants.pdf.

Ojeleye, O. (2010). *The politics of post-war demobilization and reintegration in Nigeria*. Surrey and Burlington: Ashgate.

Özerdem, A. (2009). *Post-war recovery: Disarmament, demobilization and reintegration*. London and New York: I. B. Tauris.

Özerdem, A. (2012). A re-conceptualisation of ex-combatant reintegration: 'Social reintegration' approach. *Conflict, Security & Development, 12*(1), 51–73. https://doi.org/10.1080/14678802.2012.667661.

Paffenholz, T., & Spurk, C. (2006). *Civil society, civic engagement, and peacebuilding*. Social Development Paper no. 36. Washington D. C.: The World

Bank. Retrieved from http://siteresources.worldbank.org/INTCPR/Resources/WP36_web.pdf.

Pandey, N. N. (2009). Security sector reforms in Nepal: If not now, when? *South Asian Survey, 16*(2), 253–271. https://doi.org/10.1177/097152310901600206.

Paris, R. (1997). Peacebuilding and the limits of liberal internationalism. *International Security, 22*(4), 54–89.

Paris, R. (2004). *At war's end: Building peace after civil conflict.* Cambridge: Cambridge University Press.

Paris, R. (2010). Saving liberal peacebuilding. *Review of International Studies, 36*(2), 337–365.

Paris, R., & Sisk, T. D. (2009). Introduction: Understanding the contradiction of postwar statebuilding. In R. Paris & T. D. Sisk (Eds.), *The dilemmas of statebuilding: Confronting the contradictions of postwar peace operations* (pp. 1–20). Abingdon and New York: Routledge.

Portes, A. (1998). Social capital: Its origins and applications in modern sociology. *Annual Review of Sociology, 24*, 1–24.

Porto, J. G., Alden, C., & Parsons, I. (2007). *From soldiers to citizens: Demilitarization of conflict and society.* Aldershot and Burlington: Ashgate.

Pouligny, B. (2004). *The politics and anti-politics of disarmament, demobilization and reintegration programmes.* Paris: Science-Politique/CERI.

Pugh, M. (2005). The political economy of peacebuilding: A critical theory perspective. *International Journal of Peace Studies, 10*(2), 23–42.

Putnam, R. D. (1995). Turning in, turning out: The strange disappreance of social capital in America. *PS: Political Science & Politics, 28*(4), 664–683.

Putnam, R. D. (2000). *Bowling alone: The collapse and revival of American community.* New York: Simon & Schuster.

Ramsbotham, O., Woodhouse, T., & Miall, H. (2005). *Contemporary conflict resolution: The prevention, management and resolution of deadly conflicts* (2nd ed.). Cambridge and Malden, MA: Polity Press.

Richmond, O. P. (2009). Beyond liberal peace? Responses to "backsliding". In E. Newman, R. Paris, & O. P. Richards (Eds.), *New perspectives on liberal peacebuilding* (pp. 54–77). Tokyo, New York and Paris: United Nations University Press.

Richmond, O. P. (2014). The Impact of socio-economic inequality on peacebuilding and statebuilding. *Civil Wars, 16*(4), 449–467.

Rummel, R. J. (1981). *Understanding conflict and war. Vol. V.: The just peace.* Beverly Hills, CA: Sage.

Saferworld. (2010). *Common ground? Gendered assessment of the needs and concerns of Maoist Army combatants for rehabilitation and integration.* London.

Samii, C. (2010). *Military integration in Burundi, 2000–2006.* Department of Political Science, Columbia University. https://files.nyu.edu/cds2083/public/docs/samii_burundi_ssr100608.pdf.

Sarantakos, S. (2005). *Social Research* (3rd ed.). New York: Palgrave Macmillan.
SIDDR. (2006). *Stockholm Initiative on Disarmament Demobilisation Reintegration: Final report*. Stockholm: Ministry of Foreign Affairs, Sweeden. http://www.regeringen.se/content/1/c6/06/43/56/cf5d851b.pdf.
Sideris, T. (2003). War, gender and culture: Mozambican women refugees. *Social Science & Medicine*, 56(4), 713–724. https://doi.org/10.1016/S0277-9536(02)00067-9.
Specht, I. (2010). *Socio-economic reintegration of ex-combatants*. London: International Alert.
Stark, L. (2006). Community acceptance of former child soldiers: Literature review and summary analysis. *Community Psychologist*, 39(4), 48–51. https://docs.google.com/viewer?a=v&pid=sites&srcid=Y3BjbGVhcm5pbmduZX-R3b3JrLm9yZ3xyZXNvdXJjZWxpYnJhcnl8Z3g6MjA3Nzg2ZjA3YTRh-NDYzNQ.
Subedi, D. B. (2012). Economic dimension of peacebuilding: Insights into post-conflict economic recovery and development in Nepal. *South Asia Economic Journal*, 13(2), 313–332. https://doi.org/10.1177/1391561412459387.
UN. (1999). *Disarmament, demobilization and reintegration of ex-combatants in a peacekeeping environment: Principles and guidelines*. New York: Department of Peacekeeping Operations (DPKO). http://www.somali-jna.org/downloads/DD&RUNPKO.pdf.
UN. (2000). *Disarmament, demobilization and reintegration of ex-combatants in a peacekeeping environment: Principles and guidelines*. New York: UN Department of Peacekeeping Operations/Lessons Learned Unit.
UN. (2006a). *Disarmament, demobilization and reintegration* (Report of the Secretary-General to UN General Assembly, A/60/705, 2 March 2006). New York.
UN. (2006b). *Integrated disarmament, demobilization and reintegration standards*. New York: United Nations (UN). Retrieved from http://pksoi.army.mil/doctrine_concepts/documents/UNGuidelines/IDDRS.pdf.
UN. (2010a). *The operational guide to the integrated disarmament, demobilization and reintegration standards (IDDRS)*. New York: United Nations, UN Inter-agency Working Group on Disarmament, Demobilization and Reintegration.
UN. (2010b). *Second generation disarmament, demobilization and reintegration (DDR) practices in peace operations*. New York: UNDPKO, Office of Law and Security Institutions, DDR Section. Retrieved from http://www.un.org/en/peacekeeping/documents/2GDDR_ENG_WITH_COVER.pdf.
UNDP. (1994). *Human development report 1994*. New York and Oxford: United Nations Development Programme (UNDP) and Oxford University Press.
UNDP. (2005). *Practice note: Disarmament, demobilization and reintegration of ex-combatants*. Retrieved from http://reliefweb.int/sites/reliefweb.int/files/resources/2795101D27F8E4EBC125742800328C0F-undp_dec2005.pdf.

UNDP. (2007). *Early recovery.* Retrieved from http://www.undp.org/content/undp/en/home/ourwork/crisispreventionandrecovery/focus_areas/early-recovery.html.

Upreti, B. R., & Vanhoutte, P. (2009). Security sector reform in Nepal: Challenges and opportunities. In H. Born & A. Schnabel (Eds.), *Security sector reform in challenging environments* (pp. 165–187). Geneva: LIT Verlag.

Varshney, A. (2003). *Ethnic conflict and civic life: Hindus and Muslims in India.* New Haven and London: Yale University Press.

Verhey, B. (2001). *Child soldiers: Preventing, demobilizing and reintegrating* (Africa Region Working Paper Series No. 23). Washington, DC. Retrieved from http://www.worldbank.org/afr/wps/wp23.pdf.

Verkoren, W. (2005). Bringing it all together: A case study of Cambodia. In G. Junne & W. Verkoren (Eds.), *Postconflict development: Meeting new challenges* (pp. 289–294). London: Lynne Rienner.

Verkoren, W., Willems, R., Kleingeld, J., & Rouw, H. (2010). From DDR to security promotion: Connecting national programs to community initiatives. *International Journal of Peace Studies, 15*(2), 1–32.

Visoka, G. (2016). *Peace figuration after international intervention: Intentions, events and consequences of liberal peacebuilding.* London and New York: Routledge.

Wallensteen, P., & Sollenberg, M. (2001). Armed conflict, 1989–2000. *Journal of Peace Research, 38*(5), 629–644. https://doi.org/10.1177/0022343301038005008.

Webel, C. (2007). Introduction: Towards and philosophy and metapsychology of peace. In C. Webel & J. Galtung (Eds.), *Handbook of peace and conflict studies* (pp. 3–13). Oxon and New York: Routledge.

CHAPTER 2

Why People Choose to Become a Combatant?

Combatants, who were recruited and trained by the Maoists, were the backbone of the Maoist war in Nepal. Although recruitment of combatants is a universal phenomenon in armed conflicts and civil wars, why people decide to take up arms and become combatants or fighter has always remained a puzzle. As such, there is the lack of consensus in social sciences with regard to the question of why people eventually choose to become combatants, endangering their life. While being a combatant involves a radical shift in one's worldview, it also often changes people's identity, making them isolated and disconnected from the mainstream society. And with exception in places where fighters or combatants are seen as a hero or a public savior (Bougarel, 2006; Metsola, 2006), in other places combatants are seen as a threat to durable peace, and are seen negatively as becoming a combatant ultimately changes one's identity which carries negative connotations and public imagery in post-conflict societies.

Because the reintegration phase of a Disarmament, Demobilisation and Reintegration (DDR) programme aims at bringing ex-combatants back to family and society where they belonged to in the pre-war recruitment phase, this process should, practically and theoretically, seek to address causes and drivers of armed recruitment so that remobilisation of ex-combatants in armed conflicts in future is prevented (Subedi, 2014). In other words, if post-conflict reintegration of ex-combatants is successful then the cycle of war recruitment and violence is minimised or prevented. It is precisely for this complex and often interlinked relationships

© The Author(s) 2018
D. B. Subedi, *Combatants to Civilians*, Rethinking Peace and Conflict Studies, https://doi.org/10.1057/978-1-137-58672-8_2

between war recruitment and reintegration that analysing war recruitment dynamics is fundamentally necessary and, in fact, an important entry point to think about what kind of DDR programs works or does not work. In other words, without understanding the drivers of armed recruitment and addressing these drivers through programs such as DDR, peacebuilding remains far from being effective.

This chapter examines the military structure of the Maoist armed conflict and the drivers and dynamics of recruitment in the armed conflict, with a particular focus on structural, environmental and mobilising factors that turned civilians to become combatants either voluntarily or involuntarily. While this chapter acknowledges that structural and environmental factors pushed many young people to join the Maoists People's Liberation Army (PLA), the roles and agency of the armed conflict mobiliser, hence the Maoists, and the strategies, tactics, methods they used to attract combatants cannot be overlooked. A critical analysis of combatant recruitment is relevance and necessary for reintegrating ex-combatants effectively in post-conflict period.

THE MILITARY STRUCTURE OF THE ARMED CONFLICT

When the Maoist armed conflict started in January 1996, it relied on the strength of a couple of dozens of Maoists cadres who carried out attacks on the police posts and government building in the hills of the Rukum and Rolpa districts in the mid-western region. It would be fair to state that no one would have then imagined that a small force of radical Maoists fighters armed with old riffles confiscated from rural elites and local police posts would eventually become a full-fledged non-state military that would be capable to challenge the state's security apparatus and the military establishment. Not only was the Maoist force rather small in its size, but it was also opportunistic in nature in the sense that in early days of the armed conflict, the Maoists mobilised roaming and mobile guerilla forces that operated on a typical guerrilla warfare based on "hit and run" strategy (Kumar, 2006, pp. 96–97).

It was perhaps because of the size of the force that the Maoists were initially less confident in winning the war with the state security forces. This 'war psychology' was instrumental in making the Maoists to take a strategic defensive position until first few years. The strategic defensive position had two pertinent effects on how the war had unleashed.

First, in addition to using the guerrilla warfare tactic, the Maoist fighters limited their attacks to the police rather than the military. The strategic calculation was that police was ill-equipped in fighting a guerrilla warfare not only in terms of training and capacity but also logistics such as age-old riffles and guns that needed urgent upgrading. Notably, the Nepal police is basically trained to enforce law and order and deal with community security and policing matters rather than being prepared for fighting insurgencies and protecting national security issues which was officially mandated to the Royal Nepal Army (RNA). Thus by averting confrontations with the RNA but selectively attacking at rural police posts in the mid-western hills, the Maoists were at least successful in spreading the war propaganda, terrorise the public and gain national and international media attentions.

Second, in the formative years of the insurgency, the targets of the loose and dispersed Maoist fighters in rural areas were mostly concentrated on rural elites and middle class intellectuals such as teachers, journalists, government officials and leaders of other political parties, mainly the Nepali Congress (NC) and the Communist Party of Nepal-United Marxist and Leninist (CPNUML). The strategic significance of the attacks on the middle class rural intellectuals who opposed or likely oppose the Maoists radical ideology was to eliminate political and intellectual opposition and coerce public to stock political capital needed to expand and consolidate the Maoist base.

The CPNM's Fourth Extended Central Committee meeting, held in April 1998, decided to establish an organised military wing of the party. The decision was partly an outcome of war propaganda and coercion that encouraged the Maoists to consolidate power needed to challenge the state in strategic and military terms. Hence, the decision marked an important turning point in the armed conflict because it would be going to change the "offence - defense balance" between the Maoists and the state security forces and alter local, national and international perceptions towards the Maoists' strength.

In the early days of the armed conflict, or when the Maoists had maintained defensive position, the government in Kathmandu dismissed the armed conflict as a law and order problem. Instead, it decided to mobilse special police operations to contain the threat, although the operations had counter effects because it pushed victims of security operations to the folds of Maoists in the pursuit of protection (this is elaborated later in this chapter).

By the end of 2002, the PLA had created a fully-fledged military structure by consolidating combatants into nine divisions and twenty nine battalions, as well as a number of temporary battalions, companies, platoons, and squads (Kumar, 2006; Sharma, 2004). Additionally, the Maoists had also mobilised unarmed militias, reportedly numbered between 50,000 and 100,000 (Kumar, 2006). Unarmed militias were not part of the regular force but they were available to support the PLA as or when needed, for example, during attacks and battles.

The exact number of PLA combatants was always elusive during the war, partly due to the strategic reason because a disclosure would reveal the Maoists' real military strength. An ex-Maoist fighter stated to the author in Kathmandu in January 2013 that the Maoists always gained from war propaganda and rumors about its military strengths, which always appeared to be exaggerated than its real strength. Delving into the detail of the exact military strengths of the Maoists is beyond the scope of this chapter. Nonetheless, the question that arises is what made the Maoists so successful in recruiting committed insurgents who fought ferociously with the state security forces including the military. The remaining of the sections of this chapter deals with this question.

Why People Join Armed Conflicts as a Combatant?

In social sciences, there is an on-going debate whether participation in armed conflict is an individual rational choice or a collective action driven by the agency of the participants. Argument and counter-arguments differ along philosophical and ideological viewpoints adopted to anlayse and interpret armed conflict and its mobilisation. One line of thinking, however, suggests that recruitment to and participation in civil war is phenomena driven by structural and environmental factors and conditions, which unleash grievances in conflict contexts. While there is more or less consensus on the role and impact of structural factors behind war recruitment, what constitutes these structural factors lacks consensus. Some argue that poverty is identified as a major structural condition that drives the recruitment of children and youth into armed conflict (McConnan & Uppard, 2001, p. xx). Others, however, contend that while poverty can create a general vulnerability for rebel recruitment, it is not necessarily the only determining factor, since not all children who are poor become combatants (Brett & Specht, 2004, p. 3).

Brett and Specht (2004, p. 3) further argue that the combined influence of three levels of environmental factors—poverty, the personal history of combatants, and trigger factors—become instrumental in the individual's decision to become a combatant.

On the other hand, Gates (2002) argues that geography as a physical structure and the source of spatial marginality presents an important variable to explain recruitment, management and control of rebels because hilly terrains, remote places and forests provides an advantage for rebel organisation to recruit and mange rebels, either voluntarily or forcefully. Similarly, ethnic composition of a country and low levels of gross domestic product (GDP) per capita are also considered to be important structural conditions in conflict-related recruitment (see Eck, 2008). Elbadawi and Sambanis (2002) maintain that ethnic, religious and socio-cultural factionalisation and grievances are important determinants of civil war with notable public support and participation in various capacities including as a combatant.

In a synthesis report on the causes of conflict in the third world, Douma, Frerks, and Van de Goor (1999) state that poverty and economic inequalities may not always have a positive correlation with conflict. They argue that poverty can occasionally function as a mobilising factor if it coincides with the exclusion and marginalisation of ethnic, linguistic, and religious minority groups by a state system, which perpetuates discriminations, inequalities and socio-economic marginalisation. Douma et al. (1999, p. ii) make a distinction between the categories of "pivotal factors" and "mobilising factors" of conflict, maintaining that while pivotal factors lie as the root cause of conflict and appear in almost all phases of conflict, there are mobilising factors concerning issues relating to individuals and groups that might be instrumental in mobilising and recruiting people in armed conflict.

Structural and environmental conditions that drive participation in armed conflicts are linked to the notion of grievance in armed conflict (Collier & Hoeffler, 2002). As opposed to the notion of greed in civil war, which facilitate opportunistic modes of war participation, grievance is rooted in the perceptions of identity, relative deprivations and exclusions, therefore, war participation is less opportunistic at least in economic terms (Collier & Hoeffler, 2002). While the distinction between greed and grievances provides useful insights to why people join armed insurgency, this perspectives overlooks the factors such as politics and ideology as a vital tool in rendering insurgencies feasible, especially where power and a quest for systemic change in the existing structures of power are at the stake (Marks, 2006).

In many insurgencies that become armed revolutions, such as the Revolutionary Armed Forces of Colombia-People's Army (FARC-EP) in Colombia and the Maoists in Nepal, ideology, indoctrination and political radicalisation played a critical role not only in garnering public support but also in recruiting committed rebels (Eck, 2010; Khanal, 2007; Saskiewicz, 2005). Therefore, a focus on the agency of armed groups and individual combatants offers an alternative perspective to understand how ideology becomes a tool of war participation, radicalisation and mobilisation.

From a realist perspective, war participation and mobilisation must be seen in the light of how public see the nexus between conflict and security. In other words, war participation can also become an outcome of counter-effects of actions and behaviours of insurgent organisations as well as the state security forces. Studies show that while an insurgent organisation's forceful and coercive behaviour triggers involuntary recruitment of rebels, violence and repression by state actors, such as police and the army, can also convert victims into rebels (see Hossain, Siitonen, & Sharma, 2006; Mehta & Lawoti, 2010). Goodwin (2001) provides an illustration of how repressive security actions and responses of authoritarian regimes became a catalyst for transforming popular public resistance into violent and radical armed revolution in Southeast Asia during the 1940s and 1950s, in Central America during the 1970s and 1980s, and Eastern Europe in the late 80s. Armed revolution and public participation in it is not only the public's violent response to poverty and inequality, but is also a ramification of brutal and indiscriminate use of force by the state.

STRUCTURAL AND ENVIRONMENTAL FACTORS AND WAR PARTICIPATION IN NEPAL

In the Nepali context, structural factors and conditions are useful for explaining people's participation in the insurgency. But the available explanations take multiple directions. For example a number of socio-cultural factors such as gender inequality (Gautam, Banskota, & Manachanda, 2001), caste-based and ethnic discriminations and grievances (de Sales, 2003; Leve, 2007; Onesto, 2003), as well as income inequalities between social groups and geographical regions, have been identified as key causes of the armed insurgency.

Other scholars have taken a political economy approach in explaining grievances pertinent to the Maoist insurgency. Continuity of unemployment, poverty and regional development disparities, even after the democratic transition in 1990, was one of the factors that disrupted state–society relations between the centralised state and disenfranchised masses of people in rural areas (Mahat, 2005). This continuity fuelled grievances of deprived people who could not experience tangible changes in their lives, even if the political system had changed in Kathmandu after 1990.

The history of the five decades of development programmes failed to uplift rural poor who eventually supported the insurgency (Sharma, 2006; Upreti, 2009). While the extent of underdevelopment and the state's inability to deliver basic services in the rural areas, particularly in the remote hills of the west and far-west regions, increased people's distrust with the state system, the situation was concurrently ripe for a revolution to take a root. Thus, a poor governance system perpetuated by conservative bureaucracy is often cited as a catalytic factor for the insurgency (Muni, 2003). Subsequently, the political economy of the country, which failed to enable large numbers of rural people to experience change and development, partly served as a driving factor of the Maoist insurgency.

Inception and expansion of the armed conflict is also largely ascribed to several structural and environmental factors and conditions which can be understood in terms of socio-economic inequalities, having both vertical and horizontal dimensions (Murshed & Gates, 2005). While vertical inequalities in the Nepalese context can be understood in terms of unequal income distribution and possession of wealth, horizontal inequalities can be explained in relation to various ethnic and religious groups and sub-groups' inequalities, resulting in their marginalisation in the discourse of development and the political processes. In this regard, the grievances and discontent of ethnic and indigenous groups, *Madhesi* people,[1] religious minorities and *Dalits* are all forms of horizontal inequality which have shaped the discourse of contentious politics in contemporary Nepal (Gellner, Pfaff-Czarnecka, & Whelpton, 2008; Hangen, 2009; Lawoti, 2010).

---

[1] The term *Madhesi* refers to the people from Madhesh or the Terai, both indigenous and non-indigenous people who have their own language and normally follow either Hinduism or Islam.

The caste system in Nepal is a hierarchical and exclusionary social system of differential Hindu-ritual status and practices that has stratified society into the high-caste group (the *Brahmins*),[2] the next highest group (the *Chhetris*) and several low caste groups, including the *Dalit* groups such as the *Kami, Damai, and Sarki* (Hangen, 2009; Hofer, 2004). Economically, this stratified caste system presents barriers against certain groups benefiting from occupational mobility. Consequently, certain high caste people have had the advantage of being able to take control of productive resources through the power exercised by the conventional norms of this caste system.

Several studies support this proposition. For instance, high-caste people possess the conventional productive resources, such as land and businesses and have greater access to political and public services (Bennett, 2005; ILO, 2005). The incidence of poverty among *Brahmins* and the *Chhetris* stood at 19%, compared to 47, 44 and 41% among the *Dalit*, Hill *Janajatis* and Muslims (Alexander, Gunduz, & Subedi, 2009, p. 17) respectively. Nearly 76% of the Terai *Dalits* have never attended school (Bennett, 2006), while only 2% of primary school teachers were *Dalits* before 2005 (ILO, 2005). The civil service is largely dominated by high caste *Brahmins, Chhetris* and *Newars*, and this trend grew steadily between 1989 and 2000 (Gurung, 1998). Similarly, nearly 80% of the Terai *Dalits* and 75% of Hill *Dalits* are landless, and a vast number of ethnic group members have little land of their own, meaning that they have to rent their land (Wily, Chapagain, & Sharma, 2008).

Ethnic groups in Nepal, which are currently known as "indigenous nationalities", have their origins in the Terai, Hill and Mountain regions, and according to the 2001 census, these groups comprised 36.4% of the Nepali population. Of these, five groups were in the Mountains, twenty-seven groups in the Hills, and twelve in the Terai (Wily et al., 2008, p. 53). Some ethnic groups appear not to have been accounted for in these figures; the total ethnic population may in fact be as much as 42% (Whelpton, Gellner, & Pfaff-Czarnecka, 2008).

Ethnic discontents and grievances have increasingly shaped contentious politics in contemporary Nepal, particularly after the regime change in 1990. Responding to growing ethnic demands, the democratic constitution promulgated in 1990 declared the country to be a multi-cultural

---

[2] The *Bhramins* are also called *Bahuns*; therefore, both terms are used in this volume.

and multi-ethnic state and, for the first time, recognised ethnic languages as "languages of the nation" (Whelpton et al., 2008). Despite these demands, however, no political reservation was made for ethnic groups and the land rights of these groups went unrecognised (Lawoti, 2005). The long-debated principle of reservation targeting ethnic and minority groups was eventually recognised by the government in 2003 (Whelpton et al., 2008). Many groups, nevertheless, remained marginalised, and unable to access political and economic resources, despite the attempts of democratic governments in the post 1990 period to address the growing frustration of ethnic groups.

The armed conflict broke out amidst caste-based discriminations, ethnic consciousness and simmering frustrations and grievances among *Dalits*, ethnic groups and indigenous nationalities. This fragile situation provided the Maoists with an opportunity to mobilise ethnic groups, particularly the Kham Magars, the Tharus and the Madhesis (de Sales, 2003; Lawoti, 2010; Thapa, 2012). Incorporating the ethnic dimension into what was well known as a "class-based" insurgency, the CPNM made a remarkable shift in its war mobilisation strategy. The duality of class and ethnicity-based mobilisation was easily accepted, because the distinction between ethnic group and caste is somewhat blurred in the Nepali context and some ethnic groups, such as the *Newars* "have a deeply complex caste system" (Hangen, 2009, p. 26).

The CPNM achieved further success in tapping ethnic discontent by setting up a number of ethnicity-led organisations recognised as being affiliated with the CPNM (Whelpton et al., 2008). The *Newar Jatiya Mukti Morcha*, the *Tharuwan Mukti Morcha* and the *Dalit Mukti Morcha* were ethic organisations that worked as mediators between the CPNM and ethnic groups. The Maoists' promise to establish an independent ethnic federal unit was an appealing political rhetoric for groups who were optimistic about achieving political and cultural rights through a federal system of government. Consequently, the idea of ethnic federalism first proposed by the Maoists played a key role, not only in expanding the ethnic support base of the conflict, but also in increasing political awareness, allowing the Maoists to radicalise people and attract them to the war. The following sections explore these dynamics.

As the discussion here clearly reveal that grievances of ethnic, low-caste and marginalised people served political opportunity structures while structural inequalities fuel the grievance. Therefore, war participation in Nepal appears to be phenomena driven by an intersectionality of social and political opportunity structures, and structural inequities. But beyond these factors, did the war mobiliser have any role to play? What role the insurgent organisation and the state played in the recruitment dynamics? To understand these questions, this chapter argues we cannot fully understand the war recruitment and participation dynamics without closely examining the war mobilisation and political radicalisation strategies employed by the Maoists during the armed conflict.

IDEOLOGY AND THE ARMED CONFLICT: RHETORIC AND REALITY

The Maoists articulated three broad objectives of their armed resistance: to wipe out the capitalist class and the state system that had traditionally existed; to abolish the Monarchy that protected and promoted feudalism; and to establish a democratic republic ruled by the people (Mahat, 2005).

Similar to many other grievance-based insurgency, the Maoist armed conflict was founded on a political ideology that served as a vehicle for armed conflict mobilsation. It is claimed that the armed conflict was based on the lessons and philosophy of the revolutionary ideas of Marxism, Leninism and Maoism (CPNM, 1995). While the CPNM basically picked up the Marxian idea of "class struggle" and Leninism's idea of peasant-worker alliance and mass insurrection (Chamlagai, 2006), Mao Zedong's vision of the People's New Democracy (PND), class enemy, Protracted Guerrilla War (PGW) and Permanent Revolution (PR) equally dominated the ideology and strategies of the armed conflict.

Regardless of the rationale provided for the armed struggle, the combination of armed violence with political agendas and emancipatory rhetoric tended to integrate the idea of revolutionary statebuilding through the use of violence. It was an attempt to control over the state system by challenging the legitimate use of force by the state (Bhattarai, 2014; Kievelitz & Polzer, 2002). Thus, the armed struggle was an extension of politics by other violent means.

Five years after the initiation of the armed conflict, the National Congress of the CPNM, held in February 2001, reviewed its ideological base and the war strategy in order to build the future programme of the insurgency (Subedi, 2013). Realising the need to contextualise its ideology according to the social, economic and political realities of Nepali society, the CPNM promulgated "Prachanda Path", the homegrown political ideology of the CPNM, and the term coined after the name of the party chairman, Comrade Prachanda (Subedi, 2013). The Prachanda Path synthesised and contextualised Lenin's model of armed insurrection in urban areas and Mao's model of protracted war in rural areas, although the CPNM's urban mobilisation differed from the Lenin model insofar as it involved unarmed protests by students, workers and civil society organisations.

By integrating these revolutionary principles, the Prachanda Path provided guidelines for developing both political and military wings of the revolution, which resulted in the formation of the PLA. Similarly, in synthesising ideological, political and military ideas, the Prachanda Path sought to adopt the "mass line" as a core mobilising principle (Kiran, 2003). The central idea of the "mass line" was framed as to understand and organise the aspirations of oppressed, indigenous, lower class and downtrodden men and women and, with their help, develop the armed conflict with the goal of making the masses the masters of political power. However, given the Maoists frequently coerced local people to gain their support and sympathy (Subedi, 2013) also means that the idea of mass line also appeared to be the rhetoric and propaganda of war mobilisation. In other words the Prachanda Path was used as an instrument of political radicalisation and an ideological basis for popularising the so-called emancipatory goals of the insurgency that attracted many to become fighters.

What must, however, also be acknowledge that Prachanda Path also combined dialogue and diplomacy with the armed struggle, thus it constructed a redefined ideological direction, preparing the ground for the CPNM to enter into political competition and peace dialogue while continuing to revolutionise the party (Chamlagai, 2006; Subedi, 2013). In other words, Prachanda Path created a revolutionary rhetoric for social and political change rather than systematically theorising revolution in the Nepalese context. Indeed, when the armed conflict ended and the Maoists entered into the peace process, the much-hyped narratives of Prachanda Path was left behind officially. Therefore, it was merely an ideology created for the radicalisation process in which the role of Maoists as mobiliser of armed conflict is expressed and the explanation of war participation could be found.

Ideology, Radicalisation and Armed Recruitment

The author has claimed elsewhere that the Maoists supporters and combatants turned to the armed conflict not just because they were poor, marginalised and unemployed, but because they were motivated by the political teaching they received from the Maoist party workers (Subedi, 2013). In the early days of the insurgency, the CPNM recruited a limited number of leaders who were known as "whole time" (WT) party workers, popularly known as "whole timers". The whole timers received regular salaries and subsistence allowances and were entrusted to (a) identify potential impact groups or communities; (b) be in regular touch with them; and (c) conduct political teachings in communities so as to attract them in the insurgency. As part of political radicalisation process, the Maoists whole timers as well as leaders selectively reached out to rural intellectuals and educated people, such as teachers, unemployed youth, ethnic leaders and *Dalits, Madhesi* and women.

The CPNM mobilised a number of WT party workers as motivators who moved from village to village in order to spread knowledge, information and awareness about Maoism, the war and its relevance in Nepal.

Political teaching as a method of radicalisation targeted people at individual and collective level. While individual level radicalisation process was conducted in person-to-person contact over the period of time, collective radicalisation happened at the community level. Several Maoists ex-combatants interviewed by the author in Kathmandu and Dhangadi in December 2011 stated that they first came in contact with the Maoists mobilisers in collective political awareness campaigns in their villages.

Both personal and collective motivation campaigns selectively targeted towards ethnic and indigenous communities, poor villages and *Dalits*. This strategy was based on the perception and, in fact, that was a reality that people from marginalised communities could be easily radicalised and convinced to join the war as combatants.

An ex-combatant from the *Dalit* community from Sankhuwasabha district said, "I joined the Maoist army because I was motivated that the pro-poor agendas of the armed conflict could liberate people like me who have been oppressed by high-caste people for a very long time". Another female ex-combatant from Sunsari district stated[3]:

---

[3] Interviewed in November 2011.

I decided to become a combatant because I was impressed by the political teaching of Shanti "didi" (sister) (who was killed in an army encounter). I believed in the Maoist philosophy because I was taught that only the "Jan Yuddha" (People's War) could end all forms of feudalistic exploitation and oppression.

Another ex-combatant, who was studying in grade 11 in Dhangadi, recalled how the political teaching and village to village campaign inspired rural people to join the insurgency[4]:

One or two people from the party (Maoist) used to come and give lectures about the philosophy of Marxism and Maoism. Their lectures used to be very instigative. They cited several examples from the Chinese Cultural Revolution and the Russian Communist Revolution. Issues such as redistribution of land, the dismantling of the kingship, "Sanghiyata" (federalism), and the elimination of social and economic inequalities were often the main topics of discussion. Books and other literature on communism were also distributed to the participants.

A significant number of interviews with ex-combatants echoed similar opinions and perceptions, which support the proposition that the indoctrination campaign was instrumental in politically radicalising unemployed and disillusioned masses of young people in rural areas.

Thus, the nexus between social exclusion and marginalisation, and radicalisation suggest that public grievances towards prevailing structural inequalities is dangerous from peace and stability point of view because it provides incentives for radicalisation and violent extremism whether that is opportunistic and criminal in nature or one with a political goal.

The language of political teaching would be highly instigating, sensitising and radically motivating, often focused on the dynamics of marginalisation, discriminations and oppression by the state and its feudalistic social, political and economic structures (Subedi, 2013). Ex-combatants in Dang and Chitwan districts told the author in January 2013 that the political teaching and the language of political radicalisation was selective, often citing examples from famous dictums of Mao, Marx and Lenin. The dream of liberated and emancipated 'New Nepal' in which feudalistic and oppressive systems would be eliminated by people's power certainly

[4] Interviewed in December 2011.

appeared highly attractive and influential to the people. People were soon ready to fight a decisive war with the state to take control of the state power and realise the dream of what was called a New Nepal.

When it comes to political ideology, it is notable that the Maoists benefited significantly from pre-existing communist movements in their war-related recruitment. The communist movement has a long history in Nepal, starting in the early 1950s, although the movements had been deeply fractured in the past, and today there are multiple divisions and factions / groups within the communist parties in Nepal. In the well-known movement organised by young communist cadres in the Jhapa district in 1971, several prominent land lords were punished and five of them were beheaded in a so-called class annihilation campaign (Kc, 2003, cited in Khanal, 2007). Other than this movement, most activities of the Nepali communist movement were non-violently concentrated on the grass-roots mobilisation of peasants and workers from rural areas. Consequently, the movement had already produced many sympathisers and workers before the Maoist insurgency began. Khanal (2007, p. 86) states that "without the pre-existing support groups and activists already trained in communist ideologies, it was difficult to imagine the rapid spread of the Maoists". With an aim to tap on this group of communist sympathisers as a resource, the Maoists' motivation campaigns were largely directed towards those who were either supporters of the communist worldview or were already activists in one communist movement or another (Subedi, 2013).

Collective Motivation Campaigns

The Maoists also organised large-scale political meetings attended by hundreds of people. While most villagers attended mass meetings voluntarily, usually out of excitement, several of them were brought in forcefully too.[5] This statement was further corroborated by the interviews with ex-combatants in Dhangadi (Kailali) and Birtamod (Jhapa). Bringing people into the campaigns involved intensive coordination at different levels between districts and villages, normally coordinated by WT workers and the CPNM's local committee members. An ex-combatant interviewed in Birtamod, Jhapa revealed that combatants also played a role in forcefully bringing people to mass campaigns, and added that they often made it mandatory

---

[5] Interview with a human rights activist in Dhangadi, 2011.

for the villagers to attend mass meetings while disobedience could lead to punishment. In several places, Maoist-affiliated ethnic organisations also mobilised people to attend such campaigns.

The Maoists normally advertised a mass gathering a few days before the event and ordered people from the villages and the surrounding neighbourhoods to attend. Apart from villagers, students were also brought to mass meetings, often forcefully. For instance, according to focus group participants in Dhangadi district, schools were forced to shut down so that school children could attend the mass gatherings. "Some people even walked all day and night to attend the mass gathering because of the Maoists' orders", said a journalist in the Kailali district.[6]

Mass gatherings were normally addressed by high-ranking leaders of the CPNM. Future political agendas of the CPNM, such as the elimination of kingship and the need for a constitutional assembly and ethnic federalism, were key issues in the speeches. Similarly, using nationalism as a motivational tool, the mass gatherings often strongly criticised Indian expansionism and American hegemony, identified by the Maoists as the new enemies of the Nepali people and their sovereignty. By portraying the international non-government organisations (INGOs) as creators of foreign dependency, the public were encouraged to support the Maoists' People's Government and its economic vision of communitarianism, although during interviews many ex-combatants could not properly explain what the vision was like.[7]

Cultural Campaigns for Political Radicalisation

The CPNM also formed a separate cultural unit with the responsibility of performing cultural programmes in order to attract people towards the war. Cultural programmes presented stories of war and narratives of the revolution through stage performances, which included songs, traditional folk dance and creative plays. Interviews confirmed that cultural programmes were powerful tools of political motivation or even political radicalisation

---

[6] Interviewed in December 2011.

[7] The Maoists had reportedly formed the revolutionary People's Government in several districts of the mid-west and far-west. By mid-January 2001, they had formed such governments in the Rolpa, Rukum, Salyan and Jajarkot districts (Tiwari, 2001). In most parts, the Maoists' "base areas" were under the control of the People's Government, which was an alternative form of power structure that replaced the political, economic, justice and military system of the state.

because they delivered political messages in the form of entertainment and emotional performances. Recalling how political teaching was embedded in cultural performances, an ex-combatant from Jhapa, who initially worked as a cultural team member and who later joined the PLA, said:

> We often picked up stories from the war – fighting, killing, victory, the future depicted as an emancipated world, the elimination of inequality and so on – and presented them through revolutionary and patriotic songs and dance.

Political Radicalisation in Schools

Public schools proved to be important for recruitment to the PLA. The CPNM aspired, or to put it more accurately, made a propoganda to replace the existing educational system with what was called People's Education. In several so-called "base areas", including Sindhuli, Rukum Rolpa, Pyuthan and Jajarkot districts, the CPNM instigated People's Education, although it was also found that most 'base areas' did not exist in reality.[8] Facets of People's Education included the banning of the national anthem and the institution of a minute's silence in morning assemblies to pay tribute to the Maoist martyrs.

The majority of ex-combatants interviewed mentioned that they first came into contact with the Maoist people and learnt about war at their schools. Shneiderman and Turin (2004, pp. 98–99) provide an account that also highlights "the Maoist's use of the school as a primary forum for the dissemination of their ideology among young people, and as a recruiting centre for new members". Since the Maoists used school grounds as their preferred meeting sites (Shneiderman & Turin, 2004), some scholars go as far as to claim that schools had been both "actual and ideological battlegrounds" in the insurgency (Standing & Parker, 2011, p. 182).

An ex-combatant interviewed in Dhangadi mentioned that,

> The Maoists formed CPNM's student unit committees in every class and organised regular sessions to teach the philosophy of Marxism, Leninism, Maoism and Prachanda Path. They explained to the students the historical need for the armed revolution for societal changes.

---

[8] Interview with a civil society activist in Kathmandu, November 2011.

As part of the so-called political awareness-raising, teachers and students were forcefully taken to mass meetings for the purpose of furthering their indoctrination. A teacher retired from a primary school in Sindhupalchowk district reported that he received political teaching for several days. Such teachers who returned from indoctrination were forced to advocate the Maoists' philosophy in their communities. He further mentioned that many teachers became workers and supporters of the war, either because they received a political role in the CPNM, or because it was their survival strategy for avoiding physical threats emanating from not supporting the Maoist ideology and actions at the local level.

Peer Pressure as a 'Knock on Effect'

Political motivation and radicalisation as a tool of war mobilisation produced 'knock on effect' in the war recruitment through peer and social network because a significant number of people followed their peers to the war. What was notable about war participation in Nepal was that many combatants were in regular contacts with their families, friends and relatives. In fact in many occasions when there was a recession or at least no battle in the offing, combatants were allowed to visit families and relatives or moved from one location to another with direct contacts with villagers. This facilitated continuous social contacts between combatants and their social networks. This decision was in a way tactical because it would serve two purposes. First, when combatants visited families and communities, it would be less economic burden to the PLA because in most cases villagers fed combatants although it was involuntary in many cases. Second, the social contacts also meant that combatants themselves played a role of a motivator. In other words, people joined the insurgency following peer and social network but without known anything about political ideology and the goal of the armed conflict.

War, Heroism, Empowerment and War Participation

When civilians became fighters and combatants, their social identity was (re)constructed by war. The new identity was in fact the lynch pin of a war family, which is a building block of the war system. Being a part of the war family and the war system in rural Nepal where the state's presence was minimum, combatants enjoyed a sense of freedom and liberation while at the same time being hailed as heroes by local villagers. This changed identity and the way it was perceived locally was also a source of empowerment for combatants. One female ex-combatant shared her feeling of empowerment when villagers cheering when the PLA combatants marched across a village diligently received her. It is an irony that war and violence is a source of disempowerment for some but for others like combatants it can be a matter of social recognition and empowerment. This perceived sense of heroism and empowerment associated with war participation motivated many young people to join the insurgency without knowing what they were going to achieve in future.

Violence as a Weapon of War Mobilisation

The state of coercion, violence and insecurity caused by both the insurgent organisation and the reactive state is a common phenomenon of the insurgency in Nepal. A close examination of this typical phenomenon demonstrates how the public experience of violence by both sides of the conflict triggered people's participation in the war, both voluntary and involuntary. The following sub-sections capture these dynamics.

Use of Coercion and Threats for Recruitment

Forced recruitment into the armed conflict was common across the country, although a civil society leader interviewed in Dhangadi said that this practice was more rampant in the west and far-west regions than in the central and eastern parts of the country. The "one house-one guerrilla" campaign launched by the CPNM between 1998 and 2002 in the west and far-west hills is an example of forced recruitment (Mehta & Lawoti, 2010). High school graduates and unemployed youth were major targets of such recruitment campaigns. Nepal (2005, cited in ICG, 2005, p. 10) highlights a similar phenomenon known as the "shoe campaign", in which the Maoists placed a pair of shoes outside the door of a house as an indication that a member of that particular household was expected to join the PLA. These two campaigns created what is known as a culture of terror (see Pettigrew, 2004) in the everyday life of people trapped in the war zones. The only way to escape the culture of terror was either through migrating or becoming a member of the war family—a social network generated through participation in war.

Forceful recruitment and abduction of school children soared, particularly after the formation of the PLA (Mehta & Lawoti, 2010; Sharma, 2004). Recalling his experience of abduction, a VLMR interviewed in Dhangadi stated:

> One day, they (Maoists) came to take students to attend a mass meeting in the next village. There were twenty students in our group and we walked all night to arrive in Acham district the next morning. Then they separated us from the group. Five of us were put in a small group and then taken to a political training camp where we were given political teachings for a month. I was then only 13.5 years old. We cried a lot and pleaded with them to take us back home. We were told to go back if we could do so, on our own. But we did not know the way back; neither had we any money. The political training was in the jungle. For food and shelter, they sent us to villages. People in the village were poor; however, they fed us with whatever they had because of the orders from the PLA. Disobedience could lead the villagers to physical punishment.

While most of the abducted school children were trained to become PLA fighters, a number of them were also assigned to non-combatant roles such as militia, messengers and cultural unit members. The CPNM's denial of forced recruitment, along with the secretive nature of militia recruitment, makes it difficult to estimate the exact number of forcefully recruited combatants. Nonetheless, several reports state that the forceful recruitment of children as well as adults was a common characteristic of armed recruitment in the armed conflict (Becker, 2007; Coalition to Stop the Child Soldier, 2004; UN, 2006).

Political Violence by the State and War Participation

In May 1998, the NC led the newly appointed government and authorised the infamous police operation called "Kilo Sera II" in the Maoist influenced districts of Rukum, Rolpa, Salyan and Jajarkot in the mid-western region, Gorkha district in the western region and the Sindhuli district in the central region. The operation involved a "search, kill, and destroy" strategy which resulted in the killing of many innocent people (Thapa & Sijapati, 2005, p. 92), further encouraging antagonism towards the state in the already disturbed Maoist hinterlands. Many innocent victims of the "Kilo Sera II" operation, who survived, eventually chose to join armed conflict in order to take revenge on the state (Mehta & Lawoti, 2010).

In the infamous *Khara* incident, in response to the killing of a policeman by the Maoists in the Khara village of the Rukum district, the police set fire to more than 200 houses and indiscriminately killed dozens of Maoist leaders, supporters and innocent civilians in February 2000 (Human Rights Server, 1997). The incident proved to be terribly counter-productive for the government, because the agonised victims, their relatives and sympathisers eventually joined the Maoists with the aim of taking revenge for these atrocities.[9]

In countless other incidents, the police and the army allegedly arrested and tortured women, children and old people for a variety of reasons. While some were tortured because the police wanted to extract information about the Maoists' activities, many others were accused of spying against the police, providing the Maoists with food and shelter, attending the Maoists' mass gatherings and cultural programmes, and so on. Many women were gang-raped by security forces if they refused to provide information about their men and family members in the PLA.[10] If a family member was in the PLA, it was quite likely that the entire family of the combatant experienced violence at the hands of the state. Many ex-combatants reported that they joined the insurgency (a) to fulfil the unmet dreams of their family members who were killed by the police and army, and (b) to take revenge against the state security forces for their atrocities and brutality.

There was an upsurge in unlawful killings including extrajudicial executions by police and security forces after the launching of the "Kilo Sera II" operation. There was a decline in such killings after February 2000, owing to pressure on the government to comply with international human rights standards and human rights laws (Amnesty International, 2002). Nonetheless, violence began to soar sharply again in February 2000 after King Gyanendra's regime imposed a state of emergency and mobilised the RNA to crack down on the war.[11] According to a CPNUML leader interviewed in the Morang district, "whenever there was sharply increasing repressive behaviour of the state, the timing generally coincided with a significantly increased recruitment trend in the PLA".

---

[9] Interview with a civil society activist in Kailai, December 2011.

[10] Interview with a human rights activist in Dhangadi, December 2011.

[11] Interview with a political analyst in Kathmandu, November 2011.

How Did Political Radicalisation Work?

Political teaching leading to political radicalisation, whether carried out individually or collectively, involved informal participatory learning and sharing opportunities for villagers. It created rare opportunities for everyone to speak on political, social and economic issues, and acted as an empowerment process for villagers. "Speaking in front of high caste people on political issues was beyond my imagination. The Maoists' teaching sessions transformed me from a timid *Dalit* youth to a bold combatant", asserted an ex-combatant originally from the Sankhuwasabha district. The workers and leaders of the CPNM, who were involved in political teaching and motivation, tried their best to relate to and associate themselves with people's everyday lives in order to win public confidence in the Maoist movement. This not only created an emotional bond between the CPNM workers and villagers; the way in which the political, economic, and social issues directly concerning their everyday lives were addressed in political teachings, helped to increase public confidence in the armed conflict.

The CPNM must have been aware of the reality that mere indoctrination would not work without being combined with slogans of revolutionary economic development, poverty alleviation and improved employment. As such, radicalisation was further augmented by the grievances of people who were victimised by structural violence by the state. Thus, the idea of systemic changes promulgated by the CPNM was promised, and inequalities and structural violence were being openly discussed within the agendas of the insurgency. However, on the negative side, personal motivation and village gatherings often concentrated on discussing pro-poor but somewhat unrealistic agendas, such as reallocation of the entire land system, redistribution of property and jobs for all. In several places, the CPNM confiscated land and distributed it to poor landless people or used it for communal farming. The revolutionary idea of land and property redistribution and the rhetoric of employment for all made people confident and hopeful of the CPNM's intentions.

In a similar fashion, the CPNM also heavily incorporated local development agendas in their indoctrination campaigns. They encouraged people to initiate local development works such as constructing roads, building irrigation channels, managing community forests, and so on.

The party even encouraged people to dismantle the local government system, seize its resources and use them locally for development works, as decided by the locals. Thus, in engaging people more directly in local development decision processes, the CPNM created hope for a new Nepal. Further, in encouraging people to stop paying school fees and land taxes, as well as all other forms of tax payable to the government in the Maoist hinterlands, the indoctrination campaigns served not only to provide an economic relief package to the poor, but also to create a popular positive image of the Maoists as liberators from all forms of social and economic oppression.

The CPNM challenged the traditional values, systems and norms embedded in the rigid caste, gender and religious hierarchies of Nepalese society. The CPNM organised mass campaigns to eliminate the untouchability of the *Dalits*, encouraged inter-caste and inter-ethnic marriages and punished those who stopped *Dalits* from entering Hindu temples and sacred places.[12] The CPNM introduced the idea of ethnic federalism and popularised the belief that it would provide autonomy and self-governing opportunities for ethnic and indigenous nationalities.

Similarly, political teaching also challenged traditional gender roles and hierarchies and encouraged women to step outside of traditional household roles and take part in the people's war, equally, with their male counterparts. Thus, by combining revolutionary agendas of social transformation with political teaching and radicalisation, the CPNM was successful in attracting committed rebels.

Forced and involuntary recruitment worked well because it was intrinsically linked to radicalisation and indoctrination. A deliberate indoctrination process often followed coercive and unwilling recruitment. Abductees were often taken to training camps where indoctrination was aimed at instilling communist worldviews into their minds and radicalising individuals to the extent that they would be willing to attain martyrdom. The transformation of a forcefully recruited ordinary individual into a ferocious fighter involved a sizeable investment for which radicalisation provided insurance.

For many people who became the victims of the repressive and brutal behaviour of the security forces, the war provided a safety and security net. Many ex-combatants mentioned that being part of the war network

---

[12] Although Dalits also traditionally follow Hinduism, they are not allowed to enter Hindu temples because of caste-based discrimination prevailing in the society.

provided a sense of security. Indeed, turning individuals into combatants involved a process that fragmented them from their family and social networks and reintegrated them into a "war family". It was this network of the war family that offered the combatants a sense of belonging and security. Therefore, people found it safer to remain with the Maoists than to be on the side of the government, mainly because of the former's control over the lives of villagers in remote hills, economically, politically and militarily. Further, the victims of the repressive behaviour of the state cultivated hatred towards the state and many felt that their deep desire for revenge against the police and the army could be fulfilled if they joined the war as PLA fighters. Thus, the state's repressive and violent response to the armed conflict exacerbated relationship between the state and society, and created further favourable conditions for the Maoists to recruit committed fighters.

Conclusions

A number of existing studies on rebel recruitment have highlighted the salient role of structural conditions and factors as key drivers of armed recruitment into situations of armed conflict. This chapter has demonstrated that the CPNM achieved significant success in recruiting a large number of rebels by radicalising them through their political teaching and indoctrination campaigns. This was accomplished in a context where structural factors and conditions, including grievances, created favourable conditions for the CPNM's use of indoctrination as a part of their recruitment campaign. Nonetheless, public experiences of insecurity and violence caused by the Maoists, as well as the state forces, also triggered people's participation in the war.

In this chapter, various methods of political radicalisation have been explored. These included personal motivation and political teaching, village campaigns, mass gatherings and cultural performances, and indoctrination in schools. Furthermore, two additional dimensions regarding public insecurity pertinent to armed recruitment were found. Firstly, public experience and perceptions of insecurity emerging from the coercive behaviour of the Maoists spurred people to join the war. Secondly, the state's repressive response to the insurgency in terms of the security operations of the police and army led to situations that pressured people into joining the insurgency, either as a survival strategy or to take revenge against the state security forces for their actions.

After having discussed the motivation that drove people's participation in the armed conflict as combatants, the next chapter will discuss the peace process and the mechanism applied to transform combatants into civilians. In particular, it will highlight how the process of bringing the combatants back to the community as civilians unfolded in Nepal's peace process and what impacts politics in the transitional period had on DDR of the Maoist combatants.

References

Alexander, L., Gunduz, C., & Subedi, D. B. (2009). *What roles for business in post-conflict economic recovery? Perspectives from Nepal.* London: International Alert.

Amnesty International. (2002). *Nepal: Spiralling human rights crisis.* London. Retrieved from http://nepalconflictreport.ohchr.org/files/docs/2002-04-02_report_ai_eng.pdf.

Becker, J. (2007). *Child recruitment in Burma, Sri Lanka and Nepal.* Retrieved from https://www.files.ethz.ch/isn/45674/2007_Child_Recruitment.pdf.

Bennett, L. (2005, December 12–15). *Unequal citizens: Gender, caste and ethnic exclusion in Nepal.* Paper presented at the New Frontiers of Social Policy Conference, The World Bank, Arusha. http://www.k4health.org/sites/default/files/Gender,casteandethnicexclusioninNepal.pdf.

Bennett, L. (2006). *Unequal citizens: Gender, caste and ethnic exclusion in Nepal.* Kathmandu: The World Bank. Retrieved from http://documents.worldbank.org/curated/en/745031468324021366/Executive-summary.

Bhattarai, P. (2014). *Third-party coordination in conflict resolution: Views from Third-party practitioners in the maoist armed conflict of Nepal and the moro conflict of the philippines.* University of Otago.

Bougarel, X. (2006). The shadow of heroes: Former combatants in post-war Bosnia-Herzegovina. *International Social Science Journal, 58*(189), 479–490.

Brett, R., & Specht, I. (2004). *Young soilders: Why they choose to fight.* Colorado and London: Lynne Rienner.

Chamlagai, A. N. (2006). Maoist insurgency: An ideological diagnosis. In L. R. Baral (Ed.), *Nepal: Facetes of insurgency* (pp. 13–30). New Delhi: Adroit Publishers.

Coalition to Stop the Child Soldier. (2004). *Child soldier global report 2004.* London: Coalition to Stop the Child Soldier. Retrieved from http://www.essex.ac.uk/armedcon/story_id/child_soldiers_CSC_nov_2004.pdf.

Collier, P., & Hoeffler, A. (2002). *Greed and grievance in civil war.* Retrieved from http://economics.ouls.ox.ac.uk/12055/1/2002-01text.pdf.

CPNM. (1995). *Theoretical premises for the historic initiation of the people's war.* Retrieved from http://www.bannedthought.net/Nepal/UCPNM-Docs/1995/TheoreticalPremisesForPW-9509.pdf.

de Sales, A. (2003). The Kham Magar country Nepal: Between ethnic claims and Maoism. In D. Thapa (Ed.), *Understanding the Maoist movement of Nepal* (pp. 59–88). Kathmandu: Martin Chautrai.

Douma, P., Frerks, G., & Van de Goor, L. (1999). *Causes of conflict in third world: Synthesis report.* The Hague: Netherlands Institute of International Relations.

Eck, K. (2008, March 26–30). *Indoctrination in rebel recruitment: A mechanism for mass mobilization.* Paper presented at the 49th Annual International Studies Association Convention, San Francisco, USA. http://humansecuritygateway.com/documents/ISA_indoctrinationrebelrecruitment.pdf.

Eck, K. (2010). Recruiting rebels: Indoctrination and political education in Nepal. In M. Lawoti & A. K. Pahari (Eds.), *The Maoist insurgency in Nepal: Revolution in the twenty-first century* (pp. 33–51). New York: Routledge.

Elbadawi, I., & Sambanis, N. (2002). How much war will we see? Explaining the prevalence of civil war. *Journal of Conflict Resolution, 46*(3), 307–334. https://doi.org/10.1177/0022002702046003001.

Gates, S. (2002). Recruitment and allegiance: The microfoundation of rebellian. *Journal of Conflict Resolution, 46*(1), 111–130. https://doi.org/10.1177/0022002702046001007.

Gautam, S., Banskota, A., & Manachanda, R. (2001). Where there are no men: Women in the Maoist insurgency in Nepal. In R. Manachanda (Ed.), *Women, war and peace in South Asia: Beyond victimhoom and agency* (pp. 214–251). New Delhi: Sage.

Gellner, D. N., Pfaff-Czarnecka, J., & Whelpton, J. (Eds.). (2008). *Nationalism and ethnicity in Nepal.* Kathmandu: Vajra Publications.

Goodwin, J. (2001). *No other way out: States and revolutionary movements, 1945–1991.* Cambridge and New York: Cambridge University Press.

Gurung, H. B. (1998). *Nepal: Social demography and expression.* Kathmandu: New Era.

Hangen, S. (2009). *The rise of ethnic politics in Nepal: Democracy in the margins.* Hoboken: Routledge.

Hofer, A. (Ed.). (2004). *The caste hierarchy and the state in Nepal: A study of the Mulki Ain of 1854.* Kathmandu: Himal Books.

Hossain, M., Siitonen, L., & Sharma, S. (2006). *Development cooperation for conflict prevention and conflict resolution.* Helsinki: University of Helsinki.

Human Rights Server, (1997). *Hundreds of houses have been burnt and dozens are killed.* Retrieved from http://www.humanrights.de/doc_en/archiv/n/nepal/news/260200_hundreds_of_houses_burnt.htm?act=closearchivinfo.

ILO. (2005). *Dalits and labour in Nepal: Discrimination and forced labour.* Kathmandu: International Labour Organisation in Nepal.

Kc, S. (2003). *Nepal ma Communist Aandolan ko Itihas (History of Communist Movement in Nepal): Part 2.* Kathmandu: Bidhyarthi Pustak Bhandar.

Khanal, S. (2007). Committed insurgents, a divided State and the Maoist insurgency in Nepal. In M. Lawoti (Ed.), *Contentious politics and democratization in Nepal* (pp. 75–95). Los Angeles, London, New Delhi and Singapore: Sage.

Kievelitz, U., & Polzer, T. (2002). *Nepal country study on conflict transformation and peace building.* Eschborn, Germany. Retrieved from.

Kiran, C. (2003). Philosophical concept of Prachanda Path. Retrieved from http://www.bannedthought.net/Nepal/Problems-Prospects/k_conceptof_pp.html.

Kumar, D. (2006). Military dimension of the Maoist insurgency. In L. R. Baral (Ed.), *Nepal: Facets of Insurgency* (pp. 85–117). New Delhi: Adroit.

Lawoti, M. (2005). *Towards a democratic Nepal: Inclusive political institutions for a multicultural society.* New Delhi, London and Thousand Oak: Sage.

Lawoti, M. (2010). Ethnic dimensions of the Maoist insurgencies. In M. Lawoti & A. K. Pahari (Eds.), *Maoist insurgency in Nepal: Revolution in the twenty-first century* (pp. 135–155). London and New York: Routledge.

Leve, L. G. (2007). 'Failed development' and rual revolutions in Nepal: Rethinking subaltern consciousness and women empowerment. *Anthropological Quarterly, 80*(1), 127–172.

Mahat, R. S. (2005). *In defence of democracy: Dynamics, and fault lines of Nepal's political economy.* New Delhi: Adroit Publishers.

Marks, T. A. (2006). Ideology of insurgency: New ethnic focus or old Cold War distortions? *Small Wars and Insurgencies, 15*(1), 107–128. https://doi.org/10.1080/09592310410001677014.

McConnan, I., & Uppard, S. (2001). *Children—Not soldiers.* London: Save the Children.

Mehta, A. K., & Lawoti, M. (2010). Military dimensions of the "People's War": Insurgency and counter-insurgency in Nepal. In M. Lawoti & A. K. Pahari (Eds.), *The Maoist insurgency in Nepal: Revolution in the twenty-first century* (pp. 175–194). London and New York: Routledge.

Metsola, L. (2006). Reintegration of ex-combatants and former fighters: A lens into state formation and citizenship in Namibia. *Third World Quarterly, 27*(6), 1119–1135.

Muni, S. D. (2003). *Maoist insurgency in Nepal. The Challenge and the response.* New Delhi: Observer Research Foundation.

Murshed, S. M., & Gates, S. (2005). Spatial–Horizental inequality and the Maoist insurgency in Nepal. *Review of Development Economics, 9*(1), 121–134. https://doi.org/10.1111/j.1467-9361.2005.00267.x.

Nepal, K. (2005). *The Maoist service provision in parts of mid and far West Nepal*. Kathmandu: Centre for Professional Journalism Study.

Onesto, L. (2003). Report from the People's War. In D. Thapa (Ed.), *Understanding the Maoist movement of Nepal* (pp. 151–180). Kathmandu: Martin Chautari.

Pettigrew, J. (2004). Living between the Maoists and the army in rural Nepal. In M. Hutt (Ed.), *Himalayan people's war: Nepal's Maoist rebellion* (pp. 261–283). Bloomington and Indianapolis: Indiana University Press.

Saskiewicz, P. E. (2005). *The revolutionary armed forces of colombia—People's Army (FARC-EP): Marxist-Leninist insurgency or criminal enterprise?* (Master of Arts), Naval Post Graduate School, Monterey, California.

Sharma, K. (2006). The political economy of civil war in Nepal. *World Development, 34*(7), 1237–1253. https://doi.org/10.1016/j.worlddev.2005.12.001.

Sharma, S. (2004). The Maoist movement: An evolutionary perspective. In M. Hutt (Ed.), *Himalayan people's war: Nepal's Maoist rebellion* (pp. 38–57). Bloomington and Indianapolis: Indiana University Press.

Shneiderman, S., & Turin, M. (2004). Path to Jana Sarkar in Dolakha District: Towards an ethnography of Maoist Movement. In M. Hutt (Ed.), *Himalayan people's war: Nepal's Maoist rebellion* (pp. 79–111). Bloomington and Indianapolis: Indiana University Press.

Standing, K., & Parker, S. (2011). The effect of the 'people's war' on schooling in Nepal, 1996-2006. *Education, Citizenship and Social Justice, 6*(2), 181–195. https://doi.org/10.1177/1746197911410376.

Subedi, D. B. (2013). From civilian to combatant: Armed recruitment and participation in the Maoists' conflict in Nepal. *Contemporary South Asia, 21*(4), 429–443. https://doi.org/10.1080/09584935.2013.856868.

Subedi, D. B. (2014). *Post-conflict recovery and peacebuilding in Nepal: Exploration of economic and social reintegration of Maoist ex-combatants* (Doctoral Thesis), University of New England, NSW, Australia.

Thapa, D. (2012). The making of the Maoist insurgency. In S. v. Einsiedel, D. M. Malone, & S. Pradhan (Eds.), *Nepal in transition: From people's war to fragile peace* (pp. 37–57). New Delhi: Cambridge University Press.

Thapa, D., & Sijapati, B. (2005). *A Kingdom under siege: Nepal's Maoist insurgency, 1996–2003*. London: Zed Books.

Tiwari, C. K. (2001). *Maoist insurgency in Nepal: Internal dimensions* (Paper No. 187). Retrieved from http://www.southasiaanalysis.org/papers2/paper187.htm.

UN. (2006). *Report of the Secretary-General on children and armed conflict in Nepal*. New York. Retrieved from.

Upreti, B. R. (2009). *Nepal from war to peace: Legacies of the past and hopes for the future*. New Delhi: Adroit.

Whelpton, J., Gellner, D. N., & Pfaff-Czarnecka, J. (2008). New Nepal, new ethnicities: Changes since the mid 1990s. In D. N. Gellner, J. Pfaff-Czarnecka, & J. Whelpton (Eds.), *Nationalism and ethnicity in Nepal* (pp. xvii–xlviii). Kathmandu: Vajra Publications.

Wily, L. A., Chapagain, D., & Sharma, S. (2008). *Land reform in Nepal: Where is it coming from and where is it going?* Kathmandu: DFID Nepal. Retrieved from http://www.landcoalition.org/sites/default/files/publication/797/nepal_law_book.pdf.

CHAPTER 3

The Peace Process and Management of Maoist Arms and Armies

An interesting fact to note is that the Maoist armed conflict in Nepal was initiated at the time of an historical democratic change. In the 1990s, Nepal could not remain unaffected by the post-Cold War waves of what Samuel Huntington (1993, p. 40) calls "the third wave of democracy". The country transitioned from decades of the highly centralised and undemocratic *Panchayat* system with the absolute monarchy to a multi-party democracy with a constitutional monarchy in 1990. Within few years of the democratic system in the place, the country, however, confronted with an armed conflict, the Maoist revolution in the twenty first century.

With the three broad objectives of their armed resistance—to wipe out the capitalist class and the state system that had traditionally existed; to abolish the Monarchy[1] that protected and promoted feudalism; and to establish a democratic republic ruled by the people (Mahat, 2005)— the Maoists combined armed violence with political agendas and emancipatory rhetoric which appeared to look like revolutionary statebuilding through the use of violence. In other words, it was an attempt to control the state by capturing the state mechanisms and challenging state militarily to counter the legitimate use of force by the state (Bhattarai, 2014;

---

[1] There was an active Monarchy in Nepal until the 1990s. After the success of the People's Movement in 1990, the then King was ready to share power with parliamentary political parties and remain as a constitutional Monarch. However, the King still held some powers, such as Chief of Command of the then Royal Nepal Army.

© The Author(s) 2018
D. B. Subedi, *Combatants to Civilians*, Rethinking Peace and Conflict Studies, https://doi.org/10.1057/978-1-137-58672-8_3

Kievelitz & Polzer, 2002). Thus, to some extent, the armed conflict was an extension of politics by violent means.

Despite initial hope amongst the people that their lives would significantly improve after the restoration of multiparty democracy in 1990, the nascent democracy up until the time of the insurgency had failed to fulfil the expectations of the Nepalese people due to the lack of people-centric economic and development policies, a high level of political corruption, the unheard voices of people from disfranchised groups, and exclusion and discriminations based on caste, gender, ethnicity, and place of residence (Crossette, 2005; Kievelitz & Polzer, 2002; Sharma, 2009). Thus, as also noted in the previous chapter, the perceived and actual political failure in the multi-party system introduced in 1990 and its concomitant negative impacts on the devolution of development, good governance, and social inclusion were carefully chosen by the Maoists to politically radicalise and then mobilise poor, discriminated against and marginalised young people from the margins of the state (Subedi, 2013). The consequence was a bloody armed conflict for ten years, resulting in more than 13,000 deaths, more than 1500 forced disappearances, approximately 200,000 involuntary internal displacement and damages to the property worth billions of rupees (Upreti, 2009).

The recruitment of the People's Liberation Army (PLA) fighters and their ability to fight a ferocious war in the hilly and rough terrain of remote Nepal made it difficult for the parties to conflict, hence the PLA and the state military, to see a victory even in a distant future. This led to a perception, what Zartman (2001, p. 8) calls, 'mutually hurting stalemate' (MHS). The concept of MHS is a central tenants of the conflict ripeness theory which states that when the conflicting parties find themselves locked in situation from which they cannot achieve a victory, then the deadlock is painful to the conflict parties, albeit may be in unequal degrees, that they are likely to adopt an alternative policy option that could include third party intervention, mediation or peace negotiation (Zartman, 2001; Zartman & Berman, 1982). To a certain extent, the perception of MHS prompted the Maoists and the governments to engage in peace negotiations, although, as Subedi and Bhattarai (2017) argue, the peace process was also strategic on the parts of the actors of the conflict including the Maoists, facilitated by organisational and political opportunity structures that made the Comprehensive Peace Agreement (CPA) possible in 2006.

In war to peace transition, Disarmament, Demobilisation and Reintegration (DDR) programmes are often negotiated in a peace deal.

Because DDR of ex-combatants is inherently a political process that affects and is affected by processes and outcomes of post-conflict peacebuilding and statebuilding, it is agreed that understanding the complex relationship between the political economy of peace and DDR can provide us with better insights into how post-conflict politics can facilitate, but also impede, outcomes of a DDR programme (Bleie & Shrestha, 2012; de Zeeuw, 2008; Muggah, 2009; Özerdem, Podder, O'Callaghan, & Pantuliano, 2008; Subedi, 2014a).

This chapter first critically analyses the failed peace negotiations and the evolution of the peace agreement in Nepal. In the light of the peace process, the chapter then unpacks contentions and confrontations surrounding the management of Maoists arms and armies, with an exclusive focus on the mechanisms, management, processes, key actors, and their needs and interests with respect to DDR and the peace process.

From Failed Peace Negotiations to the Peace Agreement

Before the CPA was signed between the CPNM and the government on 21 September 2006, three rounds of peace talks had failed to yield a durable peace negotiation. The failure is ascribed partly to the lack of adequate preparations and also the lack of trust and confidence between the government and the Maoists (Upreti, 2006). When the Maoists began to control local areas by attacking on government buildings and police posts and forcefully displacing political opposition in the hills of western and mid-western regions, the government, for the first time, began to realise the need for a political dialogue in order to address the insurgency which was until then considered a law and order problem by the political elites in Kathmandu (Upreti, 2009). In the face of the difficulty in containing the insurgency and maintaining political and administrative existence of the government in the Maoist hinterlands, the then Nepali Congress Prime Minister Krishna Prasad Bhattarai, who headed the government after the 1999 election, formed a high level negotiation team led by a Nepali Congress (NC) party leader, Sher Bahadur Deuba. Although, the then Home Minister Ram Chandra Poudel had reportedly met the Maoist leaders and the government had also released some Maoists leaders from the prison, the peace talk could not mature partly due to internal political rifts in the ruling party, hence the NC, and also the lack of broader political support to the peace negotiation (Mishra, 2012).

In July 2001, the newly appointed Prime Minister Deuba declared a ceasefire and nominated a negotiation team to reinitiate the peace talks. The team held two rounds of talks with the Maoists, in Lalitpur and Bardia districts in August and September 2001 respectively. Although a third round of negotiation was scheduled for November in the same year, the CPNM in the meantime attacked an army barrack in Dang and ceased a large number of modern weapons, which significantly increased the Maoists' military capacity in the following years. The ceasefire collapsed. Rather than willing to genuinely engage in the peace talks, it appeared that the Maoists had used the ceasefire as tactic to consolidate its military strengths (Subedi, 2014c). Consequently and to some extent ironically, the first round of the peace talks intensified the conflict rather than mitigating it.

Lokendra Bahadur Chand replaced PM Deuba in October 2002. PM Chand then formed a new negotiation committee. The government committee and the CPNM signed the 22-point code of conduct (CoC), followed by the first round of negotiation meeting held in April 2003. A clause of the CoC would limit the movements of the military within five kilometres of army barracks (Mishra, 2012); a decision that would directly and indirectly favour the CPNM to expand its movement and control over the territories. Being under the pressure from the top military leaders, the newly crowned king Gyanendra did not like this very clause and eventually dismissed the PM. The peace process collapsed for the second time.

The political situation was becoming fluid, unstable and uncertain with many changes in the government between 2002 and 2006. Surya Bahadur Thapa was appointed as the new PM who replaced Lokendra Bahadur Chand. As soon as Thapa assumed the office, one of his priorities was to resume the peace talks with the Maoists. Accordingly, he appointed two peace negotiators, Kamal Thapa and Prakash Chandra Lohani. However, the Maoists responded to the call by demanding the government's commitment to implement the previous agreements (mainly the code of conduct) and release 300 Maoists cadres who were in the prison at that time (Mishra, 2012). The Maoists also stressed their desire to talk with the *Malik* (the master, hence the king), not with the king's representatives. This statement provides a testimony of the degree of centrality of power in the palace and a clue to who held the key to the political settlement. Nonetheless, two rounds of peace talked were held in Nepalgunj and Dang (Hapure village) in August 2003. In the meantime, the government military killed 18 Maoists and two civilians in Doramba village in the Ramechapp district (Subedi, 2014c).

Consequently, the Maoists quit the peace talks unilaterally. All out armed conflict resumed again.

Except the two civil society negotiators, Padma Ratna Tuladhar and Daman Nath Dhungana who had a low-key status mainly as an observer, the peace talks did not involve external negotiators. In the absence of external mediators, the climate of trust in the peace process was murky; both sides tended to maintain strategic and tactical positions and sought to utilise ceasefire either as power bargain or consolidate war-capacity.

When the armed conflict escalated with more confrontations and battles between the PLA and the state security forces, it coincided with the assassination of the entire family of the then king Birendra in June 2001. Prince Gyanendra was then crowned as the new king following the infamous royal massacre.

After ascending to the throne, king Gyanendra turned to be an ambitious ruler, willing to concentrate power in his hands by gradually involving in the direct ruling of the country. The new king dissolved the elected parliament in October 2002 and centralised the state power in the palace that turned the royal regime into a dictatorship, which further undermined multiparty democracy, freedom of speech, and civil liberty. He dissolved the parliament on the recommendation of the Prime Minister Sher Bahadur Deuba on 22 May 2002. The king then postponed the election of the local bodies scheduled in July in the same year. While the king's increasingly undemocratic moves began to turn political parties from allies to opponents of the palace, the king's increasing control over the then Royal Nepal Army (RNA) and mobilisation of the military to suppress the Maoist insurgency further antagonised the Maoists with the palace.

In the meantime, the mainstream political parties organised a "five party alliance" to stage collective protest against the king. Thus the changing landscape of realpolitik at the center sowed the seed for a struggle between democratic political parties and undemocratic palace, which lead to the mass uprising in 2006 (Sijapati, 2009; Subedi & Bhattarai, 2017). In the meantime, being mindful of potential risks that the king would face arising from the opposition of political parties, he attempted to take the political parties in confidence by reinstating parliament he had dissolved. Newly reinstated Prime Minister Shear Bahadur Deuba rallied to form an all-party government, reportedly in the instruction of the king, but failed to garner support from major political parties except the Communist Party of Nepal-United Marxist and Leninist

(CPNUML). The NC decided not to join the government but continued their protest on the streets for restoration of democracy. The NC termed the government as another conspiracy and the continuation of regressive action, and argued that the formation of the new government was yet another attempt to strengthen the king's autocratic regime by other means (Subedi & Bhattarai, 2017). As a result, there was a political deadlock and unfolding chaos, which provided motivations for the king to ban on the political parties and introduce an emergency on 1 February 2005.

The emergency resulted into mobilisation of the military throughout the country. This gave rise to increased numbers of arrests of the politicians, civil society leaders and journalists, and arbitrary detentions, tortures and violations of human rights by the state security forces (Amnesty International, 2002). The mobilisation of the military increased direct confrontation between the Maoists and the state security forces—a situation that in part forced the CPNM to rethink its war strategy. Consequently, in April 2005, the Maoists held the Plenum in Rolpa and decided to continue the military offensive strategy while at the same time support the Seven Party Allliance (SPA) in its nonviolent movement against the palace (Subedi & Bhattarai, 2017). The Rolpa Plenum is a notable example of the view that an armed group considers to adopt nonviolent strategy as some point of the armed struggle.

Several bilateral and multilateral meeting followed between Maoists and the SPA members. At the end, the political parties accepted to go for the election of the Constituent Assembly (CA)—a key demand that the Maoists raised as a bottom line to accept a peace negotiation—while Maoists decided to accept competitive democracy. Thus the strategic interest of the Maoists and the SPA converged in ways that resulted into signing of the 12-points agreements between them in November 2005 (Jha, 2014). The agreement, which was largely driven by a common enemy perception that is the commitment to fight a common enemy—the King and his direct rule—was the point of departure for the 2006 peace agreement.

The CPA and Management of Maoist Arms and Armies

The CPA of 2006 brought about a number of simultaneous changes in the dynamics of conflict and national level politics in the country: it ended the armed conflict, turned the CPNM from a rebellious organisation to a major political party, dethroned the monarchy, induced a discourse of social inclusion and social justice, created a wave of federalism, and established a foundation for a republican political system. With such historical and multiple changes, the conflict-ridden country of Nepal arrived at a critical juncture where demilitarisation of state and society through dismantling the structure of the PLA and reintegration of the PLA fighters was one of contentious peace agendas to be dealt in the ensuing peace process.

Nepal's CPA document is remarkably progressive in the sense that it has envisioned optimal transformation of the country in economic, security and political terms. In economic terms, it has envisioned economic transformation, scientific land reform and agrarian revolution in "New Nepal". In political terms, the CPA is a blue print that seeks to institutionalise social inclusion in political participation and political decentralisation in the form of federalism. In security term, the issues were more complex for the fact that the CPA provided guidance, in principle, for democratic civilian control over the forces, especially the military, which was until then largely under the direct control of the King who acted as the Supreme Commander of the RNA.

The political concern to bring the military as a potential spoiler of the peace process is amply reflected in the CPA document. It stipulates that the Council of Ministers shall control, mobilise and manage the Nepali Army (NA) in accordance with the new Military Act and the Interim Council of Ministers shall prepare and implement the detailed action plan for the democratisation of the NA on the basis of political consensus and the suggestions of the committee concerned of the Interim Legislature (GoN, 2006). Although democratisation of army was an ambiguous idea and in fact contested by the military establishment, democratisation would ideally include, among other things, to bring the military to a right size (although what would be a right size was never deliberated throughout the peace process) and democratic restructuring of the military in accordance with the principles of inclusion, democracy and human rights.

The CPA document raised equally grave concerns about the military structure of the CPNM and, therefore, included broad provisions for management of the Maoists arms and armies. This included the provisions to encamp the Maoist combatants in seven cantonments and store their arms and ammunitions within the cantonments sites, which were to be monitored by the United Nations Missions in Nepal (UNMIN) (GoN, 2006).

Mechanisms and Processes

Management of the Maoists arms and armies in the peace process was politically negotiated and was based largely on the consensus among the CPNM, key political actors, the government. These agreements were made at different times but most notably in the 22 Point Understanding between the CPNM and the SPA on 22 November 2005, the 25 Point Ceasefire CoC between the CPNM and Government on 25 May 2006, the 8 Point Agreement between CPNM and the SPA on 16 June 2006, and the Summit Meeting of the Seven Party Alliance and the CPN (Maoist) reached on 8 November, 2006.

Further, following the signing of the CPA, the CPNM and the government agreed to invite the United Nations (UN) to support and monitor the peace process. Accordingly, the government and CPNM sent separate invitations to the UN Secretary General, requesting the UN to support the peace process. The requests however included different expectations from the CPNM and the government. The government requested the UN take on the role to "decommission" the Maoists arms and armies. Contrarily the Maoists condemned the idea of "decommissioning" and instead requested that the UN carry out the role of a third-party monitor. These two different positions between the key actors of the peace process hints towards their growing misunderstanding at the beginning of the peace process.

In response, the UN Security Council passed the Resolution 1740 to mandate a small non-military political mission, the UNMIN, on 23 January 2007. The UNMIN was tasked with a mandate to (a) monitor management of arms and armed personnel of both sides, the government and the Maoists, through a Joint Monitoring Coordinating Committee (JMCC); (b) provide technical support for the planning, preparation and conduct of the election; and (c) provide a small team of electoral monitors to review all technical aspects of the electoral process.[2]

Following the peace agreement, the GoN and the CPNM also signed the Agreement on the Monitoring of the Management of Arms and Armies (AMMAA) on 28 November 2006. Officially, signing of the AMMAA marked the beginning of the DDR programme, as it expedited confinement of the Maoist Army and the NA into cantonments and army barracks respectively.

[2] See http://www.un.org/News/Press/docs/2007/sc8942.doc.htm.

The process of disarming and demobilisation of the PLA ex-combatants received momentum only when the UNMIN began verifying and registering the Maoist arms and armies in early 2007. The government set up the Special Committee (SC), chaired by the Prime Minister and represented by the major political parties, in October 2008. The SC was the highest authority entrusted with the responsibility of forging political consensus and agreements on contentious issues relating to arms and armies, as well as building modalities for adjustment and rehabilitation of the PLA combatants.

According to the provision made in the AMMAA, a JMCC was formed, consisting of nine members, which included a chair by an UNMIN representative, two Vice-Chairmen, one each from the PLA and the NA, and six members, two each, from the UN, PLA and NA. Its major functions were to assist the parties in implementing the AMMAA, to serve as a dispute resolution mechanism for any operational dispute and complaints about the AMMAA, and to assist in confidence building of the parties, particularly the PLA and NA. The Joint Monitoring Teams (JMTs), which comprised one international monitor and a monitor each from the PLA and NA, were deployed to assist the JMCC.

The UNMIN's mandate, which was extended three times between 2007 and 2010, ceased in January 2010. Upon the UNMIN's exit, its responsibility for monitoring and supervision of arms and armies shifted entirely to the Army Integration Special Committee (AISC) consisted of eight members from political parties including the Maoists. Headed by the prime minister, the AISC was the highest authority, which designed the modality of the rehabilitation and reintegration package as well as the integration of some of the PLA ex-combatants into the (NA). A technical committee was set up to assist the AISC with expertise and technical input to design integration modality and a reintegration scheme. But, as major political parties nominated the members of the technical committee, it was more political rather than technical.

Combatant Verification Process

Verification of ex-combatants is an important starting point for any DDR programme, as it determines intended target group and beneficiaries of DDR. In the Nepalese case, the verification process was carried out by the UNMIN, with support from registration experts of United Nations Development Programme (UNDP) and UNICEF child protection officers. Initially, when the CPNM consolidated the PLA combatants in seven cantonments and 21 satellite cantonments, 32,250 combatants were registered for verification. However, by the time the verification completed in Division One, almost 40% of the registered combatants were absent (Martin, 2012).

The verification process included scrutinising PLA identity cards, birth certificates and education certificates together with interviews with individual combatants. At the end of the verification process concluded by UNMIN in December 2007, a total of 4008 PLA ex-combatants were declared "disqualified" for either being minors (child soldiers) under eighteen years of age, or having been recruited by the Maoists after the signing of the cease fire agreement on 25 May 2006. Out of the total number of ex-combatants, 2973 were identified as minors or child soldiers, while 1035 were recruited after the cease-fire agreement. The "unverified" combatants, also called "disqualified" ex-combatants, were later collectively categorised as "Verified Minors and Late Recruits" (VMLR). A total of 19,602 PLA combatants had been verified while 8640 had left cantonments before the verification process.

Disarmament: Collection and Verification of Weapons

As part of the disarmament process, the UNMIN registered a total of 3475 weapons of the PLA and stored them in containers inside the Maoist cantonments in early 2007. The keys of the containers were, however, retained by the respective PLA divisional commanders. On the NA side, a total of 2855 weapons were put into containers and placed inside the army barracks. Like the PLA, the army retained the keys to the containers. Thus, disarmament in the Nepali context was applied to both parties to the conflict, the PLA and the NA. On the part of the Maoists, it was a "blanket disarmament", meaning it was the PLA, not individual combatants declared their weapons and registered for disarmament. The impact of this blanket disarmament on the peace process is discussed in the next chapter.

Although the state had managed to provide security for Maoist senior leaders, the CPNM demanded that their own security would be provided by the PLA. Accordingly, due to what was called a "dual security provision", a small number of armed combatants were mobilised outside the cantonments to provide security for top Maoist leaders.

The ex-combatants turned "security providers" were allowed to use the verified and registered weapons of the Maoist army; therefore, these ex-combatants were, in reality, never disarmed.

The Demobilisation Process

As part of the demobilisation process, the UNMIN screened the ex-combatants for verification in two rounds, first in March and then again in June 2007. In the first round, as also noted above, a total of 32,250 combatants were registered for verification. At the end of the second round, a total of 19,006 combatants (15,756 men and 3846 women) were declared qualified for entitlement associated with being recognised as ex-combatants, and a total of 4008 combatants were "disqualified", whereas, a total of 8640 ex-combatants did not appear for verification interviews in this second round. Both verified and unverified ex-combatants were housed in seven main cantonments and twenty-one satellite cantonments across the country (see Fig. 3.1 for the location of cantonments). It was a camp-based mass demobilisation. Its effectiveness and impacts on the peace process is discussed in the next chapter.

According to the understanding reached at the CPA, the verified combatants received regular allowances from the government, whereas the so-called "disqualified" ones, who were later termed VMLR, were later discharged from the cantonments (more about discharge and rehabiliation of VMLRs is discussed in Chapter 6 in this volume). Since the encamped ex-combatants were looked after by the state, the government then began financing two parallel armies from the state's coffers.

The Rehabilitation/Reintegration and Army Integration Process

On 1 November 2011, the major political parties, the NC, the CPNM, and the CPNUML, and a leader of the United Madhesi Democratic Front (UMDF)[3] signed the SPA that resolved the reintegration impasse, as the agreement came up with three different policy options. The ex-combatants were given the choice of options between a voluntary retirement with a cash package, a rehabilitation package, or integration into the NA. The cash package was categorised into four levels: those

---

[3] This is a constellation of the political parties from the Terai region of Nepal.

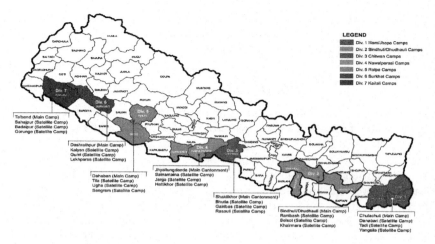

Fig. 3.1 Map of Nepal with locations of main and satellite cantonments (*Source* Designed by the author, 2013)

falling in the lowest rank received NRs 500,000[4] while the three remaining higher categories received NRs 600,000, NRs 700,000, and NRs 800,000, respectively, in ascending order.[5] The idea of rehabilitation consisted of an accompanied and facilitated rehabilitation package worth a minimum of NRs 600,000 to a maximum of NRs 900,000, including a provision for educational support and vocational training opportunities. The Secretariat of the AISC conducted an update and regrouping of the ex-combatants in November–December 2011. Its purpose was to register ex-combatants' choices against the available policy options. An officer in the AISC who was interviewed in January 2013 reported that by the end of the process, out of 19,602 verified combatants, 2456 ex-combatants were missing; therefore, only 17,146 ex-combatants presented at the time of the update and regrouping while ninety four deaths were reported. Out of these 17,146 ex-combatants, 15,602 opted for voluntary retirement, only six preferred to accept the rehabilitation package, and 1444 registered their interest in army integration (see Table 3.1 for facts and figures of the ex-combatants). As voluntary retirement

[4] One US dollar is roughly equivalent to Nepali rupees 100.
[5] Interview with a government official, Kathmandu, January 2013.

Table 3.1 Facts and figures of the Maoist ex-combatants (*Source* Fieldwork, 2012 and 2013)

Categories	Male	Female	Total
Number of combatants present during the first round of the registration process in 2007			32,250
Number of combatants who left the cantonment before the second round of verification in 2007			8640
Number of combatants who participated in UNMIN's second round of verification in 2007			23,610
Number of Minors (under the age of 18 by the time of the cease fire agreement on 25 May 2006)	1987	986	2973
Number of late recruits (recruited by the Maoists before the ceasefire agreement signed in May 2006)	804	231	1035
Total Number of Verified Minors and Late Recruits (VMLRs)	2791	1217	4008
Number of combatants verified by the UNMIN in December 2007	15,756	3846	19,602
Number of missing combatants during the re-grouping process in November and December 2011			2456
Number of deaths reported between 2007 and 2011			94
Number of combatants available for re-grouping	13,494	3558	17,052
Number of combatants opting for voluntary retirement			15,602
Number of combatants opting for army integration	1340	104	1444
Number of combatants opting for the rehabilitation package	6	0	6

and army integration dominated the final stage of DDR, reintegration and rehabilitation remained almost off the agenda in the entire DDR continuum, although a United Nations Interagency Rehabilitation Programme (UNIRP) was implemented in early 2010 targeting the disqualified or VMLR ex-combatants.

Management of the Arms and Armies: DDR or SSR?

The term DDR was deliberately excluded in the CPA, AMMAA and other documents pertaining to the peace process. Instead, *Byabasthapan ra Samayojan* (Management and Integration) was the official term used to refer to management the PLA combatants. The CPNM rejected the use of the term DDR in the peace process and proposed a new model consisted of "Camping, Monitoring and Reconstruction" (CMR) of the PLA (Ananta, 2006). Though this model was never officially formalised, it implies here that the Maoists were more interested in putting ex-combatants in camps (camping), monitoring (by a third party, preferably the UNMIN), and finally restructuring the army and the security sector so that the ex-combatants could be absorbed into the government security forces.

In the meantime, given the emphasis on restructuring the army, including combatant-army integration, the process to reintegrate ex-combatants in communities also involved some aspects of security sector reform (SSR). Therefore, management of ex-combatants could not be fully understood in insolation from a newly emerging discourse on SSR in post-conflict Nepal (see Acharya, 2009; Budathoki, 2009; Dhungana, 2007; Pandey, 2009; Upreti & Vanhoutte, 2009). Although SSR rather than DDR was top of the agenda on the peace negotiation table, the fact that only less than 8% of the total ex-combatants opted to reintegrate into the army (Subedi, 2014a) means that the management of ex-combatants eventually had limited significance from the SSR point of view. A statement by a political analyst who was interviewed in Kathmandu in January 2013 further elaborates this point:

> In the current context when army integration induced almost insignificant changes in restructuring and democratising the army, as it has been discussed, the final outcomes of ex-combatants' management has had too little significance as a SSR. Actually, after accomplishment of integration/reintegration, the debates about SSR and democratisation of the army have mysteriously disappeared from public as well as academic discussions.

Irrespective of the use of terms, the process and mechanism for the management of ex-combatants, nonetheless, involved all elements of the DDR programme, in one way or other. Therefore, the DDR programme in Nepal can be regarded as "unconventional" DDR for several reasons.

Firstly, contrary to many other contemporary DDR programmes, it did not significantly involve any external intervention or outside actors, although the UNMIN was involved in disarmament and demobilisation of ex-combatants as well as in monitoring and supervision of both the Maoist and government arms and armies. A context-specific modality was developed outside the established DDR frameworks. It is, however, equally important to note that a twelve point agreement reached between the SPA[6] and the CPNM in New Delhi, India, on 21

---

[6] The members to the SPA included the Nepali Congress (NC), Communist Party of Nepal United Marxist and Leninist (CPNMUML), Jana Morcha Nepal (People's Front), Nepal Workers and Peasants Party, Nepal Sadhbhawana Party (Anandi Devi), and Samyukta Bam Morach (United Leftist Front).

November 2005 was the foundation for the peace agreement (Einsiedel, Malone, & Pradhan, 2012). The Indian establishment facilitated the agreement; therefore, Nepal's peace process is arguably an "India led process". To this effect, it provides a reason to observe an outsider's (hence India) interest in the peace process, including rehabilitation and reintegration, plus army integration. As such, India's role and its influence must be acknowledged when studying Nepal's DDR programme. However, such engagement was subtle, invisible and did not involve direct intervention and participation (both in technical and financial terms). As a result, Nepal's DDR programme obviously did not comprise a large-scale formal peacebuilding mission led by outsiders, as has been the case in many DDR programmes elsewhere.

Secondly, though disarmament of the insurgent organisation and the provision of cantonments were organised, to a certain extent, in accordance with the United Nations Integrated DDR Standards (IDDRS) (Rynn & Green, 2008), it significantly lacked the third and perhaps most crucial element, reintegration, in the DDR continuum (this will be elaborated in chapter five and seven). Even in the case of disarmament, the weapons of the PLA were collected and stored inside the cantonments, meaning that the Nepali process followed "weapons storage" rather than an established disarmament model in which weapons are collected and decommissioned. Thirdly, there was extremely limited space for the engagement of the external actors; therefore, even though the leadership and institutional arrangement was obviously led by the national government, local ownership and inclusion remained questionable because of the fact that it was an extremely closed political process happening at the central level.

BUSINESS AND CIVIL SOCIETY ENGAGEMENT

A notable feature of liberal peacebuilding is that it aims to expand the space for the engagement of non-stake actors like civil society and the private sector. The assumption is that creating and supporting a functional civil society is a key to counter-balance the state's hegemonic behaviour and ultimately strengthen peace through market reforms and democratisation (Mac Ginty, 2011). Accordingly the business sector not only thrives under a liberal peace projects but also is also expected to assume bigger roles in pacebuilding, for instance, providing jobs and employment opportunities to ex-combatants. In reality, however, despite some exceptions, the private sector is often hesitant to recruit ex-combatants mainly due to some ex-combatants' records of violence in the past (International Alert, 2006).

In a similar vein, the function of the civil society as a watch dog of human rights, good governance and service is considered to play critical role in consolidation peace (Paffenholz & Spurk, 2006). However, in post-conflict societies, which are often divided along political, ethnic and ideological lines, it would be almost impossible to find a neutral and impartial civil society. In a country like Nepal where the civil society also competes to control political space, colluding with politicl parties, defining the civil society and its characteristics becomes rather complicated in Nepal. The liberal peacebuilding projects often tend to engage with non-government organisations (NGO), both local and international, which function as a synonymous of the civil society. However, it can be contended that NGO-isation of the civil society only takes a reductionist view.

Regardless of the ambiguities and criticism associated with the roles of civil society and the private sector, their role in Nepal's elite-led peace process was remarkably side-lined. Apart from some private vocational training centres involved in providing skill development trainings to VMLRs under the UNIRP (Subedi, 2014b), the business sector and the civil society was not given space to play facilitating roles in the DDR programme. In fact, inclusion of civil society and the private sector in planning and implementing the DDR could have been desirable, but it was almost non-existent.

UNMIN's Role as an External Actor

Unlike a fully-fledged military mission, the UNMIN was a small political mission with a limited mandate. However, from the beginning, the public, including the mainstream political parties, had high expectations from the UNMIN. A mismatch between the expectations and the UNMIN's narrow mandate made the presence of this sole international agency in the peace process unpopular from the very beginning. Between 2007 and 2011, upon the request from the GoN, the UN Security Council extended the UNMIN's tenure seven consecutive times.[7] However, when the CPNM-led government refused to extend their term, the

---

[7] Interview with a staff in the Army Integration Special Committee Secretariat, Kathmandu, December 2011.

UNMIN departed in January 2011, leaving behind a controversial history of its engagement in the Nepali peace process. Some respondents stated that the UNMIN would have needed to be more prudent in recognising and dealing with political sensitivities while engaging with the former insurgent organisation, such as in the case of verifying PLA ex-combatants. A number of respondents, however, asserted that the UNMIN's popularity was also, to a certain extent, hampered by the political parties' differences in understanding the UNMIN's role in the peace process. More discussion about why UNMIN's role was either unpopular or was controversial is provided in Chapter 5 in this volume.

National and local ownership is always a crucial issue in DDR programmes, partly because DDR programmes are often led by external actors with very limited buy-in from insidious actors. From the ownership point of view, the UNMIN's exit created an opportunity for the government and key political actors to play more critical and responsible roles in DDR. However, several non-combatant interviewees in Kathmandu expressed that the UNMIN's exit, in the meantime, marked an absence of a credible external actor that could at least leverage some moral pressure to concerned political actors, both the Maoists and the opposition, to reach an agreement on reintegration in a timely manner. "After UNMIN's departure, a possibility of benefiting from the UN's technical expertise on integration and reintegration virtually ended", said a NGO worker in Kathmandu.[8] In the absence of the UNMIN, the Maoists also felt more vulnerable, particularly from the risk of the state reneging on them. Yet, there was a counter argument in the civil society circle in Kathmandu where some people thought that UNMIN's presence would not be necessary, especially given the fact that it was increasingly unpopular in later days because of its pro-active involvement and influence in political decisions (this dynamic will be elaborated later).

CONCLUSIONS

This chapter has situated DDR of Maoist ex-combatants in the historical context of war to peace transition in Nepal. The 2006 CPA was an outcome of the strategic choice by the mainstream political parties or

---

[8] Interviewed in November 2011.

the SPA and the CPNM, primarily driven by their desire to fight the common enemy—the royal palace. This context suggests a view that the peace process in Nepal was highly political process in which management of the PLA combatants became a highly centralised process. An immediate impact of the political peace process could be seen as the tensions between the government (including major political parties) and the CPNM regarding whether managing ex-combatants would follow an DDR model or SSR model.

Although the term DDR was never used in the key documents in the peace process, managing PLA combatants included several aspects of a standard DDR programme. Disarmament partly followed weapon collection although it was a blanket disarmament. Demobilisation included cantonments, which aimed to facilitate collective demobilisation of those confined in the cantonments. In spite of the reintegration programme included a provision of a reintegration package, an overwhelming number of ex-combatants preferred the cash option. Thus the combination of different options including the cash option, army integration and a reintegration package at least two effects. On the one hand, it reflected how the DDR was politicised, that tended to pacify ex-combatants and depoliticise DDR rather than transforming causes of conflict and drivers of combatant recruitment. On the other hand, management of Maoists arms and armies appeared to look like a "unconventional DDR programme", designed partly incorporating the elements of the DDR model as developed in the UNIDDRs and partly it adopted a so-called homegrown model emerged out of political negotiations.

The discussion made in this chapter begs a question: how did the politics in war to peace transition affect management of Maoist arms and armies? The next section takes a closer look at this question.

REFERENCES

Acharya, N. (2009). The Nepalese Army. In B. Sapkota (Ed.), *The Nepali security sector: An almanac* (pp. 121–138). Geneva: Geneva Centre for Democratic Control of Armed Forces (DCAF) and National Peace Campaign (NPC).

Amnesty International. (2002). *Nepal: Spiralling human rights crisis*. London. Retrieved from https://www.amnesty.org/en/documents/asa31/016/2002/en/.

Ananta. (2006, August 20). *Hatiyar Byavasthapan Ko Bahas Ra Rajnitik Nikas Baare* [Debates on arms management and political outcomes]. Sanshleshan.

Bhattarai, P. (2014). Third-party coordination in conflict resolution: Views from third-party practitioners in the Maoist armed conflict of Nepal and the moro conflict of the Philippines. University of Otago.

Bleie, T., & Shrestha, R. (2012). *DDR in Nepal: Stakeholder politics and implications for reintegration as a process of disengagement*. Tromso: Centre for Peace Studies, University of Tromso.

Budathoki, S. (2009). Mainstreaming the security sector reform agenda in Nepal. In R. Bhattarai & R. Cave (Eds.), *Changing security dynamics in Nepal* (pp. 39–65). Kathmandu: Saferworld/Nepal Institute for Policy Studies (NIPS).

Crossette, B. (2005). Nepal: The politics of failure. *World Policy Journal, 22*(4), 69–76.

de Zeeuw, J. (Ed.). (2008). *From soldiers to politicians: Transforming rebel movements after civil war*. Boulder and London: Lynne Rienner.

Dhungana, S. K. (2007). Security sector reform and peacebuilding in Nepal: A critical reflection. *Journal of Peacebuilding & Development, 3*(2), 70–78.

Einsiedel, S. v., Malone, D. M., & Pradhan, S. (2012). Introduction. In S. v. Einsiedel, D. M. Malone, & S. Pradhan (Eds.), *Nepal in transition: From people's war to fragile peace* (pp. 1–36). Cambridge and New York: Centre on International Cooperation (CIC) and Cambridge University Press.

GoN. (2006, November 21). *Comprehensive peace accord concluded between the government of Nepal and the Communist Party of Nepal (Maoist)*. Kathmandu: Government of Nepal.

Huntington, S. (1993). *The third wave: Democratization in the late twentieth century* (Vol. 4). Norman: University of Oklahoma Press.

International Alert. (2006). *Local business, local peace: The peacebuilding potentials of the domestic private sector*. London: International Alert.

Jha, P. (2014). *Battles of new republic*. New Delhi: Aleph.

Kievelitz, U., & Polzer, T. (2002). *Nepal country study on conflict transformation and peace building*. Eschborn, Germany. Retrieved from http://nepalconflictreport.ohchr.org/files/docs/2002-00-00_report_gtz_eng.pdf.

Mac Ginty, R. (2011). Hybrid peace: How does hybrid peace come about? In S. Campbell, D. Chandler, & M. Sabaratnam (Eds.), *A liberal peace? The problems and practices of peacebuilding* (pp. 209–225). London and New York: Zed Books.

Mahat, R. S. (2005). *In defence of democracy: Dynamics and fault lines of Nepal's political economy*. New Delhi: Adroit.

Martin, I. (2012). The United Nations and support to Nepal's peace process: The role of the UN mission in Nepal. In S. v. Einsiedel, D. M. Malone, &

S. Pradhan (Eds.), *Nepal in transition* (pp. 201–231). Cambridge and New York: Centre on International Cooperation and Cambridge University Press.

Mishra, B. P. (2012). *Revisiting the Nepalese peace process*. Kathmandu: Human Development and Peace Campaign (HUDEP) Nepal.

Muggah, R. (Ed.). (2009). *Security and post conflict reconstruction: Dealing with fighters in the aftermath of war*. London and New York: Routledge.

Özerdem, A., Podder, S., O'Callaghan, S., & Pantuliano, S. (2008). *Reinsertion assistance and the reintegration of ex-combatants in war to peace transitions* (Thematic Working Paper 4). Bradford: Center for International Coopearation and Security, Bradford University.

Paffenholz, T., & Spurk, C. (2006). *Civil society, civic engagement, and peacebuilding*. Social Development Paper no. 36. The World Bank. Retrieved from http://siteresources.worldbank.org/INTCPR/Resources/WP36_web.pdf.

Pandey, N. N. (2009). Security sector reforms in Nepal: If not now, when? *South Asian Survey, 16*(2), 253–271. https://doi.org/10.1177/097152310901600206.

Rynn, S., & Green, O. (2008). *Disarmament, demobilization and reintegration in Nepal: Mini case study*. Centre for International Cooperation and Security.

Sharma, R. K. (2009). *Changing realities and challenges for the peace process of Nepal. 2, 25*. Paper presented on Globalisation and Peace Building 2006. Swedish Network of Peace, Conflict and Development Research, Sweden.

Sijapati, B. (2009). *People's participation in conflict transformation: A case study of Jana Andolan II in Nepal*. Kathmandu: Future Generations Graduate School and Social Science Baha.

Subedi, D. B. (2013). From civilian to combatant: Armed recruitment and participation in the Maoists' conflict in Nepal. *Contemporary South Asia, 21*(4), 429–443. https://doi.org/10.1080/09584935.2013.856868.

Subedi, D. B. (2014a). Dealing with ex-combatants in a negotiated peace process: Impacts of transitional politics on the DDR programme in Nepal. *Journal of Asian and African Studies, 49*(6), 672–689. https://doi.org/10.1177/0021909613507537.

Subedi, D. B. (2014b). Discontents and resistance of 'unverified' ex-combatants and challenges to their rehabilitation in Nepal. *Agrarian South: Journal of Political Economy, 3*(2), 203–237.

Subedi, D. B. (2014c). *Post-conflict recovery and peacebuilding in Nepal: Exploration of economic and social reintegration of Maoist ex-combatants* (Doctoral). University of New England.

Subedi, D. B., & Bhattarai, P. (2017). The April uprising: How a nonviolent struggle explains the transformation of an armed conflict in Nepal. *Journal of Peacebuilding & Development, 12*(3), 85–97.

Upreti, B. R. (2006). *From armed conflict to the peace process*. New Delhi: Adroit.

Upreti, B. R. (2009). *Nepal from war to peace: Legacies of the past and hopes for the future.* New Delhi: Adroit.

Upreti, B. R., & Vanhoutte, P. (2009). Security sector reform in Nepal: Challenges and opportunities. In H. Born & A. Schnabel (Eds.), *Security sector reform in challenging environments* (pp. 165–187). Geneva: LIT Verlag.

Zartman, W. I. (2001). The timing of peace initiatives: Hurting stalemates and ripe moments. *The Global Review of Ethnopolitics, 1*(1), 8–18.

Zartman, W. I., & Berman, M. (1982). *The practical negotiator.* New Haven: Yale University Press.

CHAPTER 4

The Dilemma of DDR

This chapter examines the dilemma of Disarmament, Demobilisation and Reintegration (DDR) by analysing the relationship between transitional politics and the outcomes of the DDR programme. In particular, three major themes are discussed. These include "power-sharing, fragmented politics and conflicting needs and interests of the political actors", "vagueness of the peace agreement documents" and "the Maoists' political will to participate in DDR", and their effects on the process and outcomes of DDR.

DDR is inherently a political process; therefore understanding the complex relationship between politics of peace in a transitional phase and DDR can provide us with better insights into how post-conflict politics can facilitate, but also impede, outcomes of a DDR programme (de Zeeuw, 2008; Muggah, 2009; Özerdem, Podder, O'Callaghan, & Pantuliano, 2008; Subedi, 2014). The characteristics of politics in war to peace transition, including the dynamics of power sharing between key political actors, and the process and outcomes of political negotiation for peace can have significant impacts on how ex-combatants are disarmed, demobilised and reintegrated. Ball and van de Goor (2006), therefore, argue that a DDR programme should be tailored to the local political context. In a similar fashion, Knight (2008) suggests that it is important to understand DDR as a continuation of the political dialogue, not just a programmatic undertaking.

A DDR programme may work well if all the key actors involved have a shared vision of the agreed outcome of a DDR programme,

© The Author(s) 2018
D. B. Subedi, *Combatants to Civilians*, Rethinking Peace and Conflict Studies, https://doi.org/10.1057/978-1-137-58672-8_4

especially if this happened at the time of the peace negotiation (Berdal & Ucko, 2009). It is essential for a DDR programme to be clear about whether it is intending to tackle post-conflict security issues, whether it is just a condition of peace agreement implementation or is DDR also geared towards contributing to post-conflict peacebuilding. Unlike peace agreement implementation, peacebuilding takes on a holistic approach to peace and seeks to address both direct and structural causes of violence (Galtung, 1996). Building a common understanding amongst the key political actors about a shared outcome for DDR may require political flexibility and negotiating capacity. However, such flexibility may be rare in a contentious transitional political setting. It may not be possible without strong political will (Rolston, 2007), which, according to Berdal (1996) is a chief criterion for the success of a DDR programme.

Political will, nonetheless, is a dynamic concept that might keep on changing along the line of changes taking place in terms of power configuration in the post-peace negotiation period. Perhaps more importantly, political will can be strategic and tactical, which can be determined by how power is distributed among key actors and the extent to which the former insurgent organisation is provided space in power sharing and political processes (Berdal & Ucko, 2009). This suggests to look at the dynamics of power-sharing as an important variable in understanding the linkages between transitional politics and DDR. Power-sharing is a complex concept, which often has its contextual meaning and significance. For the purpose of this chapter, the notion of power-sharing explained by Glassmyer and Sambanis (2008) is relevant. They describe power-sharing as a formal arrangement intended to distribute political positions, and it also entails a "sharp departure from previously exclusionary systems of political participation, if the new system formally includes minority groups associated with the rebels to participate in elections where previously this was not allowed" (Glassmyer & Sambanis, 2008, p. 371).

If the DDR programme is conceived at the time of peace negotiations, it is more likely to generate key political actors' willingness and commitment to DDR (Berdel & Ucko, 2009). Nevertheless, Muggah and Baare (2009) argue that inclusion of the provision of DDR in a peace document does not necessarily mean that the parties involved in the peace negotiation may remain committed to DDR. As Muggah and Baare (2009) and Muggah, Berdal, and Torjesen (2009) argue, changes in strategic needs and interests of DDR actors, the insurgent organisation and the shift in the balance of power over time, might significantly determine the government, political actors and insurgent organisation's level of interest, will, and commitment to DDR. In practice, as a peace process unfolds, the degree of political understanding and the culture of consensus building by actors involved can be altered by the changing dynamics of power and power-sharing between and within key political actors. Therefore, understanding the shifting patterns of strategic and tactical needs and interests of key political actors provides useful insights into the whole situation, enabling comprehension of the way these actors support, or do not support, the processes of a DDR programme.

A fundamental problem regarding the political will and commitment to DDR, particularly on the part of an insurgent organisation, is the security dilemma associated with the giving up of arms and also other accompanying perceived security threats (Muggah et al., 2009). Glassmyer and Sambanis (2008, p. 365) describe this as a problem of "time-inconsistency of a peace agreement", which refers to a situation where the demobilised combatants can run the risk of being reneged on by the government; therefore, unless a strong and credible security guarantee is available, a rebel organisation might not be fully committed to disarm and demobilise its combatants. In the absence of a credible security guarantor, disarmament and demobilisation reduces the power and bargaining capacity of an insurgent organisation; therefore, it can cause an attitudinal problem which may result in an insurgent organisation's limited will and commitment to surrender all of its weapons and demobilise all of its combatants (Glassmyer & Sambanis, 2008). While such an attitudinal problem continues to undermine the success of DDR and poses a threat to a peace process, Torjesen and MacFarlane (2009) argue that enabling the armed group to hold onto their weapons provides them with security insurance, and this is likely to increase their motivation and commitment to participate in a DDR programme.

Alongside the DDR programme, many peace agreements have a provision to integrate ex-combatants into the state security forces (in short "integration"). In the Asian context, former combatants were integrated into the state security forces in the Philippines and East Timor (Hall, 2009). Integration has become a strategy to avert agreement failure and address an insurgent organisation's attitudinal and commitment problem (Walter, 2002). Glassmayer and Sambanis (2008, p. 365), who call this strategy a "self-enforcing" agreement, argue, however, that

that rebel-military integration is essential but not a sufficient strategy to enhance an insurgent organisation's will and commitment to permanently terminate armed conflict. They argue that ex-combatants' integration into the state security forces mainly serves an economic function in resource poor countries, as integration can create jobs for ex-combatants, but this may not necessarily build trust.

A fundamental contradiction, however, is that while DDR involves politics in one way or other, its ultimate goal includes social and economic outcomes such as how ex-combatants rebuild relationships with their families, relatives and communities and how they are able undertake economic activities such as jobs and entrepreneurships. Political outcomes of DDR programmes; however, can be strategic, which may not necessarily strengthen social and economic outcomes expected by ex-combatants and their families from a reintegration process. As this volume shows, when political processes of DDR do not achieve social and economic outcomes, the DDR programme not only become ineffective but also creates tensions between ex-combatants and the state.

Power Sharing and DDR Dilemma

The question of how political power of key actors, and power sharing between them influences the outcomes of a peace process provides an important analytical lens to understand how ex-combatants are dealt with in war to peace transition.

As discussed in the previous section, driven by the perception of the "common enemy"—the palace, a functional alliance between two friends, the Seven Party Alliance (SPA) and the CPNM, was instrumental in forging a culture of political consensus that culminated in the peace agreement in 2006. The way the Maoists joined the interim government in April 2007 is an example of how power-sharing and consensus-building functioned in the early days of the peace process. Similarly, the Interim Constitution of Nepal 2007 formalised consensus politics; for instance, several articles of the Constitution made a provision to select a key position, such as the prime minister as decided upon "political consensus" and "mutual understanding" among key political parties. As such, many political actors tended to interpret much of the political process between 2006 and 2015, when the New Constitution was promulgated, politically according to the spirit of consensus building as stipulated in many peace documents including the Comprehensive Peace Agreement (CPA), the Interim Constitution and various agreements between key political actors.

The culture of consensus was, however, gradually weakening as the parties entered into the peace process. One such issue that fragmented political consensus immediately after the peace process was the management of Maoist arms and armies. For instance, the Nepali Congress (NC) and CPNUML would want to separate the Maoist arms and armies before the Constitution Assembly (CA) election that was planned to set up a new Assembly in which the CPNM was going to contest for the first time. On the other hand, CPNM would want an election before disarming their force—the People's Liberation Army (PLA). The question of power was central to their differing positions. For the NC and CPNUML, a CA election with the PLA still heavily armed was a big threat, while for the CPNM, the PLA was still a major source of power. Apart from the question of power, the contention around this issue also reveals fragility of political trust among key actors.

The other issue of distrust relates to dealing with the palace in the post-CPA period. Perceiving the palace and its loyal army as a threat, the CPNM wanted to formally abolish the monarchy and declare the country a Republic before the CA election scheduled for November in the same year.[1] Yet, the SPA in the coalition government wanted the elected government that would be formed after the election to make a decision on this critical issue. Despite the fact that the SPA collaborated with the CPNM, the SPA perhaps held the view that removing the monarchy, who was then the supreme commander of the army, before the CA would antagonise the military that might have serious impacts on the election and, in a worst case scenario, could potentially jeopardise the peace process. As a result of the unfolding climate of distrust, the CPNM left the consensus-based coalition government in September 2007. It was because of these two issues that the CA election was postponed twice before being finally held much later on 15 April 2008. These incidences had a considerable effect on the peace process as they had sowed seeds of suspicion, which subsequently evolved into an erosion of trust between the Maoists and the SPA.

Political cooperation and consensus-based power-sharing continued to disintegrate after the CA election, which altered the balance of power

---

[1] The election was postponed then and finally held only on 15 April 2008.

in the national political landscape. This was because the outcome of the election formally transformed the Maoists from being a former insurgent organisation to becoming the largest political party after the 2008 CA election. The election resulted in the scaling down of two of the previously large parties, the NC and the CPNUML, to second and third positions in the Constitution Assembly respectively.

In the meantime, the political change induced by 2006 *Jana Andolan* II established the discourse of social inclusion in the national politics, which gave rise to social and political movements led by ethnic organisations and indigenous groups. The political space created by the discourse of social inclusion was quickly dotted by fringe political parties. The political movement that erupted in the Terai in 2007 seeking greater political inclusion of the Madhesi people in the national polity ended up with a promise of federalism to the leaders from Terai/Madesh by the then Prime Minister Girija Parasad Koirala. Thus the growing political space in the margins of the state facilitated to establish new regional parties drawn from the Terai, which then became decisive political actors in national politics particularly between the first and second CA elections. In the meantime, formation of a new alliance by the Terai-based parties, known as the United Madhesi Democratic Front (UMDF), increased the collective bargaining power of these parties and diminished the strength of the SPA in the national politics.

Following the first CA election in 2008, there was a lack of an absolute majority by any party, which needed to form a government. The lack of majority in the CA led to increasing power bargaining that made the transitional politics remarkably vulnerable to the frequent making and breaking of governments. For instance, since the first post-CA government formed by the CPNM in August 2008, eight subsequent coalition governments and one interim government under the chairmanship of the Chief Justice were formed between 2008 and 2017.

The instability of governments after 2008 CA election had a discernible effect to the peace process including management of the Maoists arms and armies. To clarify, as a ramification of alternation in the balance of power represented in the CA, the power-sharing mechanism that existed up until the CA election and facilitated consensus building around the peace process all of a sudden shifted to power contestation in the post-CA period. As a result, inter-party contests for power sharing increased, deflecting political attention away from the peace process and the political compromises needed for timely accomplishment of the reintegration and rehabilitation of ex-combatants.

A growing number of intra-party rifts and factions was another dimension present at the time, which repeatedly made political power-sharing a contentious issue. As a result, the culture of consensus-building among key political parties, which was a driving force behind the peace process until the first CA election in 2008, began to wither away. In this regard, the NC had two factions led by the former Prime Minister, Sher Bahadur Deuba, and President Sushil Koirala. The CPNUML was also divided between two factions, with each being led by the President and former PM, Madhav Kumar Nepal, and the former Deputy Prime Minister, Khadga Prasad Oli. The Maoists were ideologically divided between the establishment faction and hard-line faction led by President Puspa Kamal Dahal (Prachanda) and the Vice-President, Kiran Vaidhya, respectively, who officially split off into two parties in June 2012.[2] Ideologically, the hard-line faction had minimum faith in constitutional politics; whereas, the establishment faction had increasingly started to accept the norms of democratic republicanism. The division in the Madhesh-based parties was rather extreme. A total of six Madhesh-based parties from the Terai were registered with the Electoral Commission at the time of the CA election in 2008. The Madhesh-based parties have, however, fragmented into eighteen splinter parties as of July 2012. Intra-party rifts of an unprecedented scale and proliferation of new political actors had ultimately resulted in further conflicts of interests that had hampered the smooth process of navigating the peace process. Rather, such divisions had remained one of the major causes of battle for making and breaking governments. For example, after the resignation of the CPNUML Prime Minister, Madhav Kumar Nepal in June 2010, the parliament could not elect a new prime minister for another six months even after voting up to seventeen times in the parliament. Such a delay provided testimony to the divided politics within Nepal and how it had shifted attention away from the peace process, including reintegration and rehabilitation of ex-combatants, to power bargaining.

---

[2] A journalist interviewed in Dhangadi, in December 2011 further said that there are two other small factions in the Maoists. These factions are led by Vice-President Dr. Baburam Bhattari and the Vice president Narayan Kaji Shrestha. At present both groups are within Prachanda's establishment faction.

Thus, the DDR dilemma was an outcome of the changing landscape of power sharing, inter-partly contestation for power and intra-party political rifts in the national politics after the 2008 CA election.

Conflicting Needs, Interests and Priorities and the DDR Dilemma

Conflicting needs, interests and priorities of the key political actors further marred the culture of compromise among them. For instance, for the NC, the CPNUML and some Terai-based parties, completion of rehabilitation of the ex-combatants and dissolution of the PLA were preconditions for moving to the next step of the peace process. The dominant perception of threat that underpins this sort of precondition was that unless the PLA is demobilised and rehabilitated, it would robustly empower the CPNM and always present a security threat to the peace process.

By contrast, for the CPNM, retaining the PLA until finalisation of a new draft of the constitution and agreeing on the modality of state restructuring (based on the principle of federalism) were strategic priorities. The Maoists' willingness to accomplish reintegration and rehabilitation of the ex-combatants only after completing other aspects of the peace process was driven by their deteriorating confidence in the peace process and lack of trust in its opponents who were then running the government. The political psychology of the NC and CPNUML was that the CPNM's sweeping victory in the 2008 CA election and its increasing political power in the national and local political spaces could ultimately threat the formers' political existence. The CPNM's rejection of the dissolving of the PLA until what they called the "logical end" of the peace process also engendered deep suspicion towards the Maoists' intention and commitment to a democratic political culture.

Amidst growing suspicion and lack of trust, sharp political differences over a modality of combatant-army integration sparked contentious debates. For instance, the CPNM relentlessly pushed for integration as maximum number of ex-combatants as possible into the Nepal Army (NA), rather than reintegrating them into the communities. Conversely, other key political parties preferred to keep the numbers integrated into the army to a minimum. As net collateral damage, these differing positions made the DDR programme dysfunctional, which, in turn, caused the ex-combatants to languish in cantonments for more than five years. In fact, until the seven-point agreement signed on 1 November 2011 created a breakthrough in releasing ex-combatants from the cantonments, the conflicting needs, interests and priorities of key political actors regarding the process and outcomes of DDR was a bottle neck to dealing with the ex-combatants effectively and timely in the peace process.

Strategic Political Will and Continuation of Conflict

Having signed the CPA, the CPNM had officially expressed its willingness to disarm, demobilise and reintegrate its combatants; however, several unfolding incidents demonstrated that the CPNM was caught up in a dilemma about participating in the DDR process. For instance, assuming that a conventional DDR programme would turn the combatants into civilians in the long-run through rehabilitation and reintegration, the Maoists did not accept the unfolding process as part of a DDR programme. Perceiving that a DDR programme would lead to neutralising and dismantling their armed forces like a defeated rebel group (Gautam, 2009), the CPNM favoured Security Sector Reform (SSR) and army integration.

Combatant-army integration, however, would require the CPNM to redefine its relationship with its erstwhile enemy—the army—and ascertain that the army was under the civilian control. Therefore, in the name of civilian control of the army, as soon as the CPNM headed the government after the CA election in 2008, the prime minister, who was also the head of the PLA in the recent past, sacked the army chief, General Rukmangat Katwal, in May 2009, and replaced him with General Kul Bahadur Khadka, who was more loyal to the Maoists. Thus the rhetoric of civilian control used to contain the military resurfaced as the continuation of conflict between the PLA and the army. Also at the heart of the entire issue was the question of the future of PLA. The top leaders of the NA, especially the Chief of the Army Staff (CoAS) General Katwal, were strongly opposing integration of any Maoist combatants in the ranks and file of the military (Jha, 2014; Subedi, 2014). On the other hand, the CPNM would want to install a military leadership, which would be more flexible to facilitate and in fact welcome planned combatant-army integration process in line with the demand of the CPNM.

The decision was, however, technically faulty, because, according to the provision in the Interim Constitution, the decision to sack the Chief of the Army should have been passed by a majority in the Council of Ministers. But, with the intention of staying out of the controversial decision, the CPNUML ministers in the coalition government headed by the CPNM boycotted the meeting. Prime Minister Prachanda continued with the decision to sack the army chief even if he failed to secure majority support in the meeting of the Council of Ministers. In response, all other eighteen parties appealed to President Ram Baran Yadav to step up and scrap the prime minister's decision. Adhering to the constitutional provision, the president instantly reinstated the army chief, leaving the Maoists' attempt to take control of the army unfulfilled. The Maoist-led government's inability to shake the leadership of the army and the president's bold action made the CPNM further suspicious and insecure about its potential rival constituencies. In effect, this further demotivated the CPNM to fully participate in the DDR programme.

From the beginning of the peace process, there were a considerable number of highly radical voices within the Maoist party, which defined the peace agreement as "historical mistake" on the part of the CPNM.[3] Such radical voices coming from different layers of the Maoist party including from the PLA was putting pressure to the Maoist leadership to keep possibility of "protracted people's war" open in order to capture the state. It was also partly because of this intra-party pressure that the CPNM was not fully committed and motivated to enter into the DDR programme until late 2011.

The Peace Documents: Vagueness and Lack of a Shared Outcomes Relating to Ex-combatants

The CPA and the Interim Constitution of Nepal are the two guiding documents that provide a basis for navigating the peace process. Section Four of the CPA and Clause 146 of the Interim Constitution of Nepal 2007 stipulate that the Council of Ministers should form a special committee to supervise, integrate and rehabilitate the combatants of the Maoist Army, and also states that the functions, duties and powers of the committee should be determined by the Council of Ministers. These historical documents, however, failed to provide clear guidelines or a framework and timeframe for reintegration and rehabilitation.

---

[3] Interview with an ex-combatant in Dhangadi, Kailali, December 2011.

The key political parties involved in striking the peace deal might have deliberately left the CPA ambiguous in relation to a future plan and the modality of reintegration. This was partly because entering deeply into carving out the modality of a DDR programme could severely jeopardise the nascent peace negotiations. The vagueness, therefore, made it easier for the political parties to reach an agreement. According to an Non-Governmental Organisation (NGO) worker interviewed[4]:

> Any efforts to draw a concrete modality of DDR at the time of peace negotiation would sweep away the Maoists' confidence in the peace process and drive them away from the peace process.

Therefore, postponing the details of the contentious issue for future deliberations was, perhaps, a wise choice made by the signatories to the peace deal. However, in the ensuing peace process, the lack of clarity about the DDR programme itself surfaced as a bone of contention in a context where political consensus and compromise amongst political parties was being increasingly hijacked by fragmented and polarised transitional politics.

The ambiguity of the terms triggered sharply contradicting and conflicting interpretations of rehabilitation and reintegration. A case in point is the way the term "adjustment" (*Samayojan*) of ex-combatants, as it is mentioned in the CPA, was interpreted. From the beginning of the signing of the peace deal, there was a perceived gap between the CPNM and its opposition in interpreting the term. The CPNM interpreted it as adjustment of the ex-combatants into the army; therefore, it continued to bargain for army integration as an agenda for the peace process. Although other major political parties implicitly accepted "adjustment" as "army integration", they were not clear about where and how the adjustment could be made: whether the adjustment could be done in the army, or in other security forces, such as the police and armed police, or by creating a new security apparatus that could be assigned to look after the security of physical infrastructure and natural resources, such as forests and rivers.

This dilemma was rooted in the ambiguity of the peace negotiation document; it consequently not only divided the political community, but also altered the direction of the rehabilitation and reintegration

---

[4] Interviewed in Kathmandu in October 2011.

programme. Its ramification, both at the political and technical levels, remained increasingly unclear as to whether the focus of dealing with the ex-combatants should have been geared towards SSR at the macro level or towards social and economic reintegration at the micro level. This dilemma could have been resolved if there had been an agreement on the shared outcome of the DDR programme at the political level before the programme actually started. It would have certainly steered rehabilitation and reintegration of ex-combatants in a more realistic direction and its outcome would have addressed one of the most contentious issues of the peace process without unnecessary delays.

Conclusions

This chapter has drawn at least three key conclusions. Firstly, dealing with ex-combatants can become extremely politicised if a DDR programme emerges from a politically negotiated peace process where transitional politics continues to move away from a culture of consensus towards deep polarisation and fragmentation. As this chapter has shown, in fragmented and polarised transitional politics, key political actors become heavily engaged in power bargaining and power-sharing. Therefore, political consensus and agreement on the issue of reintegration and rehabilitation of ex-combatants were significantly hijacked. This can be directly related to the conflicting needs and interests of key political actors.

Secondly, lack of clarity in a peace negotiation document in terms of defining a modality, process and a time frame for a DDR programme can provide the grounds for political actors to misinterpret and manipulate the processes of DDR according to their strategic and tactical needs and interests.

Thirdly, and perhaps more importantly, it has been shown that the political will and commitment of an insurgent organisation is critically vital for a better outcome of a DDR programme. If an insurgent organisation is transformed into a powerful stakeholder in post-conflict transitional politics, it holds the capacity to significantly influence and alter the process and outcome of a DDR programme. The level of trust and capacity for compromise that exists between key political actors, the government and the former insurgent organisation determines the final outcome of a DDR programme and its scope and limitations as to how well it can contribute to a peace process.

REFERENCES

Ball, N., & van de Goor, L. (2006). *Disarmament, demobilization and reintegration: Mappping issues, dilemmas and guiding principles.* Netherland Institute of International Relations, Conflict Reseach Unit, 'Clingendael'. Retrieved from http://www.clingendael.nl/sites/default/files/20060800_cru_paper_ddr.pdf.

Berdal, M. (1996). *Disarmament and demobilization after civil wars.* Oxford: Oxford Univerity Press for International Institute for Strategic Studies.

Berdal, M., & Ucko, D. H. (Eds.). (2009). *Reintegrating armed groups after conflict: Politics, violence and transition.* London and New York: Routledge.

Cilliers, J., & Dietrich, C. (Eds.). (2000). *Angola's war economy: The role of oil and diamonds.* Pretoria: Institute for Security Studies.

de Zeeuw, J. (Ed.). (2008). *From soldiers to politicians: Transforming rebel movements after civil war.* Boulder and London: Lynne Rienner.

Galtung, J. (1996). *Peace by peaceful means: Peace, conflict, development and civilisation.* Oslo and London: International Peace Research and Sage.

Gautam, K. C. (2009). The rehabilitation and integration of Maoists combatants as part of Nepal's security sector reform. In R. Bhattarai & R. Cave (Eds.), *Changing security dynamics in Nepal.* London: Saferworld.

Glassmyer, K., & Sambanis, N. (2008). Rebel-military integration and civil war termination. *Journal of Peace Research, 45*(3), 365–384. https://doi.org/10.1177/0022343308088816.

Goodhand, J. (2004). From war economy to peace economy? Reconstruction and statebuildign in Afghanistan. *Journal of International Affairs, 58*(1), 155–174.

Hall, R. A. (2009). *From rebels to soldiers: An analysis of the Philippine and East Timorese policy integrating former Moro National Liberation Front and Falintil combatants into the armed forces.* Paper presented at the the American Political Science Association Meeting, Toronto, Canada. http://papers.ssrn.com/sol3/papers.cfm?abstract_id=1460315.

Jha, P. (2014). *Battles of new republic.* New Delhi: Aleph.

Knight, M. (2008). Expanding the DDR model: Politics and organizations. *Journal of Security Sector Managment, 6*(1), 1–19.

Knight, M., & Özerdem, A. (2004). Guns, camps and cash: Disarmament, demobilization and reinsertion of former combatants in transitions from war to peace. *Journal of Peace Research, 41*(4), 499–516. https://doi.org/10.1177/0022343304044479.

Muggah, R. (Ed.). (2009). *Security and post conflict reconstruction: Dealing with fighters in the aftermath of war.* London and New York: Routledge.

Muggah, R., & Baare, A. (2009). Negotiating reintegration in Uganda: Dealing with combatants during peace processes. In R. Muggah (Ed.), *Security and*

post-conflict reconstruction: Dealing with fighters in the aftermath of war (pp. 226–247). London and New York: Routledge.
Muggah, R., Berdal, M., & Torjesen, S. (2009). Conclusions: Enter an evidence-based security promotion. In R. Muggah (Ed.), *Security and post conflict reconstruction: Dealing with fighters in the aftermath of war* (pp. 268–284). London and New York: Routledge.
Özerdem, A. (2009). *Post-war recovery: Disarmament, demobilization and reintegration*. London and New York: I. B. Tauris.
Özerdem, A., Podder, S., O'Callaghan, S., & Pantuliano, S. (2008). *Reinsertion assistance and the reintegration of ex-combatants in war to peace transitions* (Thematic Working Paper 4). Bradford: Center for International Cooperation and Security, Bradford University.
Rolston, B. (2007). Demobilization and reintegration of ex-combatants: The Irish case in international perspective. *Social & Legal Studies, 16*(2), 259–280. https://doi.org/10.1177/0964663907076534.
Subedi, D. B. (2014). Dealing with ex-combatants in a negotiated peace process: Impacts of transitional politics on the DDR programme in Nepal. *Journal of Asian and African Studies, 49*(6), 672–689. https://doi.org/10.1177/0021909613507537.
Tesfamichael, G., Ball, N., & Nenon, J. (2004). *Peace in Sierra Leone: Evaluating the disarmament, demobilization, and reintegration process*. Washington, DC: Creative Associates International.
Torjesen, S., & MacFarlane, S. N. (2009). Reintegration before disarmament: The case of post-conflict reintegration in Tajikistan. In M. Berdal & D. H. Ucko (Eds.), *Reintegrating groups after conflict: Politics, violence and transition* (pp. 47–66). London: Routledge.
Walter, B. F. (2002). *Committing to peace: The successful resettlement of civil wars*. Princeton: Princeton University Press.

CHAPTER 5

Process and Outcomes of DDR

Even though management of People's Liberation Army (PLA) ex-combatants did not follow traditional Disarmament, Demobilisation and Reintegration (DDR) model, Chapter 3 has shown that it involved some elements of a standard DDR programme. But how the DDR process was affected by the transitional politics? Did the politics of power sharing and diminishing trust between key political actors have any effects on the way ex-combatants and their weapons were managed. Was the process and outcomes planned or expected or whether they were ad hoc and grossly unexpected? This chapter deals with these key questions. It shows that when management of ex-combatants becomes a subject of political contestation and controversy and a tool for strategic political bargain, the outcomes could be unplanned and unexpected which can have lasting impacts on the peace process in question.

Weapons Collection as Disarmament: Contention and Suspicion

The disarmament of the Maoist ex-combatants involved a voluntary weapons declaration process. Since it was intended to collectively disarm the entire force rather than individual combatants, it was, by nature, a "blanket disarmament" process. The notion of blanket disarmament operated in contrast with the "one combatant-one gun" scheme, which is generally used in a conventional DDR programme.[1] Although the government had proposed the idea of "one combatant-one gun", the CPNM refused it. The compromise on the idea of collective disarmament was partly driven by the government's perception that pushing the CPNM too much on this issue at that particular critical juncture of the peace process could upset the culture of consensus and turn the Maoists into becoming a "spoiler of peace".[2]

An enormous discrepancy between the number of registered weapons and ex-combatants surfaced as another contentious issue, which understandably raised public suspicion about the effectiveness of the entire disarmament process. The figures relating to weapons registered by the UNMIN appeared to be problematic because, according to an interviewee who had quit the Maoist party[3]:

> The CPNM looted approximately 1400 modern weapons including AK47 assault rifles from the army and police (approximately 600 from the army and about 800 from police); therefore, the PLA must have certainly possessed more than the voluntarily declared 3000 weapons.

Responding to this public contention about the gross mismatch between the number of ex-combatants verfied and the weapons surrendered, Prachanda's somewhat less convincing and unaccountable statement that "all the other weapons were flooded" implicitly reveals the CPNM's strategy to save some weapons, perhaps just in case they needed to redeploy.[4]

Disarmament involves security-related objectives and requires military expertise in collecting, storing and decommissioning weapons. As opposed to the military-centred notion, Knight and Özerdem (2004) proposed disarmament as a "social contract". This alternative thinking posits that through the submission of guns, ex-combatants and their leaders enter into a mutual social contract with the state; the state, in return, ensures safety, security and

---

[1] In this study, the term blanket disarmament refers to a process in which the entire insurgent organisation and its members are disarmed in a collective way. In contrast, the idea of disbarment based on "one combatant-one gun" refers to a process in which combatants are disarmed on an individual basis. In the latter case, individual combatants, not their organisation, have a stake and agency in the disarmament.

[2] Interview with a retired government officer, Kathmandu, November 2011.

[3] Interviewed in Kathmandu, October 2011.

[4] Interview with a journalist in Kathmandu, November 2011.

livelihood options and opportunities for ex-combatants. Disarmament based on a social contract may only be possible if combatants and their leaders have faith and confidence in a positive outcome of DDR and there was an adequate level of trust between them for this sensitive purpose.

In line with this approach, disarmament in the Nepali context embraced limited "social contract". The CPNM was either not fully confident about the outcome of the peace process or it would intend to use the peace process as a tactic to hold on to the power; therefore, it was in favour of a blanket approach which allowed it to save some weapons.[5] The political uncertainty and dwindling cooperation and trust between the SPA and Maoists would also have encouraged the latter to submit a limited number of weapons and reserve the rest for possible future use.[6]

A number of combatants and their leaders were left out of a formal DDR process because, as also mentioned earlier, they continued to have access to weapons in the name of alternative security management for the Maoist senior leaders. In DDR studies, this phenomenon raises a critical question about who should be the focus of disarmament: ex-combatants, their leaders or both? Whether a disarmament programme which emerges from a negotiated peace process can or should legitimately disarm all the insurgent leaders is a key concern that the Nepali case brings forth for further scrutiny.

Cantoned but not Adequately Demobilised

The CPNM mobilised the combatants to set up temporary cantonments long before the government released the budget for their construction. By setting up the cantonments quickly, the CPNM could better consolidate its force in one place, which otherwise might have been dispersed or involved in making a livelihood through violent means. Bringing the ex-combatants into cantonments without thorough supervision involving both the government and external actors, the CPNM benefited in two ways. Whilst it helped the CPNM to strategically demonstrate the international community its commitment to the peace process, it also provided an opportunity to the CPNM to inflate the number of ex-combatants before the verification process started (these dynamics are elaborated later).

---

[5] Interview with a political analyst in Kathmandu, October 2011.
[6] Interview with a CPNUML leader, Biratnagar, November 2011.

Cantonment is a fundamental element of DDR, as it offers several operational advantages, such as registering, screening and profiling ex-combatants before they are reintegrated (Colletta, Kostner, & Wiederhofer, 1996). It also helps in the organising of pre-discharge services, including counselling and offering opportunities to assess the political objectives of the rebelling party in terms of its willingness to reintegrate its forces (Knight & Özerdem, 2004). However, on the negative side, cantonment can also reinforce existing or new command and control structures (Knight & Özerdem, 2004, pp. 508–509).

In the Nepali context, confinement of the PLA in cantonments was just a process of "encampment", not complete demobilisation as per a conventional DDR process. The life of ex-combatants inside the cantonments was completely under the command and control of PLA commanders. Access to the cantonment for the outside actors was heavily restricted; it was subject to permission from the PLA. Therefore, there was very limited information, not only in public, but also with the government about life inside the cantonments. For instance, the combatants continued to wear their military uniforms, signs and symbols while living within cantonments. Combat training was also conducted regularly inside the cantonments.[7] As the PLA restricted the socio-economic profiling of ex-combatants for rehabiliation and reintegration purpose, the cantonments could neither offer any opportunities to ascertain individual combatant's needs, interests and aspirations towards their reintegration, nor could it offer any advantages of pre-reintegration services, such as psychosocial counselling, social and economic profiling, and mental and physical preparation for discharge. Thus, cantonments did not help in completely demobilising the ex-combatants; rather they created an opportunity for the PLA to systematically reinforce command and control structures. In other words, it was remobilisation by an "alternative system" (or route); the cantonments were functioning as military camps with perpetuation of the war-time command and control structures.

Controversy of Real and Fake Combatants

The number of verified combatants sparked deep scepticism about the CPNM's intentions when it was revealed that the Maoists had actually sent a number of real ex-combatants out and replaced them with fake

---

[7] Interview with a VMLR, Birtamod, Jhapa, November 2011.

combatants. An human rights activist interviewed in Dhangadi said,[8] "The Maoists had brought young people from villages into cantonments, promising them a job in the government army in future".

A video recording of Prachanda addressing the PLA in Saktikhor cantonment in Chitwan was leaked to the media in 2008, soon after the collapse of the Maoist government. Prachanda himself revealed that the actual number of PLA combatants was much lower and that the current figure was inflated by bringing in fake combatants. Interviews in the districts also confirmed that a number of trained hard-core combatants were sent out to work in the Young Communist League (YCL), allegedly in preparation for the next round of decisive revolutionary activity, although it was not clear what the next revolution would look like. The actual figures of those sent out to the YCL is not available, yet an ex-combatant stated that nearly four hundred PLA combatants were sent out from his battalion alone.[9] Triangulation from different sources, however, indicates that the number must be in the hundreds.

The suspicion about distinguishing between real and fake combatants was tested in January 2012 when the ex-combatants turned to YCL personnel and launched a protest against the Maoist leadership, demanding similar benefits to those who replaced them in the cantonments and were going to get a cash incentive as part of their retirement from the PLA. Thus, due to the CPNM's tactic to keep some of its forces out of demobilisation and the UNMIN's erroneous combatant verification process, the DDR programme ended up dealing with some fake combatants; whereas, a significant number of real ex-combatants remained out of the formal DDR process.

TENSIONS SURROUNDING DISCHARGE AND REHABILITATION OF VMLRS

According to the International Principles and Guidelines on Children Associated with Armed Forces, the CPNM should have immediately detached and discharged the so-called "disqualified" child soldiers

---

[8] Interviewed in December 2011.

[9] Interview with a combatant who never went to the cantonment because he was sent to work first in the YCL and then in the party office. Lalitpur, November 2011. Another interviewee interviewed in Chitwan in January 2013 said that most of ex-combatants who were absent at the time of regrouping process would have supposedly been fake combatants who never stayed in cantonments.

and late recruits from the cantonments. However, their discharge was delayed for three years because of the different attitudes and views of the CPNM and the government's on designing the modality of a rehabilitation package that was targeted to include the Verified Minors and Late Recruits (VMLRs). Eventually, in December 2010, the CPNM unilaterally discharged the VMLRs. To understand the way the CPNM suddenly decided to discharge the VMLRs would require examining how the CPNM would potentially benefit from the discharge, both strategically and politically.

Strategically, at that particular juncture when the peace process was almost frozen, by discharging the VMLRs, the CPNM demonstrated to the national and international communities that it was still committed to concluding the peace process. However, according to a retired government official, "discharging the VMLRs, the CPNM placed itself in a stronger position for making bargains in the strategically important next phase of ex-combatant army integration".[10] Politically, the CPNM was partly inspired by the assumption that the discharged VMLRs could be remobilised and re-engaged in the YCL and other political roles. To a certain extent, this assumption turned into a reality, because it was found that the Maoists had been mobilising them in contentious politics in many ways, including as members of the YCL.[11]

Discharge and rehabilitation of the VMLRs could have had less damaging effects on the peace process if the government had designed a highly attractive rehabilitation package and had been actively involved in its implementation.[12] This could have minimised the possibility of the ex-combatants being remobilised into Maoist politics and maximised the trust and supported the social contract between the ex-combatants and government in ways that would have had positive effects concerning the peace process.

[10] Interview with a civil society leader in Kathmandu, October 2011.

[11] Interview with a NGO activist in Jhapa (October 2011), a journalist in Dhangadi (December 2011) and a CPNUML leader in Kathmandu (December 2011).

[12] In monetary terms, the value of the rehabilitation package per VMLR was approximately equivalent to one hundred thousand Nepali rupees.

WHY UNMIN'S ROLE WAS CONTROVERSIAL?

Suspicion began to run high about the UNMIN's neutrality and credibility from the controversy over weapons registration and combatant verification, as discussed in Chapter 3.[13] Having been allegedly blamed for legitimising fake combatants, the UNMIN's credibility began to dwindle fast in the eyes of the government as well as the Maoist opposition, mainly the Nepali Congress (NC) and the CPNUML. A series of unfolding events and incidents further damaged its reputation. For instance, effectiveness and neutrality of monitoring and supervision of cantonments by the UNMIN began to be questioned when several ex-combatants were found moving in and out of the cantonments with weapons and some had even been involved in criminal activities outside cantonments.[14]

Amidst growing unpopularity, the UNMIN came up with a sixty-day plan for army integration, with the intention of applying leverage to move the political parties into making decisions on integration and rehabilitation. The proposal displeased the CPNUML-led government, which perceived the proposal as an intervention beyond the UNMIN's mandate.[15] Similarly, the government wanted the UNMIN to only supervise cantonments, not the army barracks. However, the UNMIN refused this proposal, asserting that doing so would be a violation of the AMMAA.[16]

The NC's and the CPNUML's criticism about the UNMIN for taking the side of the Maoists, and in being ineffective in monitoring the combatants and their criminal activities, and unnecessarily legitimising the Maoists as a political power, was partly a reflection of their animosity and political clashes with the Maoists rather than with the UNMIN. For instance, the case in point is the allowance payment system for ex-combatants that appeared as a bone of contention between the government and the CPNM, and eventually also damaged the UNMIN-government relationship. From the beginning, the ex-combatants' regular payment was being made in bulk to the Maoist party, not directly to the

[13] Interview with a retired government official, November 2011.

[14] According to the CPA Section 5, Sub-section 5.1.5, armies of neither side shall be present with arms and in combat fatigue in any civilian assembly, political meetings and public programmes. However, breaching this clause, the CPNM members and the PLA fighters were found in public places, including in the CA, on several occasions.

[15] Interview with a retired government officer, November 2011.

[16] The AMMAA stipulates that the UN mission will supervise and monitor weapons placed both in cantonments and the army barracks.

ex-combatants. When there were reports that several ex-combatants were no longer living in the cantonments and the CPNM was misusing their payment as a form of "systemic corruption", the Ministry of Peace and Reconstruction (MoPR) denied the payment in bulk; rather it proposed direct payment into individual ex-combatants' bank accounts.[17]

To alter the payment system, the ministry wanted to verify the identity of the ex-combatants against their photo taken by the UNMIN at the time of verification, so that the exact number of ex-combatants present in cantonments could be reassessed. This would be impossible without the UNMIN's involvement. However, considering the sensitivity of the issues and possible backlash from the PLA (in case re-verification was conducted before finalising the modality of the army integration), the UNMIN did not support the government's idea and also refused to share the combatants' photo identification with the ministry. It was particularly due to this incident that the trust and relationship between the Madhav Kumar Nepal-led government and the UNMIN grew extremely bitter. This contributed, to a greater extent, to the government's rigid decision to end the UNMIN's term, which led to the latter's undignified exit, long before reintegration and rehabilitation was accomplished.

Cash Was More Appealing Than Rehabilitation

As was discussed earlier, as a response to the government policy prescriptions and contrary to general public expectation, only a relatively small number of ex-combatants preferred army integration, while an overwhelming majority opted for the cash payment option. This raises a question about why the rehabilitation programme disenchanted the ex-combatants. At least four factors that explain this phenomenon have been explored.

Firstly, this would need to be seen in the broader context of how marginalisation of the reintegration and rehabilitation component of DDR could potentially benefit the Maoists politically. The reintegration and rehabilitation process could engage the ex-combatants in self-development and it would eventually transform them, economically and socially. Their transformation could sufficiently distance and detach a number of ex-combatants from the CPNM. Conversely, if they retired with a cash package, a significant number of ex-combatants could end up once again

---

[17] Interview with a government official from the MoPR, Kathmandu, October 2011.

entering into Maoist politics. The combatants' overwhelming decision to opt for a "golden handshake" left them with double benefits, because, on the one hand, it provided an immediate financial incentive to ex-combatants, and, on the other, it opened up the opportunity for them to continue an active political association with the Maoists for those who were interested to do so. Offering these benefits to ex-combatants may also be interpreted as being a ramification of the CPNM's interest and willingness to transform their ex-combatants into political workers or long-term supporters rather than economically self sufficient civilians. Secondly, a less encouraging experience from the low profile rehabilitation programme targeting the VMLRs could not sufficiently attract the ex-combatants towards a rehabilitation option.

Thirdly, being in cantonments for an unexpectedly extended period had significantly raised expectations among the ex-combatants about their futures and they became desperate to experience some kind of quick tangible benefit or compensation for their long engagement in the war. As the peace process kept on faltering, the ex-combatants became increasingly less optimistic about whether their war-time engagement was going to yield any satisfactory social, economic and political benefits in the way they had been told during the war. This was particularly in respect to the convincing promises that their organisation, the CPNM, had made to them at the time of their recruitment. Fourthly, while their economic vulnerability remained as it was at the time of recruitment in the war, desperation about securing an improved economic future was fast growing among the ex-combatants. In this situation, opting for a readily available cash incentive was more lucrative than a rehabilitation package. Finally, as also mentioned earlier, the Maoists swapped real combatants with fake ones. Therefore, the fake ex-combatants, who had no experience of the war as combatants, found the cash option to be a quick financial incentive, rather than waiting for a long-term rehabilitation/reintegration package.

CORRUPTION AND EMBEZZLEMENT OF FUNDS

Evidence from as diverse DDR contexts as Liberia, El Salvador, Haiti, Somalia, Nicaragua, the Philippines, Indonesia and Afghanistan, among others, reveals that the use of cash is a common policy option in DDR programmes. Although common, it is certainly not the perfect solution as the policy has both benefits and flaws, and these outcomes are evidenced by several positive and negative experiences from the field (Özerdem, Podder, O'Callaghan, & Pantuliano, 2008). One of the pressing issues in the cash-DDR nexus is the persistent concern about whether cash used in a DDR programme induces corruption.

The DDR literature regards corruption in two forms. Firstly corruption in a DDR programme can be understood as the 'war economy'; an illicit economy in which commanders and war lords exploit private, public and natural resources to either consolidate power or return to war conditions (Cilliers & Dietrich, 2000; Goodhand, 2004; Le Billon, 2000). Jonathan Goodhand (2004, p. 157) distinguishes combat economy from other forms of war economy and defines the later as an economic system which produces, mobilises and allocates economic resources to either for further generation of resources to wage war or to the destruction of resources in order to undermine the ability of opposing groups to wage retaliatory action.[18] The concept of the war economy provides a lens through which one may examine whether the resources used in a DDR programme are mobilised and redirected for the use of the insurgent organisation or alternatively, individual commanders and warlords.

Secondly, the diversion of resources by commanders and war lords in a DDR program is a central concern as it is the potential breeding medium for corruption and bad governance. Kilroy (2012, p. 202) asserts that corruption and bad governance violates the concept of social contract, a central idea in a DDR program.

He further argues that the diversion of funds or resources addresses the interests of selected people only and ignores the interests of a significant number of other potential beneficiaries. Diversion and misappropriation in this case can be either coercive or systemic. In coercive corruption, the forced extortion of combatants by commanders is normally the case. Afghanistan presents a case in point where the UN stopped paying cash to demobilised combatants after it was reported that the combatants with cash were extorted by their commanders (Reliefweb, 2004). Similarly, Sierra Leone proved the case where the reinsertion benefit which was 600,000 in local currency encouraged a system of corruption at the commander level (Tesfamichael, Ball, & Nenon, 2004, p. 15). Corruption in DDR is often a resultant

---

[18] The other forms of war economies are the shadow economy and the coping economy. For more, see Goodhand (2004).

phenomenon of power imbalance and asymmetries among the different actors involved, and the way the asymmetries undermine accountability and consultation (Kilroy, 2012). This could be particularly the case where power relations cannot be entirely altered or challenged in the course of implementing a DDR program that originates from negotiation. As will be discussed later, the Nepali case exemplifies this point.

Kilroy (2012, p. 204) also highlights non-participation as a form of corruption. He states that this could be the case when non-combatants join the DDR program with the assistance of commanders, fellow combatants or war lords, particularly during the disarmament process. It will be shown later that the opportunity cost of non-participation can also cause coercive corruption at the final stage of a reintegration program.

In the context of Nepal, following the PLA's decision to set up a contributory fund, every divisional cantonment, from the very beginning of the establishment of the cantonments, established a PLA fund which operated under the control of respective divisional commanders but also was subject to control from the party headquarters.[19] The fund collected a mandatory contribution of NRs 1000 from each combatant's monthly salary. Since the government paid, on average, NRs 6500 monthly to 19,600 combatants from 2007 to November 2011, this monthly deduction alone generated a fund of over NRs 1.18 billion over the five years. The regrouping of combatants conducted in November and December 2011 revealed that a total of 2456 combatants left cantonments at different times, yet the PLA had continued to draw their salaries which, according to Pun (2012a), contributed another NRs 1.34 billion to the PLA fund.

In addition, there are also allegations that the PLA fund earned a huge income through commissions received from the ration suppliers. On average, the government paid a ration allowance of NRs 2730 per combatant, per month. Although it is hard to determine and substantiate how much this contributed to the PLA fund, Pun (2012a) estimates that the PLA fund would have earned about NRs 600 million out of the NRs 3.19 billion paid by the government for the ration allowance over the five years. He adds that the contractors who supplied the rations conceded that they paid 20% commission of the total contract to the commanders.

[19] Interview with a platoon vice commander, Chitawan, January 2013.

Information and communication are vital factors in the avoidance of systematic defectiveness such as corruption and embezzlement. A lack of proper interpretation and communication available to the combatants about the purposes and aims of the PLA fund was part of the problem and an enabling factor for the corruption. The combatants who were interviewed mentioned that they were told that the PLA would use the fund transparently to support the welfare of combatants, although the combatants recall that the definition of 'welfare' was never quite clarified for them.

Partly linked to the problem of communication and transparency is the question of authority, which was frequently mentioned in the interviews. The PLA fund was operated at the sole discretion of respective commanders in the divisional cantonments. Although power and authority may be different concepts in general, in this case, they are inherently linked. Having power in terms of the rank and file hierarchy of the cantonment as well as the power coming from certain commanders' direct connections with the higher echelons of the party leadership was vital in rendering them previledges to handle the fund at their sole discretion. Over the time, the level of strife within the party regarding the use or misuse of the PLA fund increased exponentially to the extent that it had the potential to damage the reputation of its senior leaders. As a response to this mounting conflict, the CPNM had formed a three-member panel, headed by Posta Bahadur Bogati, to investigate corruption in the PLA fund, though the panel's report has not been made public yet.

In general, corruption might have different purposes for those involved in the practice. It depends upon who is involved in the corruption and what the motivating and facilitating factors are. However, looking at cantonment-related corruption from the war economy perspective, the fund had been redirected for the benefit of the organisation as well as the individual.

At the organisational level, as one commander reported, the CPNM used part of the fund to finance the activities of YCL[20]; a statement, which was confirmed by other interviewees, both combatants and non-combatants in different districts. Similarly the Maoists also needed a huge amount of resources to cover the expenses of 4008 VMLRs who were residing inside the cantonments, so part of the money was also used

---

[20] Interview with a vice-commander in Chitawan, January 2013.

to cover VMLR-related expenses and other unforeseen logistical processes to run the cantonments.[21] This can be further substantiated by the declaration of commanders who, being under fierce pressure from combatants, declared that they had sent 60% of the fund to party headquarters, under instructions from the head of the CPNM (Pun, 2012a).

At the individual level, regarding the impact of corruption, combatants have expressed their contention that certain commanders and party leaders had benefitted significantly from the PLA fund; many of the corrupt leaders had invested funds privately, in businesses including real estate, hospitals, and so on.[22] A portion of the CPNM's investment in Jana Maitri Hospital in Kathmandu allegedly comes from the PLA fund.[23] Where and how the fund was spent is the secondary question; the primary question is whether it was moral for the PLA to set up the fund in the first place and use it opaquely to furtively fund the activities of the Maoists' party.[24]

It should be admitted that these claims are, to a certain extent, based on individual combatants', and commanders' experiences as well as certain civil society leaders' assumptions. In practice, political parties do not make their balance sheets public and neither does the CPNM. This creates a significant challenge for studying corruption which relates to political parties and political military organisations like the PLA. However, despite a growing public contention both from within the PLA as well as from civil society, the CPNM has neither denied nor accepted the accusations of corruption. Instead, by forming a committee to probe the corruption cases and the party workers' and combatants' allegations that some of the Maoists leaders and commanders had become heavily corrupt could be taken to mean that the CPNM has implicitly accepted that corruption existed, regardless of its origins, severity and intensity.

The manner in which the PLA fund siphoned state funds to finance the activities of its rebellious organisation, mobilise loyal groups in

---

[21] Interview with a vice-commander in Chitawan, January 2013.

[22] Interviews with ex-combatants in Chitawan and Dang in January and February 2013 respectively.

[23] Interview with a journalist in Kathmandu, February 2013. Also see *eKantipur* news in http://www.ekantipur.com/the-kathmandu-post/2012/09/03/top-story/alleged-pla-fund-graft/239177.html.

[24] A civil society leader interviewed in Biratnagar, Morang, January 2013.

contentious politics and embezzle funds for the private use of certain commanders and leaders, nonetheless, presents a typical example of how public resources eventually generated a war economy in the politically negotiated peace process in Nepal.

As also noted in earlier in this chapter, at the time of combatant verification in 2007, the Maoists had heavily inflated the number of the PLA members by enrolling non-combatants, party workers and supporters who had never participated in the war as fighters. By bringing in non-combatants, the Maoists were able to send the trained fighters out to work in the YCL, (Martin, 2012). As a result of the non-combatants' participation in the DDR program, the authentic combatants remained outside of the process while the arms and army management process dealt with the 'fake' combatants.

This kind of non-participation of some ex-combatants in the DDR process could also be a source of corruption from the point of view of a moral and ethical standards' violation on the part of the CPNM. Nonetheless, beyond the moral issue, this form of participation-non-participation issue also undermined the social contract between the insurgent organisation and the state in that, from the beginning of the disarmament process, suspicion towards the Maoists' intentions in the peace process and a culture of mistrust between the Maoists and other political parties grew exponentially.

Non-participation in this paper is referred to the situation where a large number of combatants did not fully participate in the DDR program. In other words, the non-participants were absent from the cantonments; however, the public cost of this non-participation was excessive in that the government continued to pay the salaries of the non-participanting ex-combatants.

Non-participation affected actual participation in DDR. As the Maoists had substantially increased non-combatant participation in the DDR, some of these fake combatants left the cantonments at later stages. Thus the artificially increased participation in the beginning actually had the effect of increasing the non-participation rates later.

On one hand, by increasing non-combatants' participation in the DDR programme, the cost of management of the cantonments increased substantially. This provided an increased income for the PLA and obviously the opportunity to manipulate more resources inside the cantonments. In other words, increased participation by non-combatants simultaneously increased the volume of the war economy engendered by the PLA fund.

On the other hand, combatants from Chulachuli, Ilam, Nawalparsi and Surkhet publicly protested, complaining that that their commanders had seized the pay cheques of their voluntary retirement installments.[25] Commanders had made an informal arrangement with some of the combatants who actually had never lived in the cantonment but reappeared just at the time of regrouping in order to collect their voluntary retirement packages. According to the arrangement, the combatants were asked to hand over 40% of the cash package to the commanders. Explaining this phenomenon, a combatant asserted,

> Commanders had forged an understanding with the returnee combatants that the latter would give 40 per cent from their cash package to the PLA fund. However, at the end, combatants denied the understanding which led to a situation where some commanders used force to seize pay cheque.[26]

Another female ex-combatant added;

> Despite heavy threats, a few combatants dared to bring the cheque-snatch case out, which put moral pressure on the commanders; otherwise many combatants would lose a substantial portion of their retirement package.[27]

This informal understanding between commanders and absentee combatants was a deal calculated on the basis of the opportunity cost of the combatants' non-participation in the cantonments in the past. Denying the commanders' proposal would mean that the commander could block the absentee combatant's participation in the voluntary retirement scheme. Thus the opportunity cost of accepting the offer would be higher than the cost of being excluded from the programme. Hence, non-participation worked as a factor to increase corruption instigated by the commanders using coercive means.

Nepal's peace process is typically homegrown, with minimal involvement of the external actors. Ironically, the government as a key party in

---

[25] Interview with a journalist in Kathmandu, January 2013.
[26] Interview with a vice-commander in Narayanghat, Chitawan, January 2013.
[27] Interview with a female combatant, Kathmandu, January 2013.

the peace process could not assume stronger oversight role particularly in managing cantonments' budgetary and financial matters. The MoPR disbursed PLA salaries and cantonment related budgets to the cantonment management unit, a MoPR line agency in the cantonment sites. The MoPR did have any direct authority to oversee the way the funds were being spent in the cantonments, despite that the MoPR had the budget got audited by the office of the auditor general. This a complex and also weak oversight mechanism weaken the government oversight and authority, leaving financial management of cantonments entirely in the hand of the PLA. Despite being aware, from different informal sources, of the fact that a large number of combatants did not live in cantonments at all, the government was regularly paying their salaries of the absentee combatants. Though the peace minister from the Communist Party of Nepal United Marxist and Leninist (CPNUML) wanted to alter the system from bulk payment to the payment in individual's bank account,[28] doing so would need recounting of combatants which could not happen due to CPNM's strong opposition and to some extent UNMIN's non-cooperation.

A civil society leader said "the government could not establish its strong authority in managing cantonments so that unfortunately it just became a generous sponsor of ex-rebels' everyday life".[29] After UNMIN's exit in January 2011, the monitoring and supervision of cantonments came under the purview of the Special Committee (SC) on Supervision, Rehabilitation and Integration of Maoists combatants headed by the prime minister, however, neither UNMIN nor the SC had a clear mandate, authority and accountability to oversee any administration and financial matters inside cantonments. Thus, being the government out of management of cantonment provided the PLA favorable conditions to manipulate the public resources for private purposes.

It does not, however, mean that the government was not concerned about the corruption. The SC for Supervision, Integration and Rehabilitation of Maoists combatants demanded an investigation into the corruption case and also decided to ask the MoPR to provide details of the expenditure made for the former Maoist combatants since 2006. As noted above, the CPNM also formed a three member panel, headed by Posta Bahadur Bogati, to investigate the corruption of the PLA fund.

---

[28] Interview with ex-peace minister, Kathmandu, December 2011.

[29] Interview with a male civil society leader, Kathmandu, December 2011.

The concluding meeting of the SC on supervision, rehabilitation and integration of the Maoist combatants held on 12 April 2013 passed a proposal to conduct a special investigation through the office of the auditor general into the NRs 19.71 billion spent on PLA cantonments in the last seven years.[30] The SC member, however, remained sharply divided on the decision. While non-Maoist members in the committee supported the proposal, the Maoist supports and sympathisers rejected the plan, claiming that no investigation is needed as Ministry of Peace has had the budget audited annually.

Making a distinction between auditing and investigation in essential here to clarify the point. Auditing is regular process of checking whether public spending has complied with standard practice, norms and procedure. The office of the auditor general is responsible for auditing government expenditures. However, the question here is not auditing but investing misappropriation of funds. Corruption case therefore does not fall under the jurisdiction of auditor general but it is a task of the Commission for Investigation of Abuse of Authority (CIAA). If CIAA is not invited to investigate the case, corruption that took place in cantonments might simply be forgotten over time.

The role of a civil society is increasingly recognised in promoting good governance, economic prosperity, combating corruption, and expanding civic engagement to hold public officials accountable through fostering actions and mechanisms by citizens, communities, media, and civil society (Clark, 1990; Mungiu-Pippidi, 2010; WB, 2000). The logic of fostering dynamic relationship between civil society and the public sector partly draws on increasing recognition given to the role of civil society in modern state building.

Although the Nepali civil society play a vital covert and overt mediating role in bringing the Maoists, the seven party alliance and the government to the negotiation table, civil society had neither space nor any role in the management of the Maoists arms and army. "None of peace documents relating to rehabilitation and integration of the Maoists army have even slightly mentioned about the civil society", said a civil society leader.[31] Neither was civil society invited, in practice, to participate in any discussion on rehabilitation and integration related matters. A complete

---

[30] See http://202.166.193.40/the-kathmandu-post/2013/04/12/top-story/pla-integration-process-concludes/247508.html.

[31] Interview with a female civil soceity leader in Kathmandu, December 2011.

lack of civil society oversight mechanism lost an opportunity to hold the PLA and CPNM leaders morally accountable in handing the public funding in cantonments.

Frustration and Anger of Ex-combatants

At the final stage, as an effect of the rift between the CPN-M and the CPNM, the ex-combatants and commanders divided into two groups, reflecting a growing intra-party ideological rift. Following this division, the ex-combatants in the two groups began to confront each other within the cantonments (Pun, 2012b; Subedi, 2014). Indeed, the chain of command began to unravel and the cantonments virtually imploded in April 2012. As a response to this critical situation, the Maoist prime minister Babu Ram Bhattarai mobilised the army to take over the cantonments to avert violence and bloodshed that was likely if the situation was not tackled in time. The hard-line faction of the CPNM and the ex-combatants who supported it perceived the military intervention as a symbolic victory for the Nepal army in a circumstance where the war had ended in a win-win situation through a political negotiation.

The dramatic chaos in cantonments was a resultant phenomenon, which was based on an accumulation of ex-combatants' simmering frustrations and resentments engendered by their prolonged life of "virtual confinement to barracks" within the cantonments. A case in point is the seven-point deal. The negotiation had made a provision that the ex-combatants opting for army integration would need to qualify on the basis of their education and age. A "bridging training" for those who would be selected for army integration was made mandatory, but it failed to clarify the confusion over the issue of harmonising ranks of ex-combatants from the PLA after they were integrated into the Nepal Army. This infuriated the ex-combatants as it ruled out the possibility of bulk entry—the proposition for which the commanders had been battling. Selection criteria also might largely prevent many ex-combatants from entering the army. Decisions were made without sufficient consultations with ex-combatants and their commanders; hence the seven-point deal could not garner enough support from the wider community of ex-combatants. Rather it exacerbated intra-party political dynamics in the CPNM and worsened the ex-combatant/government relationship. In an opportunistic move, the hard-line faction of the Maoists called the outcome "surrender" and an "historical betrayal". The ex-combatants who supported the hard-line faction declined the integration proposal. In their view, it was "undignified army integration" because on one hand they had to fulfil recruitment criteria, and on the other hand, there were confusions about rank harmonisation between the two armies.

Another, and perhaps the more damaging factor, was the concern about transparency over the "PLA fund". Since the beginning, the PLA collected a fund from three sources. Firstly, the PLA fund collected a mandatory contribution of NRs 1000 from each combatant's monthly salary. Since the government paid, on average, NRs 6500 monthly to 19,600 combatants from 2007 to November 2011, this monthly deduction alone generated a fund of approximately NRs 1.18 billion over the five years. As a total of 2456 combatants left cantonments at different times, the PLA had continued to draw the salaries for these 2456 ex-combatants who were absent from their cantonments. The salaries of absentee combatants, according to Pun (2012a), contributed another NRs 1.34 billion to the PLA fund. In addition, there were also allegations that the PLA fund earned a huge income through commissions received from the ration suppliers.[32] On average, the government paid a ration allowance of NRs 2730 per combatant, per month. Although it is hard to determine and substantiate how much this contributed to the PLA fund, Pun (2012a) estimates that it would have earned about NRs 600 million out of the NRs 3.19 billion paid by the government for the ration allowance over the five years. He adds that the contractors who supplied the rations conceded that they paid 20% commission of the total contract to the commanders. How the PLA fund was handled is still a mystery and it has sparked several contentions among ex-combatants. The CPNM has formed a committee to inquire into this matter, however the report is not out yet and there are assertions that the PLA fund was massively embezzled by collusion between commanders and the party headquarters.

Ex-combatants revolted in the cantonments seeking their share in the fund while the hard-line faction of the Maoists used this inflammatory case as a tool to defame the establishment faction. Thus, the fight around the PLA fund hijacked attention away from the Maoist leadership to manage the opportunity to transform ex-combatants into security actors.

---

[32] Interview with a journalist in Kathmandu, March 2013.

In other words, because of conflicting intra-party political interests, integration of combatants into the Nepali Army could not sufficiently attract the ex-combatants who eventually felt deceived. "The war ended in "win-win", but now it had arrived at a point where the army was the winner and the PLA the looser", said an ex-combatant in Narayanpur, Chitwan.

Given that the DDR programme had missed the opportunity to properly reintegrate and rehabilitate the ex-combatants, it has left a significant number of ex-combatants frustrated, disillusioned and angry with not only the government, but also its own leadership. The future of these ex-combatants will always remain central to the future of peace in Nepal.

Conclusions

This chapter has shown that dealing with ex-combatants can become highly politicised if a DDR programme emerges from a politically negotiated peace process where the transitional politics continues to move away from a culture of consensus towards deep polarisation and fragmentation among key actors. In fragmented and polarised transitional politics, key political actors become heavily engaged in power bargaining and power-sharing. The Nepalese experience suggests that the process and outcomes of a DDR process is partly defined by the political context in which the DDR takes place and also partly by the relationships between key actors in the peace process including former insurgent organisation. The lack of political consensus and agreement on the issue of reintegration and rehabilitation of ex-combatants was a direct consequence of conflicting needs and interests of the Maoists, government and major political parties that determined the outcomes pertaining to the management of Maoists arms and armies.

References

Cilliers, J., & Dietrich, C. (Eds.). (2000). *Angola's war economy: The role of oil and diamonds*. Pretoria: Institute for Security Studies.

Clark, J. (1990). *Democratizing development: The role of voluntary organizations*. West Hartford: Kumarian Press.

Colletta, N. J., Kostner, M., & Wiederhofer, I. (1996). *Case studies in war-to-peace transition: The demobilization and reintegration of ex-combatants in Ethiopia, Namibia, and Uganda*. Washington, DC: World Bank.

Goodhand, J. (2004). From war economy to peace economy? Reconstruction and state building in Afghanistan. *Journal of International Affairs, 58*(1), 155–174.

Kilroy, W. (2012). *From conflict to ownership: Participatory approaches to the reintegration of ex-combatants in Sierra Leone and Liberia* (Doctor of Philosophy (PhD)). Dublin City University, Dublin, Ireland.

Knight, M., & Özerdem, A. (2004). Guns, camps and cash: Disarmament, demobilization and reinsertion of former combatants in transitions from war to peace. *Journal of Peace Research, 41*(4), 499–516. https://doi.org/10.1177/0022343304044479.

Le Billon, P. (2000). *The political economy of war: What relief workers need to know*. London. Retrieved from https://odihpn.org/resources/the-political-economy-of-war-what-relief-agencies-need-to-know/.

Martin, I. (2012). The united nations and support to Nepal's peace process: The role of the UN mission in Nepal. In S. v. Einsiedel, D. M. Malone, & S. Pradhan (Eds.), *Nepal in transition* (pp. 201–231). Cambridge and New York: Centre on International Cooperation and Cambridge University Press.

Mungiu-Pippidi, A. (2010). *The experience of civil society as an anticorruption actor in East Central Europe*.

Özerdem, A., Podder, S., O'Callaghan, S., & Pantuliano, S. (2008). *Reinsertion assistance and the reintegration of ex-combatants in war to peace transitions* (Thematic Working Paper 4). Bradford: Center for International Cooperation and Security, Bradford University.

Pun, K. (2012a, February 9). Combatants suspect misuse of 3 billion from 'PLA fund'. *My Republica*. Retrieved from http://archives.myrepublica.com/2012/portal/?action=news_details&news_id=41832.

Pun, K. (2012b, April 11). Why the cantonments imploded? *My Republica*.

Reliefweb. (2004). *Afghanistan: UN stop paying demobilized soldiers after extortion revealed*. Available from http://reliefweb.int/report/afghanistan/afghanistan-un-stop-paying-demobilized-soldiers-after-extortion-revealed.

Subedi, D. B. (2014). Dealing with ex-combatants in a negotiated peace process: Impacts of transitional politics on the DDR programme in Nepal. *Journal of Asian and African Studies, 49*(6), 672–689. https://doi.org/10.1177/0021909613507537.

Tesfamichael, G., Ball, N., & Nenon, J. (2004). *Peace in Sierra Leone: Evaluating the disarmament, demobilization, and reintegration process*. Washington, DC: Creative Associates International.

WB. (2000). *Helping countries combat corruption*. Washington, DC: World Bank.

CHAPTER 6

Rehabilitation of Verified Minors and Late Recruits

Verified minors and late recruits (VMLRs) made up nearly 17% of the total number of ex-combatants registered for verification and, therefore, they form an important constituency in the management of Maoists' arms and armies. However, the case of VMLRs was marginalised; some even did not consider them as ex-combatants; therefore, they ware not treated as a significant part of the Maoist arms and army management process.

This volume, nonetheless, argue that as the VMLRs were provided with a formal rehabilitation package delivered through the United Nations Interagency Rehabilitation Programmes (UNIRP) following United Nations DDR (UNDDR) standards, they should be implicitly and explicitly considered as ex-combatants by any international standard. Furthermore, the VMLRs returned to their communities with the identity of ex-combatants, sharing similar identity with verified ex-combatants and facing reintegration and community acceptance issues, plus livelihood related issues similar to the other qualified or officially recognised ex-combatants, means that VMLRs and verified ex-combatants must be seen from a similar analytical lens for research as well as DDR programme purposes. In other words, without researching the rehabilitation of VMLRs, the effort to understand the relationship between reintegration and peacebuilding in Nepal remains incomplete.

There are a number of context specific macro and micro-level factors, which may vary from country to country, and can shape and reshape the process and outcomes of a rehabilitation programme (Colletta & Muggah, 2009). Porto, Alden, and Parsons (2007, p. 137) have identified a series of issue clusters including the "long-term reintegration focus", "reintegration and vulnerability in war-to-peace transition", "strengthening social capital by targeting the community", and "reintegration and political participation". They argue that these factors need to be taken into account in delivering reintegration programmes, because these issues can either constrain or facilitate the rehabilitation of ex-combatants. Drawing on the literature and further building on the data collected from the fieldwork, micro and macro-level factors that have effects, either positive or negative, on the rehabilitation of VMLRs will be discussed in this chapter.

This chapter aims to find answers to such critical questions as: What was the nature of the rehabilitation programme? What micro and macro-level factors have affected, either positively or negatively, the process and outcomes of the rehabilitation programme? How have the ex-combatants themselves perceived and responded to the programme? What lessons can we learn in the field of post-conflict peacebuilding from efforts made to rehabilitate the VMLRs?

CHILDREN IN ARMED CONFLICT IN NEPAL

Children were one of the forefront victims in the Maoist armed conflict. Although no accurate data is available about how many children were actually victimised, the reports claim that both the Maoist and the government army used children (child-soldiers below the age of 18) in the armed conflict directly and indirectly (Coalition to Stop the Child Soldier, 2004; Pun Magar, 2004).[1]

Though the Maoists officially deny conscription of any children in the war, several children were recruited both voluntarily and forcefully in armed roles, but also to work as messengers, cooks, transporters, militias, spies and so on (Hart, n.d.; Subedi, 2013). Identification of minors who were ex-combatants is a further testimony that substantiates the claims against those who conscripted children into fighting in the Nepalese armed conflict. Unlike the Maoists, there are no credible reports suggesting recruitment of children as fighters by the Royal Nepal Army, however, interviews with human rights activists conducted in Kathmandu revealed that the government security forces used children as

---

[1] Also see http://www.hrw.org/reports/2007/nepal0207/4.htm.

spices in many places, especially in and around the Maoist hinterlands in mid-western and western hills.

Among various roles that children were forced to play by the Maoists and security forces, this volume particularly concerns with the phenomenon of child soldiers and their rehabilitation at the end of the armed conflict. This volume refers to the 1997 Cape Town Conference on Child Soldiers, which defined a child soldier as

> any person under 18 years of age who is part of any regular or irregular armed force or armed group in any capacity, including but not limited to cooks, porters, messengers, and those accompanying such groups, other than those who were purely family members. (Lee, 2009, p. 3)

Recruitment of children in the war was against the principle of the Declaration of the Rights of the Children and the UN Convention on the Rights of the Child (CRC), which were adopted in the year 1959 and 1989 respectively. Nepal is a party to nineteen different human rights instruments, including the CRC (Dahal, Kafle, & Bhattarai, 2008); therefore, it was a responsibility for the state to protect children from armed conflict and violence. In this regard, the Comprehensive Peace Agreement (CPA) has clearly stipulated that children would not be used in the violence and that both parties to the conflict, the Maoist and the government, would "immediately stop ... conscription or use of children aged 18 or below in the armed conflict" (GoN, 2006).

Unlike verified ex-combatants, VMLR ex-combatants (the category also includes child soldiers) were deemed ineligible to remain in cantonments. Therefore, the signatories of the peace agreement established that VMLRs would be released and rehabilitated into the communities without delay according to standard international norms and practices. Yet, despite the understanding, and due to a lack of an agreement between key political parties including the Maoists and the government on the modality of rehabilitation, VMLRs spent more than three years in cantonments, sharing everyday life with other verified ex-combatants.

In December 2009, the CPNM unilaterally decided to send VMLRs out of the cantonments over a disagreement on the modality and package of the rehabilitation programme. While the decision reflected the Maoists growing rift with the government on the issue of DDR, the decision was also strategic as the Maoists wanted to show the international community about their commitment to the peace process. As a result, in January and February 2010, a total of 2394 VMLRs left cantonments while the remaining 1614 were absent at the time, and they had reportedly left the country for foreign employment (UNDP, 2012).

The United Nations Interagency Rehabilitation Programme (UNIRP)

Once the VMLRs left the cantonments, concern surrounding their proper rehabilitation mounted, not only because many of these were child soldiers and this called for a humanitarian response, but also if these frustrated and unemployed ex-combatants left unaccompanied, they could be a significant threat to post-conflict security. The government then invited the United Nations (UN) agencies working in the country to design and deliver a rehabilitation package. Consequently, under the leadership of the United Nations Development Programme (UNDP), the United Nations Children's Fund (UNICEF), United Nations Population Fund (UNFPA) and International Labour Organisation (ILO) were brought together to create the UNIRP—a formal rehabilitation programme that exclusively targeted the VMLRs. The UNIRP commenced from the end of 2009 through its five regional offices based in Biratnagar, Chitwan, Kathmandu, Nepalgunj and Dhangadi. Being organised following the guiding principles of the UN Integrated Disarmament, Demobilisation and Reintegration Standards (IDDRS), the UNIRP was the only formal reintegration/rehabilitation programme targeting ex-combatants in the entire peace process in Nepal.[2]

The UN-led Rehabilitation Programme

There is a near universal proposition that child soldiering is a violation of Universal Children's Rights and is unacceptable under any circumstances (Lee, 2009). The phenomenon of the child soldier is closely interlinked to the current discourse on children's rights, which posits that children cannot and should not have agency in war participation. Although, in some armed conflicts, for example in the anti-apartheid struggle in

---

[2] For more on IDDR standards, see UN (2010a). The other verified ex-combatants deselected a rehabilitation option; instead they received a cash package.

South Africa in the 1970s and 1980s, the militant children were hailed as heroes and agents of democracy and liberation; the point being that they were not seen as victims (Bundi, 1987). All the members of the UN, except the United States of America (USA) and Somalia, have ratified the CRC. The CRC has prompted a new discourse on rights-based humanitarianism concerning the rights and protection of children from all kinds of threats, including armed conflict (Goodwin-Gill & Cohn, 1994). Along with the rise of the rights-based approach, the practice of dealing with child soldiers is shaped accordingly by the principles and practices of a humanitarian response to civil war and acute emergencies (Lee, 2009).

In the Nepalese context, because of the presence of child soldiers in the VMLR category, the rehabilitation programme was conceived to address children's rights and ensure protection.[3] However, it also involved some aspects of post-conflict recovery, because an overarching aim of the rehabilitation programmes was to transform VMLR ex-combatants into civilians, through creating economic opportunities and enabling social environment.[4]

The rehabilitation package consisted of the four options: (a) vocational skills training (VST), (b) micro-enterprise (ME) development training, (c) formal education support and (d) health related training. The vocational skills training packages contained thirty-four types of training options to choose from, and included institutional and on-the-job training, with meal support, toolkits and linkages to employment and microfinance. The micro-enterprise development included thirty-nine options including business induction and skills training. In addition to the training, the VMLRs who had taken this option also received start-up support, a daily stipend, meals, tools and support for linkages to market and micro-finance support.

The rehabilitation package also included the formal education option, which allowed for educational support for a maximum of four years up to grade XII, including two years of stipend provision and stationery. A school or college that enrolled a VMLR would receive "structural support"; this was material support that could be utilised to upgrade the infrastructure of the school. Such support was considered to be an element

---

[3] Interview with a UN staff member in Kathmandu, November 2011.
[4] Interview with a staff member at UNIRP in Kathmandu, November 2011.

of a community-based approach to reintegration.[5] Similarly, the health related training included three different courses: (a) Community Medical Assistance (CMA), (b) Pathology Laboratory Assistant training, and (c) Auxiliary Nurse Midwife training (ANM) courses.

In addition to the vocational training options, the programme also included career counselling, mentoring and psychosocial support. The programme was innovative in that it included gender support for both male and female VMLRs. According to a UNIRP officer interviewed in November 2011, out of a total of 2100 beneficiaries of the programme, nearly 38% were female, including mothers. The programme thus responded to the specific needs of female participants, particularly targeting pregnant women, breast-feeding mothers and both male and female VMLRs caring for younger children.[6] It also included nutritional support for the children of VMLRs, special reproductive health allowances, and maternity and paternity allowances. According to the UNIRP staff, once the additional gender support was introduced, it considerably increased enrolment of VMLRs in the programme.[7]

There are several positive aspects of the rehabilitation programme that deserve attention. For instance, according to a UNIRP staff member, by the end of 2011, almost 67% of the total VMLRs had been registered in the programme and undergone different types of training.[8] By April 2013, almost 70% of the total VMLRs who registered in the programmes were employed or self-employed (UNPFN, 2013). This figure is certainly commendable in a country where the unemployment rate is reportedly high.[9] Similarly, the gender support component added to the rehabilitation package has several positive effects on the ground. VMLRs, especially those having children, were greatly benefitted from

---

[5] Interview with a UN staff member and a government official from MoPR in Kathmandu, October 2011.

[6] Interview with a UNIRP staff member, Kathmandu, November 2011.

[7] Interview in Kathmandu, October 2011.

[8] Interview in Kathmandu, December 2011.

[9] There is no actual figure available on the unemployment rate in Nepal. A database on unemployment rate has reported it to be 46% of the total population (see http://www.indexmundi.com/g/r.aspx?v=74). In Nepal, calculating the unemployment rate can also be complicated because of a significant overlap between unemployment and under-employment, as a large proportion of the rural population who live on subsistence agriculture remain unemployed most of the time. Interview with a sociologist in Kathmandu, February 2013.

the programme. This component particularly addressed gender concerns and needs of ex-combatants, which is a commendable effort and an innovation made by the rehabilitation programme.

However, despite the positive aspects of rehabilitation, some macro and micro level factors have remained as constraints and challenges, as discussed in the following sections.

Organisational Context and the Programmatic Approach

At the macro level, the overall political context of the peace process affects DDR in one way or another (Pouligny, 2004). Berdal (1996) argues that the willingness of key political actors in DDR determines the success or failure of reintegration programmes. The overall organisational context of a rehabilitation programme, therefore, must be examined in the light of the macro political environment of the peace process involved.

In this study, the political and organisational context was reiterated as a major concept emerged from the data. When frequently repeated concepts from the data were compared, it was found that "UNIRP operation in politicised environment", "inadequate planning", "an individual-combatant focused programmatic approach", and "the notion of disqualified combatants" emerged as major themes pertaining to the political and organisational context.

UNIRP Operating in Politicised Environment

From the outset, the unfavourable political environment and the politicisation of the issue of the Maoist ex-combatants, including rehabilitation of VMLRs, remained a key challenge to the UNIRP. In this regard, this study found two pertinent issues that had considerable negative effects on the rehabilitation programme.

Firstly, the major political parties, including the CPNM, the Nepali Congress (NC) and the Communist Party of Nepal Marxist and Leninist (CPNUML), had sharply differing views on developing the modality of the rehabilitation package. As also noted above, the deep political divisions delayed the discharge of VMLRs from cantonments for three years. The NC's position was that the VMLRs should leave the cantonments immediately after their verification and the Maoists were to initiate the process without any delay. Arguing that it was the CPNM who should be more responsible for, and accountable to, the VMLRs, the then NC-led government maintained a somewhat biased and rigid position in terms of providing a comprehensive rehabilitation package to VMLRs.

In sharp contrast, the CPNM maintained that the VMLRs should be treated the same as other qualified ex-combatants. The Maoists wanted the government (led by the NC) to design a rehabilitation package that was dignified and acceptable to VMLRs, although what "dignified rehabilitation" would mean was never clarified. The CPNUML, which held a middle-path approach to this debate, proposed that the government could offer a rehabilitation package, with a value equivalent to, or less than, one hundred thousand rupees per VMLRs.[10]

While agreement on the rehabilitation package continued to be marred by deeply divided politics, the CPNM was under mounting pressure from the international community, including the UNMIN and the Special Representative of the Secretary General (SRSG) for Children and Armed Conflict, to release the VMLRs from cantonments immediately. In the meantime, the CPNM, the Government of Nepal (GoN) and the UN signed the United Nations Security Council Resolution (UNSCR) 1612 Action Plan. Following the signing of the Action Plan, amidst the political debate about a rehabilitation package, the CPNM made a unilateral decision to discharge the VMLRs from cantonments. Starting in January 2010, the discharge process was entirely led by the CPNM. The CPNM's unilateral decision to discharge the VMLRs and the government's almost non-existent involvement in the process reflects the degree to which the rehabilitation programme was marred by politicisation.

Secondly, the UNIRP had to operate in an extremely sensitive and fragile political environment, which caused institutional and operational difficulties for the UNIRP. For instance, the rehabilitation programme was envisioned as a six-step linear process. It was expected to follow a sequence of: (1) information and consultation, (2) profiling survey of combatants, (3) discharge from cantonments, (4) orientation and counselling in the transit centre, (5) rehabilitation with technical education and vocational training support and (6) post-training support and monitoring. But the second stage (profiling survey) could not be conducted,

---

[10] Interview with an officer from the Ministry of Peace and Reconstruction in Kathmandu, October 2011.

because the CPNM did not allow the government and UNIRP staffs to collect personal information from VMLRs inside the cantonments.[11]

This rejection demonstrates the degree of mistrust and growing political animosity between the CPNM and the government, particularly when it involved collecting sensitive information about the ex-combatants and their everyday lives inside the cantonments. Due to the lack of the profiling survey, which was intended to document the existing skills of individual ex-combatants, their educational level and interests, the UNIRP could not obtain any baseline data. Without this data, the UNIRP was limited in their capacity to address the needs, interests and aspirations of the VMLRs, as well as to monitor and evaluate the progress of the rehabilitation process at a later stage.

Inadequate Planning and Preparations

The sudden unilateral discharge of VMLRs necessitated a prompt response to provide rehabilitation to the frustrated, angry and disillusioned VMLRs. There was a perception that a delay in their rehabilitation would likely lead to VMLRs' involvement in criminal activities.[12] Although the UN agencies that implemented the UNIRP had consulted with relevant stakeholders at the time of designing the rehabilitation package, the UNIRP staffs interviewed conceded that they were not given enough preparation time to design the programme.[13] A well-prepared commencement of the programme would have made a difference. For instance, a rigorous market survey taking into account the realities of the local and national economy would have been necessary before preparing the rehabilitation package; however, this did not eventuate due to time constraints. Appropriate preparation time would also have enabled the UNIRP to disseminate the information about the programme to the VMLRs beforehand, which would have informed them of the details and purpose of the programme. According to Saferworld (2010), the communication gap between the UNIRP and the VMLRs initially caused a low case-load in the programme.

---

[11] Interview with a MoPR officer, October 2011.
[12] Interview with a CPNUML leader in Kathmandu, December 2011.
[13] Interview with a UNIRP staff member, Kathmandu, November 2011.

Individual Combatant-Focused "Minimalist" Rehabilitation

Information collected during the interviews suggests that the VMLRs' rehabilitation programme was largely focused on individual ex-combatants. This study identified two factors that shaped the ex-combatant-focused nature of the rehabilitation programme.

Firstly, the UNIRP was designed partly as a humanitarian response and partly as a means of addressing the socio-economic issues and concerns of the VMLRs in an expedited manner. The programme was, therefore, specifically designed to keep the ex-combatants engaged in skills training and entrepreneurship skills development so that it would avert their remobilisation, engage them in a non-violent means of livelihood and divert their attention away from involvement in militant alternatives. From this point of view, attention on the VMLRs' families and communities remained out-focused. During the field work, many ex-combatants asserted, when they were interviewed, that although their families did not complain, many felt that some form of material support targeting ex-combatants' families would have helped them not only to recover from economic burdens, but it would have also assisted in the acceptance of ex-combatants into their respective families, which would have been a much smoother transition with the material assistance.

Experience from other contexts also suggests that some form of material support to the families of ex-combatants motivates them to receive ex-combatants back into the families (Colletta, Kostner, & Wiederhofer, 1996). However, it can be argued that providing material support to the families does not necessarily help reintegrate ex-combatants because family acceptance can vary, based on how or whether ex-combatants' conscription in the past had been consented to by their families. Some families and social networks encourage children to join the military on the basis of norms, ideology, social pressure, or even despair due to harsh economic conditions (Kimmel & Roby, 2007; Wessels, 2006). Although it was not explored in detail whether families who gave their consent for their children to join the war have a different perception of reintegration from those who did not provide consent conscription, this study has found generally that ex-combatants who joined the insurgency without family consent tended to avoid going back to their families. These dynamics suggest that we must not be overly confident that material support alone can increase acceptance of ex-combatants into their families.

It is necessary to look deeper into the past conditions of war participation and the changing dynamics of relationships between ex-combatants and their families.

Secondly, the VMLRs were not only dispersed across the regions and districts but also many of them gradually moved from their places of origin to urban areas either in search of employment or because they found it easier to live in new communities where their past identity as combatants was not known. Due to the highly dispersed population and mobile nature of VMLRs, the UNIRP had a limitation in adopting a community-centred approach in the programme.

Focusing more on harnessing the ex-combatants' vocational, technical and entrepreneurship development skills and less on social reintegration, the rehabilitation programme adopted an approach which I call bringing the VMLRs "back to work" rather than "back to the community". According to a female respondent who worked in a UN agency in Kathmandu, the "back to work" approach tended to transform the VMLRs' identity through jobs and entrepreneurship, but had actually missed an opportunity to assist them to reconnect with their families and the communities in their places of origin, as some of them were known to be experiencing various difficulties related to social stigma and rejection by the community.[14] In this regard, it was suggested that the family could help VMLRs adjust better than they could do by themselves.

Notion of Disqualified Combatants and (Non)Participation in the UNIRP

As mentioned earlier, VMLRs were initially classified by the UNMIN as "disqualified" combatants. The literal translation of "disqualified" in the Nepali language is *ayogya*, which has several negative connotations and inferences in Nepali society. For instance, to be *ayogya* means, among other things, to be virtually useless, redundant, unfit or incapable of anything good. Without knowing the implicit and explicit negative connotations of the term, the UNMIN had proved culturally and socially insensitive and naïve in categorising the ex-combatants as "disqualified" and this ultimately created an unfavourable operational environment for the UNIRP.

---

[14] Interview with civil society leaders in Kathmandu, Biratnagar, and Dhangadi in September, October, and December 2011 respectively.

The notion of "disqualified" carried stigma, humiliation and a feeling of rejection amongst the VMLRs. Use of the term was one of a few reasons why many VMLRs could not return to their villages and families. An ex-combatant in Dhangadi said, "being called 'disqualified' is humiliating and carries a lot of social stigma. I cannot go to my village because people call me 'disqualified'; it hurts me badly".[15] The notion of "disqualified" combatants, therefore, generated the VMLRs' negative perception and narratives towards the UNIRP. As a consequence, while many VMLRs rejected the UNIRP package, others became dubious about the UNIRP's credibility to support them. In both circumstances, the UNIRP initially experienced the VMLRs' rejection and non-participation in the programme, although participation in the programme increased over the time.

Post-conflict Economy

Successful rehabilitation can be significantly shaped by both micro and macro-economic environments in places where ex-combatants are to be rehabilitated (Lamb, 2011). Macro-economic factors such as structural adjustment programmes, economic reforms, a narrow industrial base, labour market saturation, high inflation and high military expenditure will affect economic rehabilitation support in areas such as vocational training and micro enterprise development (Özerdem, 2009, p. 24). At the micro-level, the function of economic reintegration is to address the restoration of a sustainable livelihood for ex-combatants which, according to Porto et al. (2007, p. 141), requires:

> Stabilisation of the macro-economic situation in the country for which the revitalisation of the national economy (strengthening of the business sector - both public and private) is extremely important, as is financial stabilisation.

Here Porto et al. (2007) state that both micro and macro-economic conditions are closely inter-linked and thus have a role to play in creating favourable conditions for a successful rehabilitation programme to work.

Unfortunately, micro and macro-economic conditions in post-conflict contexts are generally plagued by several shortcomings, such as poor employment opportunities, lack of physical infrastructure and inadequate

---

[15] Interview with a VMLR in Dhangadi, December 2011.

economic development policies, as well as informal and shadow economic activities that undermine the growth of the formal economic sector (Lamb, 2011; Upreti, 2010). Therefore, while a healthy post-conflict economy is a precondition for a successful rehabilitation programme, conversely, it is argued that more emphasis should be given to gearing up the rehabilitation programme towards linking it with post-conflict economic recovery and development initiatives (Bragg, 2006; ILO, 2009; Knight & Özerdem, 2004; SIDDR, 2006; UN, 2000).

Job creation is an important element of economic rehabilitation (ILO, 2009). In this regard, economic rehabilitation aims to either improve employability of ex-combatants through skills development training and job creation (ILO, 2009; Specht, 2010) or promote self-employment or self-entrepreneurship after receiving relevant technical education or vocational training (Body, 2006; ILO, 1997). This proposition, however, can be contested because it might work for some ex-combatants but not for others who find it extremely difficult to return to their villages or the workforce because of their involvement in atrocities and violence in the past. In other words, economic reintegration should not be taken for granted in the absence of efforts to reconcile ex-combatants as perpetrators and community as victims, or vice versa.

Furthermore, the creation of alternative livelihoods and/or jobs is exceptionally difficult in post-conflict or conflict economies where a number of unemployed young people compete for the limited numbers of opportunities available (UN, 2010b). Similarly, skill development and vocational training have risks of being "supply-driven", as the skill may not often match the demand in the market. Consequently, the chances of ex-combatants' involvement in the informal economy and the "shadow economy" may remain high (Lamb, 2011). Body (2006, p. 4), therefore, recommends selecting vocational training and technical skills for ex-combatants by taking into account an their skills, needs, age, education, and interest as well as an assessment of the local economic context. A mismatch between demand and supply in terms of training and employment can exacerbate grievances and this may push ex-combatants into a non-violent means of livelihood.

From the economic perspective, it was found that the following macro level factors must be understood if we are to make sense of the opportunities and constraints associated with the rehabilitation of VMLRs.

The Private Sector: Important Actor but Ignored

Because of its capacity to offer jobs to ex-combatants, the private sector (PS) can be an important actor to collaborate with (International Alert, 2006; SIDDR, 2006; Specht, 2010). However, often the PS itself is a victim of a fragile post-conflict economy. Creating an enabling environment to harness the capacity of the PS to navigate post-conflict economic growth and thereby create more jobs is, therefore, recommended. A reduction of barriers to doing business, access to credit, technology and technical support are some of the recommendations made by SIDDR (2006, p. 29) to motivate the PS to contribute to the rehabilitation of ex-combatants. Despite this optimism, the PS has often been hesitant to provide jobs to ex-combatants because of their obvious militarised past. Lack of trust between the PS as the employer and ex-combatants as the employees could, therefore, be a barrier to the successful rehabilitation of ex-combatants in the national or local economies.

The fieldwork revealed that apart from a few private service providers involved in delivering vocational and micro-enterprise training, the PS was not systematically involved in the UNIRP or in supporting rehabiliation of VMLRs in one way or other. As a result, the PS, although being the largest job creator, was either unaware of, or had limited knowledge about, the rehabilitation programme. When asked what role the PS could play in creating economic opportunities for the rehabilitated ex-combatants and how the sector could benefit from the UNIRP, the PS people who were interviewed expressed mixed responses. While some believed that the rehabilitation programme could solve the labour shortage in the industrial sectors where highly specialised technical skills were needed, others expressed a hesitation to offer jobs to the ex-combatants. Because of the ex-combatants' politicised and militarised backgrounds, the business people in Kathmandu as well as in districts outside Kathmandu believed that this could be problematic in the workplace.

The decision to offer a job to an ex-combatant depended on how the rehabilitation programme could defuse their politicised and militarised mind-set, and how well the ex-combatants could become detached from the Maoist party.[16] Politicised trade unions presented a major challenge to the industrial sector in Nepal (Kyloh, 2008). In recent times, the CPNM-affiliated trade union has become a major concern for

---

[16] Interview with a male businessman in Biratnagar, October 2011.

industrial relations.[17] In this context, business people also expressed concerns about the possibility that ex-combatants would retain links with the CPNM and its affiliated trade union, which could lead to the politicisation of the workplace.

As an attempt to involve the PS in the rehabilitation programme, the UNIRP interacted and coordinated with some influential business people and their umbrella organisations, such as the Federation of Nepalese the Chamber of Commerce and Industries (FNCCI). However, it did not reach out to Small and Medium Enterprises (SMEs), which occupy a major proportion of the PS in Nepal and make a huge contribution to the local and national economy, as well as in creating jobs for unemployed people locally. Building a thorough coordination mechanism involving SMEs would have provided the means to foster mutual trust and understanding between business people and former combatants. It could also provide prospective employers with an opportunity to observe the skill level and attitude of ex-combatants as potential employees.

The reputation and credibility of the training providing organisations, which were contracted by the UNIRP to deliver vocational and skill development training packages, also mattered a lot for the ex-combatants in relation to their chances of securing a job. There was more willingness to employ those combatants who graduated from the training institutes that had a strong reputation and linkages with the PS.[18] The training providers also could have played a facilitating role in linking the graduates with the potential employers. However, it was observed that many training institutions were either under-resourced or simply did not have the willingness and capacity to play a facilitating role for finding employment for trainee VMLRs. In the meantime, some training providers in the districts were sub-contracted. Saferworld (2010, p. 75) labels them "middlemen", who did not properly understand the spirit of the programme and, therefore, had very limited ownership of it. Selection of credible training institutions and contracting them to offer post-training support, such as job linkages, counselling, monitoring and follow-up could have made the outcome of rehabilitation more effective.

---

[17] Interview with a male businessman in Biratnagar, October 2011.
[18] Interview with a female INGO worker, Kathmandu, October 2011.

Urban Centric Economic Rehabilitation

Since an overwhelming majority of VMLRs who graduated from training programmes have been living in urban and semi-urban areas, particularly in the southern belt of the country, known as *Terai*, along the east and west highway, as well as in the Kathmandu valley, the economic rehabilitation of VMLRs ultimately has become "urban centric".

Two dimensions of the urban centric rehabilitation were identified: economic and social. Economically, the Terai region and Kathmandu are two major economic hubs in the country. Major industrial corridors, such as the Morang-Sunsari industrial corridor and the Bara-Parsa industrial corridor, are located in this region. Since economic opportunities are more available in the Terai region than the hills and mountains, big cities like Biratnagar, Birgunj, Butwal, Bhairahawa, Nepalgunj, and Dhangadi are lucrative destinations for workers from the employment and business points of view. Kathmandu, on the other hand, is seen as the land of opportunity. Thus, following the pathways to economic opportunities, many VMLRs who graduated from the UNIRP landed in urban and semi-urban areas.

Socially, most of the VMLRs did not wish to go back to their villages for a host of social reasons, but most important among these was social stigma attached to their perhaps flawed identity as "disqualified" combatants. Being in the city spaces under such circumstances could help them conceal their past and thereby gradually create a new civilian identity.

Rural urban migration, as well as foreign labour migration, is growing on an unprecedented scale in Nepal. On the one hand, this new trajectory of internal and international migration has been gradually creating regional imbalances in terms of the availability of human capital and business activities. On the other hand, the agricultural sector, which is the backbone of Nepal's economy, has been suffering from skilled, semi-skilled and unskilled labour shortages. The rehabilitation programme could have helped to address such imbalances by producing skilled and semi-skilled human capital in the agricultural and agro-related sectors in general. This contribution would be more valuable and meaningful for agrarian transformation, which is highly essential for economic development in post-conflict Nepal.[19] Since the Maoists rejected

---

[19] Interview with a civil society leader in Dhangadi, December 2011.

agriculture-related training components, the UNIRP lost the opportunity to contribute to human capital development in this sector. Ultimately, the rehabilitation programme ended up, in some way, contributing to an already rapidly increasing rural-urban migration.

NATIONAL AND LOCAL OWNERSHIP AND COLLABORATION

Promoting the national government's ownership and the fostering of multi-stakeholder partnerships between the government, international agencies, civil society and the PS may determine outcomes of a rehabilitation programme (UN, 2006). SIDDR (2006) makes a recommendation to promote national and local ownership of a successful rehabilitation programme. National and local ownership is also essential to avoid external intervention without recognising local contexts and realities, which may have tremendous implications for the way ex-combatants are accepted in workplaces and societies. Understanding such realities requires a good knowledge of the causes of the preceding conflict and the factors which drove people to become ex-combatants in the past. Further, ownership of the rehabilitation programme has both governance and political elements, because it requires an effective and transparent governance system and special institutional arrangements that may be contingent upon the political processes and arrangements associated with a DDR programme (Muggah, 2009).

Attached to ownership is the issue of partnership and collaboration. While the role of civil society is recommended (SIDDR, 2006), local ownership and collaboration may also depend on the initiative of the ex-combatants together with their families and the support they receive from their communities, the government and non-government organisations (NGOs), as well as other forms of external assistance (Kingma & Muggah, 2009). As mentioned earlier, partnership with the PS can positively contribute to the economic dimension of rehabilitation.

It was discovered that from the beginning, the government had limited direct involvement in the preparation and implementation of the rehabilitation programme. Apart from attending the UNIRP steering committee meetings, the government did not have any formal mechanism to participate in the implementation of the UNIRP. Thus, having been left in the hands of UN agencies, the rehabilitation programme lacked national as well as local ownership. In other words, the programme appeared to be "UN-led", rather than what it should have ideally been, a "UN-supported" process with government taking leading role in the implementation.

Three factors were identified that explained what was behind the government's minimal involvement and participation. Firstly, there was the political factor. As mentioned earlier in this chapter, the lack of political consensus on the modality and process of the VMLRs' rehabilitation actually hindered the activities that were to follow. Secondly, because of limited technical and administrative capacity, the government did not become involved in the programme as much as it should have done. Third, was a financial reason; it was perceived or interpreted as being too costly to undertake without financial assistance. The UNIRP was funded through the United Nations Peace Fund for Nepal (UNPFN). The UNPFN is a multi-donor trust fund supported by Norway, Denmark, Switzerland, the United Kingdom and Canada.[20] Because the funding did not flow through the government mechanism, this potentially minimised the government's interest as well as accountability in the programme. Channelling financial resources through the government could have arguably increased its active participation in the programme, but it may have created other problems too. Arguably, financial assistance could have encouraged the government to contribute non-financial resources such as physical and human capital, in order to assist implementation of the programme.

But some interviewee contended that the government could have actively provided this type of in-kind contribution anyway, even without the financial assistance received from the donors. At the local level, the UNIRP did coordinate with some district-level line agencies of the government, such as the Centre for Technical Education and Vocation Training (CTEVT) and the National Skill Testing Board (NSTB). Yet, several regional staff of the UNIRP stated that apart from coordinating for security-related matters with the Chief District Officer (CDO) and district police office, the UNIRP regional offices operated with virtually no coordination with the local government.

The UNIRP's technical expertise would have helped build the government's capacity in rehabilitation-related works if the government had taken responsibility for its overall implementation. This would also have ensured the VMLRs' confidence in the process; therefore, a larger role

---

[20] Interview with a UN staff member, Kathmandu, December 2011.

by the government would not only have increased national and local ownership but it would also have depoliticised the rehabilitation package.

Apart from the government's role, civil society could have also been an important actor. Engaging civil society organisations could have been critically helpful in rebuilding relationships between ex-combatants and the local community. Indeed, the UNIRP partnered with local NGOs, mostly the ones that had worked with UNICEF in the rehabilitation of children associated with armed forces and armed groups (CAFAG). This strategy worked well, as the local NGOs were socially and morally more accountable to beneficiaries than external ones. However, the NGOs were given very limited roles, such as involvement in social mobilisation and peacebuilding aspects of the UNIRP. Therefore, according to a female NGO activist,[21] civil society participation carried out through the peacebuilding elements of the rehabilitation programme was only "ceremonial", meaning that they were just fulfilling ritualistic needs, such as social mobilisation, trustbuilding, in the programme.

Saferworld (2010) recommends that community ownership could be promoted through the establishment of Community Rehabilitation Committees, which could play a lead role in the implementation of the social, psychosocial and monitoring aspects of rehabilitation programmes at the local level. This study, however, found that instead of setting up new institutions, the UNIRP could have been linked to existing institutions and local peace initiatives, for example, Local Peace Committees (LPCs).[22] As the LPC has increasingly become politicised in recent times, this could potentially increase the risk of the rehabilitation programme being a victim of further politicisation. Nonetheless, there was a need to promote agency of local government as well as civil society organisations even if the rehabilitation programmes are phased out after 2013. Therefore, proactive role of the Ministry of Peace and Reconstruction (MoPR) at the national level, and active engagement of LPCs at the local level would have increased both local and national level ownership.

[21] Interviewed in Kathmandu, October 2011.

[22] The Local Peace Committee (LPC) is a district-level as well as community-level inclusive peace mechanism. It has members from all major political parties, civil society, conflict victims and women. Its overall aims are to create an environment conducive to a just system in a transitional period through restoration of sustainable peace by resolving the remnants of conflict at the local level and systematically promoting the processes of peace and reconstruction through mutual goodwill and unity. As of April 2011, according to the Ministry of Peace and Reconstruction (MoPR), 73 out of 75 districts have established LPCs under the tutelage of the MoPR.

Ex-combatants' Personal and Social Circumstances

Ex-combatants' personal and social circumstances and background such as connections with their family and relatives, and their relationship, interaction and trust with their personal and social networks—collectively known as "social capital"—are important enabling factors for successful economic rehabilitation (Leff, 2008). Family is an important dimension in relation to an ex-combatant's personal and social circumstances. How and to what extent ex-combatants maintain their relationships with their families can have enormous effects on the success of the reintegration programme (Knight, 2008). Individual ex-combatants' family commitments and responsibilities, as well as their relationships and networks in the communities where they will be rehabilitated, can directly and indirectly inform their perceptions about the reintegration programme and their livelihood choices (Lamb, 2011, p. 17). Lamb further argues that such personal circumstances can also significantly influence their decision to participate or not in a rehabilitation programme. In this regard, it has been discovered that the following micro-level factors shaped the VMLR ex-combatants' experiences of rehabilitation.

Dependency Syndrome and Politics of (Dis)engagement in Rehabilitation

A sizeable number of VMLRs had developed a dependency on their commanders and CPNM leaders. This dependency syndrome was partly a result of the phenomenon of the VMLRs' prolonged stay in the cantonments. Having lived in the cantonments along with the verified ex-combatants for more than three years, the VMLRs not only associated themselves with the ex-combatants' war family but also substantially increased their expectations, particularly in terms of receiving the similar level of support and benefits as other qualified ex-combatants would receive. In the meantime, the PLA commanders and CPNM leaders raised their expectations and, thereby, kept on making unattainable promises to the VMLRs. For instance, a male VMLR interviewed in Dhangadi in December 2011 said:

> We (VMLRs) were always told that we would be treated equal to, meaning the same as, other fellows, the so-called "qualified" combatants. The party leaders including Comrade Prachanda and PLA commanders, always

assured us that the UNMIN had classified us as "disqualified", but that they (Maoist leaders and PLA commanders) have not done and would never do so.

Making such promises to VMLRs was indeed a tool used by the commanders to retain these ex-combatants' loyalty to their leadership at the time of their discharge. The consequence of this was that it strengthened the VMLRs' dependency on the leadership.

Such dependency is found to have had particular effects on their personal choices and decisions to participate in the rehabilitation programme; this was because in many places, commanders and the CPNM leaders discouraged, and in some places like in Dhangadi, even restricted their participation in the rehabilitation programme.[23] VMLRs from the far-west region (particularly in the Bardiya, Kailali and Mahendra Nagar districts) and eastern region (Jhapa, Morang, Ilam, Dhankuta and Taplejung districts) were more discouraged than those from the central region. It was partly for this reason that the case load from these areas was relatively low, being only around 1585 by mid-2010 (UNIRP, 2012), although this figure later increased towards the end of the same year.[24]

Following the discharge of VMLRs from the cantonments, the CPNM provided them with group accommodation, regular monthly allowances and rations. In Dhangadi district alone, the VMLRs who did not take up any rehabilitation package were accommodated in three rented houses. In several districts in the eastern region (Morang, Jhapa, Taplejung), as well as in Kathmandu, Bhaktapur and Lalitpur districts, the VMLRs lived in shared accommodation arranged by the respective CPNM district office.

During the field visit, it was observed that these groups had a strong connection with the nearby cantonments. These shared accommodation locations, in a way, looked like a "proxy-cantonment". Command and control structures perpetuated as the PLA assigned a commander who was responsible for managing the VMLRs in shared accommodation. The assigned commander retained loyalty and gained control over the VMLRs because of his/her important role in facilitating and coordinating with the PLA in the cantonments, as well as respective district

---

[23] Interview with ex-combatants, Dangadi, December 2011.

[24] Interview with UNIRP staff member in Kathmandu, November 2011.

committees of the party, in order to provide VMLRs with supplies, including rations and other necessary expenses. Initially, discouragement of the VMLRs from participating in the rehabilitation programme was, to a certain extent, inspired by the prospect of their remobilisation in the Maoists' contentious politics through its various sister organisations, most notably the Young Communist League (YCL).

Nonetheless, a number of interviews also suggested that many VMLRs could not return to their villages owing to the stigma attached to their "disqualified" status; therefore, they demanded that the party arrange for them to live in groups. Almost all VMLRs interviewed preferred to live in the group, because doing so would increase their collective bargaining capacity, not only with the party but also with the government. Further, living in groups assured them their physical safety and security, plus rendered the emotional and psychological support of their fellow combatants. A male VMLR in a FGD in Dhangadi said,[25]

> living together with fellow ex-combatants and being in constant contact with commanders has provided us with a sense of security and belonging to the PLA family of which we are and continue to be an integral part

The dynamics, however, changed over time. The ex-combatants who did not participate in the rehabilitation programme began to feel "left out". They formed a national struggle committee and began to organise struggle programmes against their own party for not taking any initiatives to provide them with an attractive and dignified rehabilitation package. The struggle committee even presented a memorandum to the government requesting it to be ready to revise and offer an attractive rehabilitation package. Dr. Babu Ram Bhattari-led government decided to provide the VMLRs with additional Nepali rupees (NRs) 200,000 in cash, although the decision was later scrapped by the Supreme Court.

Over time, those living in rented houses gradually appeared to be a burden, particularly an economic burden, for the PLA. In the meantime, the CPNM decided to dissolve the YCL,[26] which made the VMLRs, who were then branded as YCL workers, redundant. The district leaders and

---

[25] Interviewed in December 2011.

[26] YCL is the youth wing of CPNM, officially established in February 2007. Initially the YCL operated as a para military group and was accused of carrying out political violence across the country.

PLA commanders, therefore, gradually began to encourage the VMLRs to join the rehabilitation programme. In the meantime, the VMLRs who had participated in the rehabilitation programme began to show some achievements by earning modest livings on their own. As a consequence of these various factors and changing circumstances, the case load in the UNIRP programme increased dramatically at a time when the programme was planning to end.[27] Consequently, by July 2012, the net enrolment in the training and education programme of the UNIRP increased to 54%.[28]

The Rehabilitation Package: Ex-combatants' Mixed Perceptions

All the VMLRs interviewed in the field explicitly and consistently expressed that the rehabilitation package, offered by the UNIRP, was "undignified, irrelevant and inadequate". Their dissatisfaction with the package had two dimensions.

Firstly, there was a typical stereotyping of certain agricultural and labour-intensive work and jobs in Nepalese society. Such labour-intensive work attaches a perceived low social status and a lack of dignity in the hierarchical Nepali society. Partly because of this social perception and also partly because the ex-combatants themselves felt their association with the war had empowered and elevated them socially, the VMLRs considered some traditional training schemes, such as poultry farming and motorcycle repairing, to be undignified and not suitable for ex-combatants. Training packages that involved modern technology, such as mobile phone repairs, were popular among many male ex-combatants.

Secondly, the intensity and time frame of the training programme for the VMLRs was not adequate. The VMLRs came from a distinct background; they did not possess the basic requirements and competencies to join any kind of vocational and/or entrepreneurship development programme. Additionally, the training programme was fast-tracked, which made it difficult for most ex-combatants to keep pace. A female ex-combatant who was involved in tailoring training in Itahari said the following when interviewed[29]:

---

[27] Interview with a UNIRP staff member, Kathmandu, November 2011.
[28] Interview with a UN staff member, December 2012.
[29] Interviewed in October 2011.

> I was in the war for several years and then I spent an idle life in cantonments for three years. Now I am involved in tailoring training, which is very intensive and I am having difficulty in learning so many things in such a short time.

Another VMLR who was employed as a cook in a restaurant in Belbari, Morang said[30]: "the content of the training was not only inadequate but it was also out-dated". Although the UNIRP offered support to upgrade skills, many VMLRs were not aware of this provision that was introduced later as part of the UNIRP.

Due to the lack of a proper survey of the ex-combatants' aspirations and needs, and opportunities in the market, there was a mismatch between the VMLRs' expectations and the rehabilitation package offered, meaning that the lack of an adequate market survey resulted in providing traditional training schemes, which were not so appealing to many of the ex-combatants.

If examined from gender perspective, women ex-combatants have particularly different needs which make their perceptions toward the rehabilitation package distinct. Many female ex-combatants thought that they would need more financial and psychosocial supports. Those female ex-combatants who had children or were expecting children in near future would require special support to child care, because the burden of child care would limit their availability to participate in rehabilitation scheme. The UNIRP recognised and addressed this gender specific need of female ex-combatants by providing special gender support, as stated earlier in this chapter. Those ex-combatants who were able to receive the gender support had generally positive perception towards the UNIRP package.

Another area were gender specific need was strikingly visible is psychosocial support. Due to inter-caste marriage and prevalent caste-based discrimination, ex-combatants, especially female ex-combatants who had inter-caste marriage suffered from rejection in families (in-laws family as well their own maternal family) and social stigma. This had significant impact on the way in which they would be reintegrated. Although, the UNIRP included psychosocial counselling support, it could not reach out to many and needy female ex-combatants. As a result, while gender-specific support was adequately addressed and those who could not

---

[30] Interviewed in October 2011.

avail such support at the time of need were critical about UNIRP's psychosocial support element.

Participation in UNIRP: The Three Categories of VMLRs

In terms of their participation in the training programmes, this study noted three distinct categories of VMLRs: "engaged", "semi-engaged" and "disengaged". This categorisation is based on ex-combatants' narratives and a subsequent assessment of how individual ex-combatants' personal and social circumstances influenced and framed their responses in terms of participating in the UNIRP. It is acknowledged, however, that these categories are not strictly mutually exclusive because in some circumstances, some ex-combatants may fall into either or both categories. Despite this, it was found that these three categories of VMLRs provided useful insights to enable an understanding of their responses to the rehabilitation programme more clearly.

In the "engaged" category, there were VMLRs who either found the fact that they were in the grip of frustration with the CPNM or that their dependency on the PLA was not going to bring any real differences with respect to transforming their lives in the long run. Loyalty towards the CPNM was slowly fading away and war fatigue was increasing with the ex-combatants within this category. Many of them were already in contact with their families and wanted to detach themselves from the CPNM. Therefore, inspired by an aspiration and commitment to start a new career and life, they participated in the UNIRP right from the very beginning.

In the "disengaged" category, the VMLRs did not participate in the rehabilitation programme for a range of reasons, such as restrictions brought to bear on them from the CPNM and dissatisfaction in the package being offered to them. Many VMLRs were actually being paid more in monthly cash allowances provided by the CPNM for not participating in the UNIRP than what they would get from the UNIRP. Therefore, the short-term incentives of non-participation outweighed those of participation. The VMLRs in this category were found to be more politically active and highly politically radicalised by the Maoist ideology.

In between was the "semi-engaged" category. Many VMLRs wanted to settle in urban areas in order to find better opportunities in this human-populated context. For those seeking such opportunities, taking up a rehabilitation package provided a paid "window period" in which to find a new way of engaging with the idea of resettlement. Bleie and Shrestha (2012, p. 34) call this phenomenon a "springboard for finding opportunities for settling in urban areas". To a certain extent, the ex-combatants within the semi-engaged category were opportunistic by nature, including some of them who were even reportedly involved in crime. Similarly, for many VMLRs whose spouses were still confined in a cantonment, the UNIRP programme provided a good opportunity for them to buy time to wait for their spouses to be released from the cantonment. A female ex-combatant in Jhapa district said[31]:

> My husband is in a cantonment in Morang district, so I have started poultry farming in Kherkha bazar according to his advice. I will do this business until he gets out of the cantonment. Once he leaves the cantonment, we will once again plan something new.

As a result some VMLRs accessed the UNIRP more for the short-term benefits than for utilising the training and skills for a new career. The VMLRs from this category were mobile; therefore, many of them could not be located at the addresses provided by the UNIRP regional offices. I found, as a researcher, that the UNIRP lacked a thorough and rigorous monitoring system to follow the progress and movements of the VMLRs who frequently changed locations.

It is important to clarify here that these three categories have been identified based on the ex-combatants' responses to the rehabilitation programme. If factors such as their political and social participation, involvement in economic activities and criminality are taken into account, it is possible that ex-combatants might be categorised differently.

Informal Advice More Important in Selecting the Package

Although formal career counselling was available in every regional office of the UNIRP and, indeed, it was mandatory before selecting any package, many VMLRs mentioned that they made their decision based on the advice received from one or many informal sources, including peers (fellow VMLRs), spouses, family members, relatives, CPNM leaders and commanders. The ex-combatants' reliance on informal sources of

---

[31] Interviewed in November 2011.

counselling and advice was pertinent; it influenced them to select the rehabilitation package or not. When asked why they preferred to follow informal advice when career counselling was available in the UNIRP, an overwhelming number of VMLRs responded that the counselling session was too brief (often lasted for less than an hour), very formal, and, more importantly, they said that they did not have enough time to build a rapport with the counsellors.

Many followed advice from fellow VMLRs because, in doing so, it would enable them to live together with the fellow ex-combatants during their training. This also could open up the possibility of conducting a joint business, in which case the business start-up grant provided by the UNIRP could increase substantially. The VMLRs also experienced a lack of adequate information about the package, its basic requirements and future prospects, which is another reason for the ex-combatants relying on informal advice.

According to a counsellor working with UNICEF, the VMLRs had very limited trust and confidence in the UNIRP itself. The distrust increased partly because of the way the CPNM defamed the UNIRP and discouraged the VMLRs from taking up any rehabilitation package. On the other hand, ex-combatants had trust either in a member of their biological family, the war network such as fellow combatants, their spouses (in most cases their spouses had also served as combatants or CPNM party workers), and the CPNM leaders and commanders, who had much more influence than the UNIRP staff on the VMLRs' decisions and choice of a rehabilitation package.

Families and Social Network: The Missing Enabling Factors

Most ex-combatants mentioned that they were not able to visit their families regularly during the war, because either they were too busy in the war or there were security risks involved; nonetheless, they agreed that they were in contact with their family in one way or other. A female VMLR ex-combatant interviewed said[32]:

---

[32] Interviewed in Itahari, Sunsari, October 2011.

> I could not visit my family because there was a lot of spying and so I could be caught and immediately killed by the police or army, but I kept on communicating with them by phone or by sending letters that people from my area were willing to carry and deliver for me.

This, and several other similar testimonies, display that connections between ex-combatants and their families survived in one way or another during the war. Many ex-combatants re-strengthened their contacts with their families and relatives during their stay in the cantonments. Ex-combatants were granted leave from the cantonments for a previously approved period of time, so that many ex-combatants utilised this time to catchup with family and relatives. Several ex-combatants mentioned that they even discussed their future plans with their family members during this period. A sizeable number of ex-combatants did not return to the cantonments—they took up foreign employment with the support of their families and relatives. There was a significant number of VMLRs who had either no immediate family or they did not want to contact them. This category was found heavily dependent on the war network or the war family in relation to their decision-making.

Over time, the contacts established with family appeared to be beneficial in the process of many VMLRs' rehabilitation. For many VMLRs who chose micro-enterprises, the support they received from their family and social network was an enabling factor in setting up their businesses. For example, a male VMLR from Jhapa district said:

> I started a grocery retail shop in my village because of the support I received from my family; without their financial and moral support I could not even think of doing this business successfully.

Interviews with VMLRs highlighted three different types of support: moral and psychological support, physical support and financial support. In the past, the ex-combatants joined the Maoist insurgency both with and without family consent—many of them were forcefully recruited. However, regardless of how they joined, families of ex-combatants, in general, were ready to extend moral and psychological support. The families who did not provide consent for their children to join the insurgency sent the VMLRs to foreign employment abroad, mainly to the Gulf countries. Although there are no actual figures on how many

VMLRs left for foreign employment, it was found during the fieldwork that most of the VMLRs who were absent at the time of their discharge ceremony in 2010 most probably would have gone abroad for foreign labour employment with the support of their families and relatives. According to a UN staff member interviewed in Kathmandu in August 2012, many VMLRs who returned from overseas employment were later found to be interested in participating in the UNIRP package; this was towards the middle of 2012.

Many VMLRs who had started micro-enterprises significantly received physical and financial support to their families and relatives. Physical support, in general, involved helping them find a location for the business and setting up the business itself. Access to credit was a major challenge for the VMLRs, mainly because the start-up support from the UNIRP was nominal and, therefore, the VMLRs had extreme difficulties in accessing funds via the formal credit system.[33] However, many had received support from their families to access credit via the local informal credit system and savings-credit cooperatives. A female VMLR from Morang said[34]:

> The business start-up provided in the form of in-kind support by the UNIRP was inadequate. My father helped me to get a loan without which I could not sustain this business.

Contrary to a generally held perception that ex-combatants often have difficulties in receiving family support during their reintegration, the Nepali context shows otherwise. The support from families was not only easy to access but it also played a determining role in the VMLRs' economic rehabilitation. This was possible owing to the typical social reasoning of members of the Nepalese society, where parents and older family members always maintain their social obligations and moral responsibilities towards their children and younger family members, sometimes for extended periods. A male respondent said[35]:

---

[33] According to VMLR interviewees, they received up to Nepali rupees 20,000 as post-training and business-start up support, but this was paid in kind in instalment basis.

[34] Interviewed in October 2011.

[35] Interviewed in Kathmandu, October 2012.

> In general, there is not any prescribed age at which young people are to be independent, and as long as an individual family member is not economically independent, family obligations and responsibilities to look after them continue to apply until such time as they are deemed to be independent enough. It is precisely due to this typical sense of moral obligation towards one's family members that young people are often found dependent on their parents even after their marriage.

Although there was some potential for ex-combatants to benefit from the support of family and relatives, the role of social entities like family was overlooked in the rehabilitation programme. Actually, keeping in view additional expenses that might occur, the rehabilitation programme provided additional living costs to the ex-combatants who wanted to pursue education away from home. Such additional money proved a disincentive for ex-combatants' family reunions, because this provision resulted in physically detaching many ex-combatants from their families.

Local social and cultural norms can have tremendous effects on the way ex-combatants are treated in families. Although there were several cases of family rejection reported in the case of ex-combatants who underwent inter-caste marriage, overall it was reported that families were receptive and supportive in rehabilitation of the VMLRs. Family could actually become an enabling factor and this could be utilised as a resource in rehabilitation. However, because of an emphasis on a "back to work" rather than "back to the community" approach, the ex-combatants families and relatives, as resources of rehabilitation, were largely under-utilised in the case of Nepal.

Conclusions

This chapter has examined micro and macro-factors affecting rehabilitation of VMLR ex-combatants. It was found that the initiative to rehabilitate the VMLRs has taken a minimalist approach as it has concentrated on bringing about change and transformation of individual combatants rather than focusing on rebuilding relationships between ex-combatants, their families and the communities to where they returned. Even though the overall goal of the UNIRP was minimal, as it tended to bring ex-combatants "back to work" rather than "back to community", such minimalist rehabilitation is not insulated from the effects of various micro and macro-level factors as discussed in this chapter.

Overall, organisational contexts and approaches to rehabilitation were greatly influenced by the political environment and perceptions towards the child soldiers and ex-combatants who were recruited late. At the macro level, the political environment of the country had constrained the rehabilitation of VMLRs, as had the role of national and local ownership, through a lack of a sense of responsibility.

Furthermore, the identity of ex-combatants has been of vital significance because identity construction and its broader social and political implications have influenced ex-combatants' responses to the programme. For instance, as argued in this chapter, the notion of a "disqualified" combatant and the social and political construction of identity of ex-combatants around this idea had enormous implications in terms of the way this identity issue aroused tensions between the VMLRs, the government and the UNIRP; eventually affecting ex-combatants' participation in the programme in very negative ways.

Although the ex-combatants' families and communities have actually played an enabling role in helping ex-combatants in their rehabilitation, the limitation of the rehabilitation programmes not to effectively engage families and communities in the rehabilitation process, like they should have, has resulted in a missed opportunity to foster social capital between ex-combatants, their families and communities. Overall, the way the government and UN agencies dealt with the VMLRs is neither entirely a humanitarian action nor an action of post-conflict recovery. Limited political and policy attention paid to VMLRs has produced a group of frustrated ex-combatants who could readily turn to destabilising actions due to various factors at play in a post-conflict society.

After having examined the processes and immediate outcomes of the rehabilitation of unverified ex-combatants, the economic dimension of reintegration of verified ex-combatants will be examined in the next chapter. There will be particular focus on whether a cash package instead of long-term reintegration support can help ex-combatants earn a living, through improving their livelihoods and, thereby, reintegrating into society via economic means.

REFERENCES

Berdal, M. (1996). *Disarmament and demobilization after civil wars*. Oxford: Oxford University Press for International Institute for Strategic Studies.

Bleie, T., & Shrestha, R. (2012). *DDR in Nepal: Stakeholder politics and implications for reintegration as a process of disengagement*. Tromso: Centre for Peace Studies, University of Tromso.

Body, T. (2006). *Reintegration of ex-combatants through micro-enterprise: An operational framework*. Retrieved from http://peacebuildingcentre.com/pbc_documents/ReintEx-ComMicroEnt.pdf.

Bragg, C. (2006). *Challenges to policy and practice in the disarmament, demobilisation, reintegration and rehabilitation of youth combatants in Liberia* (Working Paper No. 29, pp. 1–23). Sussex Center for Migration Studies. Retrieved from https://www.sussex.ac.uk/webteam/gateway/file.php?name=mwp29.pdf&site=252.

Bundi, C. (1987). Street sociology and pavement politics: Aspects of youth and student resistance in Cape Town, 1985. *Journal of Southern African Studies*, *13*(3), 303–330.

Coalition to Stop the Child Soldier. (2004). *Child soldier global report 2004*. London: Coalition to Stop the Child Soldier. Retrieved from http://www.essex.ac.uk/armedcon/story_id/child_soldiers_CSC_nov_2004.pdf.

Colletta, N. J., Kostner, M., & Wiederhofer, I. (Eds.). (1996). *The transition from war to peace in sub-Sahara Africa*. Washington, DC: World Bank.

Colletta, N. J., & Muggah, R. (2009). Context matters: Interim stabilisation and second generation approaches to security promotion. *Conflict, Security & Development*, *9*(4), 425–453. https://doi.org/10.1080/14678800903345762.

Dahal, J., Kafle, K., & Bhattarai, K. (2008). *Search for common ground—Children associated with armed forces and armed groups program, evaluation report*. Kathmandu: Search for Common Ground.

GoN. (2006, November 21). *Comprehensive peace accord concluded between the government of Nepal and the Communist Party of Nepal (Maoist)*. Kathmandu: Government of Nepal.

Goodwin-Gill, G. S., & Cohn, I. (1994). *Child soldiers: The role of children in armed conflict*. Oxford: Clarendon Press.

Hart, J. (n.d.). *Conflict in Nepal and its impacts on children: A discussion document prepared for UNICEF South Asia*. Oxford: Refugee Studies Centre, Oxford University. Retrieved from http://www.rsc.ox.ac.uk/pdfs/workshop-conference-research-reports/CAACNepalfinalreport.pdf.

ILO. (1997). *ILO and conflict-affected peoples and countries: Promoting lasting peace through employment promotion*. Geneva: International Labor Office.

ILO. (2009). *Socio-economic reintegration of ex-combatants: Guidelines*. Geneva: International Labor Organization/Crisis Response and Reconstruction Programme (ILO/CRISIS).

International Alert. (2006). *Local business, local peace: The peacebuilding potentials of the domestic private sector*. London: International Alert.

Kimmel, C. E., & Roby, J. L. (2007). Institutionalized child abuse: The use of child soldiers. *International Social Work, 50*(6), 740–754. https://doi.org/10.1177/0020872807081901.

Kingma, K., & Muggah, R. (2009). *Critical issues in DDR: Context, indicators, targeting, and challenges.* Cartagena: Center for International Disarmament Demobilization and Reintegration.

Knight, M. (2008). Expanding the DDR model: Politics and organizations. *Journal of Security Sector Management, 6*(1), 1–19.

Knight, M., & Özerdem, A. (2004). Guns, camps and cash: Disarmament, demobilization and reinsertion of former combatants in transitions from war to peace. *Journal of Peace Research, 41*(4), 499–516. https://doi.org/10.1177/0022343304044479.

Kyloh, R. (2008). *From conflict to cooperation: Labour market reform that can work in Nepal.* Geneva: International Labour Organization.

Lamb, G. (2011). *Assessing the reintegration of ex-combatants in the context of instability and informal economies: The cases of the Central African Republic, the Democratic Republic of Congo and South Sudan.* Washington Transitional Demobilization and Reintegration Programme and the World Bank. Available from http://www.tdrp.net/PDFs/Informal_Economies_Dec2011.pdf.

Lee, A.-J. (2009). *Understanding and addressing the phenomenon of 'child soldiers': The gap between the global humanitarian discourse and the local understandings and experiences of young people's military recruitment* (Working Paper Series No. 52). Oxford: Refugee Study Centre, University of Oxford. Retrieved from https://www.rsc.ox.ac.uk/files/files-1/wp52-understanding-addressing-child-soldiers-2009.pdf.

Leff, J. (2008). The nexus between social capital and reintegration of ex-combatants: A case for Sierra Leone. *African Journal on Conflict Resolution, 8*(1), 9–38. http://dx.doi.org/10.4314%2Fajcr.v8i1.39419.

Muggah, R. (2009). Introduction: The Emperor's clothes? In R. Muggah (Ed.), *Security and post conflict reconstruction: Dealing with fighters in the aftermath of war.* London and New York: Routledge.

Özerdem, A. (2009). *Post-war recovery: Disarmament, demobilization and reintegration.* London and New York: I. B. Tauris.

Porto, J. G., Alden, C., & Parsons, I. (2007). *From soldiers to citizens: Demilitarization of conflict and society.* Aldershot and Burlington: Ashgate.

Pouligny, B. (2004). *The politics and anti-politics of disarmament, demobilization and reintegration programmes.* Paris: Science-Politique/CERI.

Pun Magar, J. B. (2004). Giving children a fighting chance: Year zero is already here for Rolpa's child militia. *Nepali Times.* Retrieved from http://nepalitimes.com/news.php?id=1481.

Saferworld. (2010). *Common ground? Gendered assessment of the needs and concerns of Maoist Army combatants for rehabilitation and integration.* London: Saferworld.

SIDDR. (2006). *Stockholm initiative on disarmament demobilisation reintegration: Final report.* Stockholm: Ministry of Foreign Affairs, Sweden. http://www.regeringen.se/content/1/c6/06/43/56/cf5d851b.pdf.

Specht, I. (2010). *Socio-economic reintegration of ex-combatants.* London: International Alert.

Subedi, D. B. (2013). From civilian to combatant: Armed recruitment and participation in the Maoists' conflict in Nepal. *Contemporary South Asia, 21*(4), 429–443. https://doi.org/10.1080/09584935.2013.856868.

UN. (2000). *Disarmament, demobilization and reintegration of ex-combatants in a peacekeeping environment: Principles and guidelines.* New York: UN Department of Peacekeeping Operations/Lessons Learned Unit.

UN. (2006). *Integrated disarmament, demobilization and reintegration standards.* New York: United Nations (UN). Retrieved from http://pksoi.army.mil/doctrine_concepts/documents/UNGuidelines/IDDRS.pdf.

UN. (2010a). *The operational guide to the integrated disarmament, demobilization and reintegration standards (IDDRS).* New York: United Nations, UN Inter-Agency Working Group on Disarmament, Demobilization and Reintegration.

UN. (2010b). *Second generation disarmament, demobilization and reintegration (DDR) practices in peace operations.* New York: UNDPKO, Office of Law and Security Institutions, DDR Section. Retrieved from http://www.un.org/en/peacekeeping/documents/2GDDR_ENG_WITH_COVER.pdf.

UNDP. (2012). *Annual progress report 2012: United Nations Interagency Programme (UNIRP).* Kathmandu: United Nations Development Programme.

UNIRP. (2012, June). *Rehabilitation update.* Kathmandu. Retrieved from.

UNPFN. (2013). *United Nations Peace Fund for Nepal: Project status update for the period of April–June 2013.* Kathmandu: United Nations Peace Fund for Nepal.

Upreti, B. R. (2010). Reconstruction and development in post-conflict Nepal. In B. R. Upreti, S. R. Sharma, K. N. Pyakuryal, & S. Ghimire (Eds.), *The remake of a state: Post-conflict challenges and state building in Nepal* (pp. 129–150). Kathmandu: NCCR North-South and Kathmandu University.

Wessels, M. (2006). *Child soldiers: From violence to protection.* Cambridge, MA: Harvard University Press.

CHAPTER 7

Economic Reintegration

This chapter examines economic dimension of reintegration of verified ex-combatants. The elements of economic reintegration programme are circumstantial and cannot be generalised. How ex-combatants experience their reintegration in economic terms (including jobs and livelihood) depend on many factors including the economic causes of the preceding conflict, the needs and capacities of ex-combatants themselves, and the overall economic conditions in the post-conflict society. Nonetheless, in a Disarmament, Demobilisation and Reintegration (DDR) programme, the emphasis of an economic reintegration programme is generally placed on improving the employability of ex-combatants through providing them with vocational training, as well as an enabling economic environment that can absorb as many ex-combatants as possible into the local labour market (ILO, 2009; Specht, 2010). The significance of economic reintegration programmes for ex-combatants and the manner in which their success or failure, ameliorates or deteriorates conditions for peace, is less debatable. What is often contentious, however, is how to choose viable and appropriate policy options to reintegrate combatants into communities in ways they do not face the same level of economic hardship which might have pushed some of them into violence.

Experience from diverse contexts such as Liberia, El Salvador, Haiti, Somalia, Nicaragua, the Philippines, Indonesia and Afghanistan, among others, reveals that cash is a common policy option used in DDR programmes. Although the relationship between economic reintegration and post-conflict peacebuilding is well established, there is very little research on the relationship between cash and economic reintegration in situations where ex-combatants return home after war with cash but without any linkages to an accompanying reintegration programme. This is the case in Nepal. Further, even in formal DDR programmes where combatants are paid cash, research and policy analysis concentrates largely on the use or misuse of cash by the recipients. There is little theoretical or empirical documentation regarding the critical questions: Can cash-based approaches reintegrate ex-combatants? What formal or informal mechanisms do ex-combatants engage with to earn a living in a bid to build a livelihood in a post-conflict society? What were the factors that facilitated or impeded the livelihood strategies of the Maoist ex-combatants in re-entering the community? This chapter deals with these critical questions, exploring ex-combatants' perceptions and experience about economic dimension of their reintegration.

This chapter contends that merely examining the use or misuse of the cash payments, as has been the research tradition in the DDR literature and policy realm, is insufficient to assess the economic reintegration of the Maoist ex-combatants in Nepal. It argues that in situations where cash is a substitute for a long-term reintegration programme, economic reintegration of ex-combatants can be understood in terms of how or whether the cash helps ex-combatants to earn a living and the way the use of cash engenders ex-combatants' perception and experience of livelihood security. The livelihood of ex-combatants, in this case, refers to basic variables that can be analysed by examining the livelihood capitals of ex-combatants. However, this chapter also maintains that reintegration schemes need to be developed by taking into account the needs and aspirations of ex-combatants, the causes and drivers of the preceding armed conflict and the political economy of war to peace transition. This chapter promotes a broader understanding, which can help to locate reintegration as a part of post-conflict recovery and peacebuilding, rather than reintegration as a means of peace agreement implementation.

Economic Reintegration from Livelihood Lens

Interviews with Maoists ex-combatants significantly suggested that economic reintegration in their experience is largely related to their livelihood security. The more ex-combatants have perceptions and experience of livelihood security—a social and economic condition in which ex-combatants have ability and access to secure livelihood options that enables them experience dignified social and economic status in the society, which further determines their civilian status over the time. The more ex-combatants experience or likely to experience livelihood security, the more they feel economically integrated. The forms of their livelihood as a means of making a living defines how and the extent which ex-combatants feel economically secure and eventually become a dignified member of the local economic system and social organisations. Therefore, to understand economy reintegration, we must first understand livelihood security through the lens of livelihood and livelihood capitals.

According to Chambers and Conway (1991, p. 7), livelihood is defined as people's

> capabilities and their means of living, including food, income and assets…a livelihood is environmentally sustainable when it maintains or enhances the local and global assets on which livelihood depends, and has net beneficial effects on other livelihoods. A livelihood is socially sustainable which can cope with recovery from stress and shocks, and provide for future generation.

The concept of livelihood is based on the Sustainable Livelihood Approach (SLA), which initially emerged as an analytical tool, as well as a school of thought, to study and respond to poverty and development in rural settings (see Carney, 1998; Chambers & Conway, 1991; Ellis & Biggs, 2001). Over time, considerable attention has been paid to studying livelihood-related issues, as well as poverty, in urban settings (Meikle, Ramasut, & Walker, 2001). Thus, the SLA has radically broadened its focus, incorporating both rural and urban livelihood-related issues and putting poor people at the heart of livelihood interventions and policy discourses.

A major contribution of the SLA is the recognition of the crucial roles of a variety of assets in determining the wellbeing and livelihoods of individual households. As the SLA emphasises, economic growth does not necessarily reduce poverty. Poverty reduction largely depends on poor people's access to different forms of capital and their capability of expanding their economic opportunities (Krantz, 2001). Thus SLA offers a broad understanding that reframes poverty as a dynamic multidimensional process. Livelihood activities of poor people in rural and urban settings are related to the availability of livelihood assets, also known as sustainable livelihood capitals: human capital, physical capital, financial capital, natural capital, and social capital, known as the asset pentagon.

According to the Department for International Development (DFID) (1999), human capital represents skills, knowledge and health, which collectively enable people to pursue particular livelihood-related activities. In this regard, constituentive elements of social capital have been widely debated. In the context of the SLA framework, social capital refers to a set of social relationships such as kinship, friendship, patron–client relations, relationships of trust, reciprocal arrangements, membership of formal groups, and membership of organisations that provide loans, grants and other forms of insurance on which people can draw to expand livelihood options. Natural capital includes natural resources such as land, forests, water, pastures, wildlife, biodiversity and other environmental resources. Physical capital involves privately owned assets such as buildings, livestock, tools, machinery, and vehicles, publicly owned infrastructural items such as roads, transport, water, energy, communications and electricity supply; and social infrastructure such as schools and hospitals. Financial capital refers to cash income and savings, readily convertible liquid capital, supply of credit, remittances, pensions and wages. The analysis of economic reintegration in this chapter concentrates on how ex-combatants were able or unable to establish and secure livelihoods, rather than just exploring the use or misuse of cash they received at the time of their release from cantonments.

Scoones (2009) has criticised the SLA for its lack of recognition of political context and power dynamics, and suggested that a rigorous analysis of political context is essential because it largely determines livelihood strategies and outcomes for poor people. Given the nexus between reintegration and politics, caution should be taken in applying the livelihood framework rigorously to study outcomes of the reintegration programme, particularly in a politicised context like Nepal. Recognising this limitation, only human capital, physical capital, financial capital, natural capital and social capital from the sustainable livelihood framework rather than the entire SLF, are adopted as an analytical tool for the purpose of this chapter.

Merits and Demerits of Cash in DDR

In the field of complex emergencies, humanitarian crisis and chronic insecurity situations, cash transfer to recipients is nothing new (Harvey, 2005; Harvey, Slater, & Farrington, 2005). Harvey (2007, p. 1) asserts that based on recent experiences, the traditional belief that cash and vouchers work only in developed states with a strong banking system can be challenged, and that "cash or vouchers are a possible response even where states have collapsed, conflict is on-going or there is no banking system". The idea here is that individual recipients of assistance are rational actors who know better how to use the money. Although the idea of cash transfers in development and humanitarian works is still subject to controversy, there are reports that cash transfers have beneficial ripple effects on the local economy, and it allows more flexibility, choice and dignity for the recipients (Harvey, 2005). The counter argument, however, contends that cash and voucher-based approaches fuel corruption, become vulnerable to insecurity, can be used for anti-social purposes, and are more difficult to target (see Harvey, 2005; Willibald, 2006). Despite the arguments and counter-arguments, aid agencies are often quite sceptical about cash transfers and are reluctant to adopt this idea, although in acute emergencies some aid agencies have agreed to provide cash rather than in-kind support.[1]

In DDR programmes, the cash transfer is used mainly in disarmament and reinsertion phases, rather as using it as an alternative to rehabilitation and reintegration (Isima, 2004). Cash and vouchers issued to ex-combatants in exchange for weapons is a common approach adopted in cooperative disarmament.[2] For instance, the United Nations (UN) has implemented weapons "buy-back" schemes in many African countries, including Liberia, Mozambique, Somalia and Cote d'Ivoire (see Tanner, 1996), in which combatants exchanged their weapons with cash. In Macedonia, a lottery system was introduced in 2003 in order to encourage ex-combatants to submit guns. Those ex-combatants who surrendered arms were provided with tickets for a lottery with chances of winning prizes like cars, scooters, computers, mountain bikes, cell phones and so on (Wood, 2003). A general rationale behind the "weapon buy back" scheme is to replace the economic value one might get by holding the gun with the cash incentives paid directly to ex-combatants.

---

[1] The US Office for Foreign Disaster Assistance (OFDA), for instance, provided aid to fund pilot "cash grant" and "cash for seed" initiatives to respond to chronic drought, famine and food insecurity situations in Ethiopia in 2003 (see USAID, 2006). The World Food Programme (WFP) has long been practising the provision of cash and vouchers to people in need of humanitarian support (see WFP, 2006, 2012).

[2] Here the term cooperative disarmament is used to refer to a disarmament process in which weapon collection is carried out in voluntary basis rather than by the force. It is cooperative in nature because cooperation of insurgent organisation and its members is vital in carrying out disarmament.

Another type of cash transfer used in DDR is known as "reinsertion support". It is a transitional support which normally includes cash payment as well as in-kind support to ex-combatants in order to enable them to cover financial and material expenses such as food, utensils, clothes, household materials and so on at the time of their re-entry into the family or community (Özerdem, Podder, O'Callaghan, & Pantuliano, 2008). Reinsertion is intended as a "safety net" for ex-combatants between their demobilisation and full reintegration phase (Özerdem et al., 2008, p. 7). Therefore, reinsertion support should not be confused with reintegration.

Although the use of cash is common in DDR programmes, its outcomes demonstrate both positive and negative experiences in the field (Özerdem et al., 2008). Losing weapons through the disarmament process, ex-combatants are likely to lose physical and economic security and if this vulnerability continues, it could raise their propensity to rearm (Swarbrick, 2007). Further combatants will be reluctant to relinquish a weapon which they perceive to be their guarantee of security (UN, 2010, p. 12). Thus, both in security and economic terms, ex-combatants have high expectations from disarmament programmes. In Liberia, ex-combatants engaged in violence and nine people were killed in December 2003 when their expectations of prompt payment after surrendering their guns were not addressed immediately (Isima, 2004, pp. 3–4). Further, "weapon-buy-back" schemes have disproportionate effects on gender. Commanders reportedly took guns away from female ex-combatants in Sierra Leone, so that the female ex-combatants were prevented from benefiting from the cash scheme, but the commanders were able to make more cash (Tesfamichael, Ball, & Nenon, 2004).

The community of ex-combatants is heterogeneous with divergent individual needs, interests and aspirations. Proponents of the cash option argue that cash can be more adaptable to the specific needs of individual beneficiaries, as this allows an individual recipient more dignity, flexibility, choice and freedom to utilise the assistance (see Özerdem et al., 2008; Willibald, 2006). Cash can also help to revive local development and have positive ripple effects on the local economy and market (see Specker, 2008; Willibald, 2006). A survey conducted in Mozambique showed that cash not only benefited individual ex-combatants, but also assisted in sustaining their extended families (Hanlon, 2004, p. 377).

On the contrary, it is contended that cash involves the inherent risk that the money can be misused for anti-social purposes, although there are exceptions. For instance, South Africa was an exception where there was no evidence of cash being spent on either alcohol or gambling (see Özerdem et al., 2008, p. 14). Some suggest that combatants who spent several years fighting war would lack the skills and capacity for utilising cash productively (Peppiatt, Mitchell, & Holzmann, 2001). Ex-combatants tend to use the money for household items and consumption; therefore, a cash payment may not necessarily enable them to earn a sustainable livelihood (Lundin, Chachiua, Gaspar, Guebuzua, & Mbilana, 2000). Beneficiaries of cash payments tend to invest the money in social and productive investments only after their basic needs are met, and thus a cash payment should only be regarded as a "transitional safety net", as it does not necessarily solve the problem of reintegrating ex-combatants into society (Özerdem et al., 2008, p. 14). As has been seen in the literature, the use of cash in DDR is common; however, the practice of using cash to replace a reintegration programme altogether is rare.

In the context of Nepal, cash was a major policy option used to reintegrate ex-combatants. What is typical about the Nepalese case is that it was used to replace formal and accompanying reintegration and rehabilitation support to ex-combatants. Although the government proposed a rehabilitation package as an option, nearly 91% of ex-combatants refused to undertake the rehabilitation scheme. As also discussed in previous chapters, while a number of political and individual factors demotivated ex-combatants to opt for a rehabilitation option (see Subedi, 2013), confusion and lack of clarity about the implementation modality was another factor for ex-combatants' disenchantment with the rehabilitation option. In other words, lack of a social contract between the state and ex-combatants resulted in ex-combatants going for the quick option of cash rather than waiting for an extended period in the rehabilitation programme. Ex-combatants received ta cash package between minimum Nepali rupees (NRs) 500,000 (roughly USD 6000) to a maximum of NRs 800,000 (roughly USD 9000), depending on their rank and file in the People's Liberation Army.[3] A cheque was issued in the name of individual ex-combatants, which was distributed by the Secretariat of the Army Integration Special Committee. It was paid in two equal instalments within two fiscal years—2011 and 2012. Since

---

[3] Interview with a government official, Kathmandu, January 2013.

the donor community,[4] which has supported the peace process in Nepal, refused to support cash payments to ex-combatants, the cash paid to them was covered by the state coffers.

Resettlement and (Mis)use and of Cash by Combatants

The way in which ex-combatants managed their post-cantonment settlement and the place where this takes place has particular implications for the use or misuse of the cash paid to them. Therefore, prior to exploring and analysing how or whether ex-combatants used the cash, an examination of their settlement pattern is necessary.

Settlement Pattern

The cash package provided ex-combatants with flexibility in terms of their initial resettlement, and thus it is one of the reasons behind why a large number of combatants did not return to their roots, or the villages in their origin, but have settled in new neighbourhoods instead. The dispersion in resettlement, from the east to the far-west regions of the country, makes it difficult to obtain an accurate figure on how many combatants actually returned to their villages. However, triangulating the data from different sources indicates that less than one third returned to their villages of origin, and the resettlement of the remainder comprised an urban, semi-urban and rural mix. In this regard, at least three distinct categories are detected.

Firstly, most ex-combatants settled in villages, and urban and semi-urban areas close to their cantonment site. They settled more densely in areas such as Shinghiya of Sunsari, Pipra-Panchim of Saptari, Padampur of Chitwan, Parroha of Rupandehi, Purandhara and Bijaruri of Dang, Rajhena and Kohalpur (Bazar and Madan chowk) of Banke, Uttarganga and Hariharpur of Surkhet, and Sandepani of Kailali. A number of combatants from Shaktikhor cantonment settled in Madhavpur, Pithuwa, Jutpani, Shaktikhor, Padampur, Chainnpur, Khaireni, and Parsa

---

[4]According to an officer from the Ministry of Peace and Reconstruction (MoPR) who was interviewed in December 2012, the donors who are supportive of the peace process in Nepal through the Nepal Peace Trust Fund (NPTF) include Switzerland, the United Kingdom (UK), Norway, Denmark, Germany and the European Union.

Fig. 7.1 Districts with high concentration of ex-combatants (*Source* Fieldwork, 2013)

of the Chitwan district.[5] Somewhere between 3000 and 3500 combatants retired from the cantonments of the sixth and seventh division and settled in Dang district alone, with dense concentrations in Bijauri and Purandhara Village Development Committees (VDCs).[6] Figure 7.1 presents a district map of Nepal showing the high concentrations of ex-combatants.

Secondly, a noteworthy number of ex-combatants moved to the big cities like Kathmandu, Lalitpur, Bhaktapur, Biratnagar, Pokhara and Nepalgunj, in the pursuit of economic opportunities.[7] Combatants who migrated, or are likely to migrate to pursue foreign labour employment also fall under this category. Thirdly, this study estimates that less than one third returned to their villages of origin. A male ex-combatant who returned to his village in the Dailekh district said that he was seeking an opportunity to migrate from his home as soon as possible, and he claimed many other returnee combatants shared his situation.[8] He added that only those who were lucky to find a role within the

---

[5] Interviews conducted with ex-combatants in Padampur, Chitwan (January 2013), Kathmandu (December 2012) and Dang (February 2013).

[6] Interview with a male journalist in Ghorahi, Dang, February 2013.

[7] Interview with a combatant in Kathmandu, January 2013.

[8] Interviewed in Kohalpur in February 2013.

Maoist parties, or were able to find positions in local organisations, such as Community Forest User Groups (CFUG), Watershed Management Groups (WSMG), the "all party mechanism",[9] or school management committees, returned to their communities of origin.[10]

Generally, combatants who did not return to their village chose to live in groups and formed closely connected communities of combatants. In the Padampur VDC in Chitwan alone about 120 families have settled in a village of nearly 250 households. Approximately 100 households have settled together with local communities in Purandhara VDCs, while more than 200 families settled in Bijauri VDC in the Dang district. Similarly, more than 100 combatants have settled with their families in the Madanchowk area, near Kohalpur. In big cities like Kathmandu, resettlement was more scattered, although ex-combatants are found living in small groups in shared houses located close to one another.

While economic factors, such as seeking better economic opportunities, partly explain the reason why ex-combatants have ended up in urban and semi-urban areas, this move can also be seen in the light of social stigma. The identity of ex-combatants has been stigmatised, particularly in the places where ex-combatants cannot produce believable justification to the local people for the violence they have committed in the past. As a result, they have decided to avoid their community of origin and resettle in a group elsewhere, as group living offered the emotional support of fellow combatants and feelings of safety and security. The group living created 'bonding capital' between/among ex-combatants, which also alienated them from rest of the community.

It was discovered that a number of ex-combatants had actually already planned their reintegration before the decision on the cash provision had been made by the government.[11] Actually, many ex-combatants had already settled their families near cantonment sites and kept them

---

[9] Since elections for local authorities have not been held in Nepal for several years, there is a leadership vacuum in local government bodies such as Village Development Committees (VDC), municipalities, and District Development Committees (DDCs). The "all party mechanism" was set up to bring representatives from the major political parties into the constitutional assembly. Though these mechanisms were officially scrapped by the Ministry of Local Development in 2012, the culture of the "all party mechanism" continues in one way or another in making local governance and development related decisions at the local level.

[10] Interview with ex-combatants in, Bujauri VDC, Dang district, February 2013.

[11] Interview with a AISC staff, Kathmandu, March 2013.

involved in some form of livelihood activities. Therefore, family settlement patterns during ex-combatants's stay in contonments also had a considerable effect on the ex-combatants' resettlement decision and location after they had been released from cantonments.

Use and Misuse of the Cash

In the resettlement process, housing and household goods are generally priorities for ex-combatants. Accordingly, this study has found that they had spent a significant portion of the cash package on buying fixed assets like a house and residential land, even in urban neighbourhoods. The combatants who returned to villages, lived in existing houses belonging to their families and found it relatively easier to resettle. However, they also spent a significant portion of the cash on household investments, including house renovation, buying clothes, utensils and food.[12]

As will be elaborated later in this chapter, many combatants spent the money on agro-based micro-enterprises, while a smaller group also engaged in other micro-enterprises. Some combatants had spent cash on foreign employment-related expenses, such as fees paid to employment placement consultants and visa medicals, visa applications and travel; education including both self-education and that of children, health of family members and repayment of loans. All combatants reported that they had spent on several items simultaneously, including household goods and consumption, in order to satisfy basic needs of their families. Triangulating the data from different sources helped to itemise spending as illustrated in Table 7.1.

The data collected from the field revealed that only a few combatants spent the money on the consumption of alcohol and purchasing technology such as expensive mobile phones and motorbikes. A government official involved in the distribution of the cash packages said that he had observed that approximately 200 out of the 500 ex-combatants who came to collect the second instalment of the cash package in Birendranagar, Surkhet, owned motorbikes.[13] Currently in Nepal, a motorbike costs between NRs 200,000 and 250,000, which means those who bought motorbikes invested nearly half of the money they received.

Investing in goods such as motorbikes is not necessarily a misuse of cash if they use this investment for productive purposes, such as a means

---
[12] Interview with a male ex-combatant in Kohalpur, February 2013.
[13] Interview, Kathmandu, February 2013.

Table 7.1 Areas and items of cash spending by combatants (*Source* Fieldwork, 2013)

Spending on non-consumption items	*Spending on consumption items*
• House and small piece of land • Agro-based micro agro-enterprises: poultry farming, vegetable farming, goat farming, dairy farming, vegetable shop • Non-agricultural micro-enterprises—tea shop, retail shop, internet café, brick manufacturing, soap manufacturing, beauty parlour • Education and health for family • Foreign employment • Savings in bank	• Household consumption (clothes, grocery, utility bills like electricity, phone, travel) • Payment of personal loans • Purchase of phone and other luxurious goods such as motorbikes • Entertainment and celebration of festivals

of transportation for employment. Upon enquiring about the usefulness of such an investment with combatants, many agreed that investment in the motorbike was not for the purpose of business or employment, and that these soon became an extra economic burden, in terms of maintenance and operation costs.

Despite such non-productive cash expenditure, there was no clear evidence of ex-combatants using the money for anti-social pursuits such as the purchase of weapons and drugs. Although the misuse of cash is not evidently clear, this does not imply that the money actually helped to reintegrate combatants economically. The critical issue is not whether combatants used or misused cash, but whether it helped them in establishing livelihoods in ways that would enable them to return to leading a productive civilian life in the post-conflict period. Using the analytic tool discussed above, the following section examines constraints and limitations on their livelihoods.

Livelihood Capitals and Constraints of Economic Reintegration

Human Capital

Human capital has the intrinsic value that it makes use of all other forms of assets (DFID, 1999). Ex-combatants also recognised the necessity of education, skills (particularly vocational skills) and health as important forms of capital necessary for earning a living.

Education and Skills

The educational background of the ex-combatants varied. Many reported that they had joined the insurgency at a school-going age, and thus lacked any higher education. Out of fifty ex-combatants interviewed, only twenty two were high school graduates and only six had a tertiary degree. At the end of the war, merely 195 combatants had a university degree (bachelors and or master) while 6500 combatants had attended only primary schools and 1200 were illiterate (Dahal, 2011). Dahal further mentions that at the time of verification, roughly 10,000 combatants had presented a School Leaving Certificate (SLC), which is proof of completion of a ten-year high school education in Nepal.

During their seven-year cantonment period, the Deutsche Gesellschaft für Internationale Zusammenarbeit (GIZ) and the Norwegian Embassy in Kathmandu supported ex-combatants with an opportunity to attend SLC exams inside cantonments, under an open education system. This opportunity enabled many ex-combatants to complete a high school education and obtain a relevant certificate. Consequently, by the end of 2011, the number of high school graduate combatants increased to approximately 14,000 (Dahal, 2011). This support certainly contributed to increased employability of combatants: however, in the Nepali context, high school graduation alone is insufficient to compete favourably in the job market. The school education system lacks a vocational or skill-based curriculum, and its value in generating employment, mainly in terms of securing a job, is questionable, although it provides a basic education. A civil society leader emphasised[14]:

> As the high school curriculum grossly lacks the practical education needed to equip students with skills and knowledge to earn a living, the school system has become a machine that produces roughly 500 000 unskilled and unemployed youth annually.

There are also huge differences in the quality of education between public and private schools in Nepal. Private schools are generally more expensive, but the public perception is that they offer a relatively better quality of education in an English medium. Socio-economic disparity,

---

[14] Interview in Kathmandu, March 2013. In the year 2012 alone, 528,257 students attended SLC exams. In the year 2011, this figure was close to 480,000.

even in basic aspects of social development, such as education is a perpetual phenomenon in Nepal. Such disparity has had lasting effects on the lives of ex-combatants who attended rural public schools, and, therefore, they perceive themselves as incompetent compared to those from private schools in urban areas. This perception not only affected the self-esteem of combatants, but it also reduced their competitiveness in the job market.[15] In this regard, successful reintegration of ex-combatants should have also focused on reducing social inequalities in Nepal, which might contribute to averting conflict and reduce an interest in joining any form of violent (re)mobilisation in future.

Ex-combatants admitted that they were in dire need of developing a vocational skill to earn a living, although, ironically, many did not select the rehabilitation option when given a choice, which included a vocational training component in addition to post-training support and a start-up grant. Many ex-combatants regretfully admitted that they lost an opportunity to acquire skills through the proposed rehabiliation programme. Other ex-combatants expressed a willingness to accept support to improve their entrepreneurship and vocational skills in areas such as agro-based micro-enterprises, heavy vehicle driving, plumbing and electricity wiring, mobile phone repair, and accounting and book-keeping for micro-enterprises. In the past, the Maoists had perceived the international community as being the target western hegemonic force, with the local Non-Governmental Organisations (NGOs) being agents of that force; this is the same force that was one of the main targets of the armed struggle. Thus, the willingness of ex-combatants to accept support from the international community and local NGOs indicates a shift in their attitude not only towards the NGOs but also the international community.

During the cantonment period, with support from GIZ, roughly 6000 combatants went through vocational training in cooking, tailoring, mobile phone repairing and driving. About 12,000 completed basic and advanced English language training, and over 6000 graduated in computer courses (Dahal, 2011). Ex-combatants mentioned that the training programmes had a positive impact on the post-cantonment lives of many ex-combatants, because those who completed the GIZ supported training successfully were self-employed. For instance, ex-combatants who were running internet cafés and tailoring centres prove the benefits of such training.

---

[15] Interview with ex-combatants in, Dang, February 2013.

Nonetheless, combatants still emphasised that they did not receive any post-training services such as access to credit, mentoring and accompaniment, counselling or start-up grants. Due to the lack of such support, which would largely determine the outcome of vocational training they received at the time of their stay in cantonment, at the next stage of setting up a small business, ex-combatants acknowledged the limitations they faced translating the training into productive entrepreneurship.[16]

Health

Ex-combatants generally rated "health" as a satisfactory element of human capital among their ranks. Apart from disabled and wounded ex-combatants, the rest did not report having any serious illness. All ex-combatants interviewed were between twenty and forty years of age, which means that they fall within an economically active section of population in a country, where the average life expectancy at birth was sixty nine years in 2011.[17]

The experience of disabled and wounded combatants is, however, pathetic and sad. It is found that five out of fifty ex-combatants interviewed were disabled; the war had caused their disability. Interviews mentioned that no additional support was provided together with the rehabilitation package to the disabled and physically impaired at the time of the fieldwork for this study. As a result, they suffered a double burden in terms of their added difficulties in gaining employment, and their need to cover additional health-related expenses. A government official interviewed, however, mentioned that disabled ex-combatants received special support separately under a conflict victim support programme run by the Ministry of Peace and Reconstruction (MoPR). Nevertheless, he further acknowledged that there are several bureaucratic hurdles that make it difficult for the ex-combatants to access the disability support. The disability support directly targeted to ex-combatants rather than channelling the support through the conflict victim support scheme would have had better impacts on ex-combatants' reintegration process.

Apart from physical health, mental health of ex-combatants is a concerning issue. A sizable number of ex-combatants reported anxiety and

---

[16] Interviews with ex-combatants, Bijauri, Dang, February 2013.
[17] See http://data.worldbank.org/country/nepal.

post-conflict traumatic disorder was a major problem with many ex-combatants but especially with female ex-combatants who experienced rejection from their in-laws families due to inter-caste marriage. It is notable that several ex-combatants in each cantonment had had inter-caste marriages which broke down over the time as the in-laws families did not accept them. As a result, female ex-combatants who were unaccepted in families due to inter-caste marriage experienced social stigma and depression, some of them even suffered from severe depression and mental health problem. This was further confirmed by psychosocial counsellor working with UNIRP in Biratnagar, Kathmandu and Dhangadi. They further stated that female as well as male ex-combatants suffered from anxiety and mental health disorder mainly due to (a) failed inter-caste marriage leading to social stigma and even depression, (b) increased economic burden on women due to divorce or inter-caste marriage, and (c) post-traumatic mental health disorders. Ex-combatants from the Western region reported higher prevalences of mental health disorder while the ex-combatants from the eastern region reported the least prevalence of such disorder. This trend is associated with rigid caste system and education leading to the process of social change in the regions. Compared to the western parts of the country, the society in the eastern parts are more egalitarian and the notion of caste hierarchy are less severe than the west. Similarly, the education system in the eastern part is more advance in the west, as a result caste hierarchies and caste-based discriminations are less severe in the east, which resulted into few ex-combatants experienced caste-based discriminations in the society. Regardless of geographic regions, support system such as financial, economic and moral support from families, relatives and kinships networks helped ex-combatants to overcome both physical and mental health problem. In other words, social capital played critical role in overcoming the mental health problems among ex-combatants including women.

A psychosocial counselor interviewed in Dhangadi stated that although the impact on mental health problem was enormous, it was either under-reported or ignored. As a result, the DDR programme which ended up distributing cash instead of a reintegration programme failed to deal with physical and mental problems of ex-combatants, which considerably impacted on economic performances of those who suffered from mental health problems in one way or other.

Life Skills

The United Nations Children's Fund (UNICEF) defines "life skills" as psychosocial abilities for adaptive and positive behaviour that enable individuals to deal effectively with the demands and challenges of everyday life.[18] This definition is adopted as a premise while exploring both combatants' and non-combatants' views and perceptions about life skills, and whether these are relevant as human capital.

Combatants responded that life skills such as communication, leadership, interpersonal and relationship skills are vital for people to become successful in entrepreneurship, jobs or businesses. However, they also stressed that they already possessed these qualities, and that they did not need assistance to cultivate such skills. This perception reflects their arrogance, which, according to a civil society leader, is a "legacy of combatant-hood" that should be transformed in order for ex-combatants to prosper as a successful entrepreneur.[19] A businessperson, in contrast, reported that combatants, in particular, needed to improve their interpersonal relationship skills and their attitude to respecting different views held by others.[20]

PHYSICAL CAPITAL

Physical capital refers to both privately owned materials as well as public infrastructures. With regard to privately owned materials, a number of combatants, who did not return to their villages of origin, invested a significant portion of the cash package in a small piece of residential land and/or a house, which secured an important element of physical capital. Combatants who started agro-based micro-enterprises reported they did not have sufficient cash to buy technological equipment and physical materials necessary to run their enterprise. Many ex-combatants were running enterprises yet lacking basic physical materials. For instance, the combatants involved in cattle farming in the Banke district did not have modern cement sheds to house cows. As a result, it was extremely difficult to shelter the cows in the rainy season. The combatants who invested in off-season vegetable farming in Bijauri VDC in the Dang district mentioned that due to the lack of an electrified deep borehole

---

[18] See http://www.unicef.org/lifeskills/index_7308.html.
[19] Interview with a civil society leader in Nepalgunj, February 2013.
[20] Interview with a private sector leader, Biratnagar, January 2013.

irrigation system, their work had become highly labour intensive with the use of manual pumps.

In the case of combatants living in urban areas, such as in Kathmandu, the need to invest in physical capital varied from person to person. Those in urban areas, mostly involved in non-farm micro-enterprises, exhibited a common difficulty and burden in relation to physical capital, as they were facing far higher costs in renting business premises.

When it comes to securing livelihoods, physical and financial capitals are strongly interrelated. A female combatant running a retail shop from a temporary shed in Kohalpur bus park could not rent a permanent space for her shop, due to insufficient financial capital. She acknowledged that a permanent shed would not only ensure safety and security for her business, but would also increase sales and profits.

With regard to public and physical infrastructure, it is noted that combatants who had decided to settle in rural and semi-urban areas occupied public land, known as *Aailani Jagga*. The settlement on public land lacked basic infrastructure, such as road networks, electricity and safe drinking water, while it is mandatory in Nepal to provide a land registration certificate and recommendation from a local government official (e.g. secretary of a VDC) in order to access these public services. Having settled on the public land, many ex-combatants lacked a land registration certificate and eventually found that obtaining a recommendation from local government was impossible, which left them virtually "disenfranchised" and unable to participate in their communities, with no access to public infrastructure and services. Similarly, the combatants who were running farm-based micro-enterprises cited poor road and transportation network as a major drawback to delivering their products to nearby markets.

Access to public infrastructure was far better for combatants residing in urban areas, who had no difficulty accessing mobile phone services, electricity, drinking water, use of city transportation, and so on. However, accessing these services was expensive and often out of their reach. Depending on the overall development condition of districts, ex-combatants experienced constraints of physical capital slightly differently across the districts. For instance, physical capital such as road, electricity or drinking water is relatively better in the Chitwan and Dang and Banke districts; however, even within these districts, ex-combatants living in remote areas or even in peri-urban areas had relatively more difficulty in accessing various aspects of physical capital.

Social Capital

Lack of support mechanisms and associated economic vulnerability led many combatants to rely on informal social mechanisms to cope with both predictable and unpredictable hardships. Relationships and networking with biological families and relatives, as well as "the war family", are two elements of social capital that have contributed to the economic reintegration of combatants.

Relationship and Networks with Biological Family and Relatives

Utilising the free time in the post-war period for catching up with families and relatives, a number of combatants reconnected with their families by improving their interactions and rebuilding relationships with biological family members and relatives during their stay in cantonments.[21] Ex-combatants often mentioned in their interviews that reconnecting with biological families was not very difficult because they had remained in contact with families during the war, through phone calls, letters and personal visits. Even the People's Liberation Army (PLA) allowed combatants to visit their families during ceasefire periods, as well as an other suitable occasions.[22]

Later when ex-combatants were released from cantonments, their renewed family relationships provided an informal support mechanism in several ways. Firstly, several combatants reported that they had received advice and moral support from relatives in selecting a resettlement location, as well as in choosing a livelihood option and investing their cash package to support their livelihood choices. For some combatants, the family network had an influence on the selection of a resettlement location. Secondly, most families warmly received the ex-combatants back, particularly those who had joined the war with the consent from family members. This acceptance provided an additional support structure in coping with economic hardships. Support in accessing credit, and facilitating access to local civil society organisations, such as *Bachat Samuha* (savings and credit groups), are examples of how family relationships generated social capital for ex-combatants.

---

[21] Interview with three male commanders in Kathmandu (January 2013), Chitwan (January 2013), and Kohalpur (February 2013).

[22] Interview with a male battalion vice-commander, Kohalpur, February 2013.

However, renewed family and social relationships also carried the obligation of reciprocity, which also had economic implications in the lives of combatants. Social capital in this regard increased their financial burden in terms of the costs of travelling to visit parents and relatives; phone calls; social and cultural events such as celebrating festivals, and obligations concerning marriages, births and death ceremonies.

Relationship and Network with the "War Family"

Their participation in the insurgency integrated combatants into the communist war system. Hazan (2007, p. 4) discusses war-induced disintegration-integration patterns in which, she argues, war has an integrative function, as participation integrates combatants into what she calls the "war family". When an individual assumes a role in a war, he or she becomes a member of the war family by a common ideology and purpose. A war family denotes a war-induced, extended grouping of people who operate together with a mutual sense of belonging and solidarity, under war-time command and control structures.

With some exceptions, the Maoist ex-combatants considered the entire PLA as a family. Therefore, as combatants resettled into communitarian settlements in various locations, this resettlement pattern facilitated the formation of new blocks or groups of war families. A significant number of ex-combatants re-established relationships and connections simultaneously with their biological families and the war family.

The war family functioned as an informal mechanism and support structure in the economic reintegration of combatants. There were several cases where the war family played a role in bringing combatants together and facilitated joint ventures among them, such as collective micro-enterprises. Thus, the war family was instrumental in forging collective action in the economic reintegration of combatants. In situations where many combatants lacked adequate financial capital or confidence to run a business, the war family became a source of accumulating capital through joint investments, as well as offering moral support from fellow combatants.

For example, ex-combatants in the Dang, Chitwan and Banke districts formed savings and credit groups, which exemplify social capital that emerged from the war family. These savings and credit groups were an informal mechanism that promoted a savings culture and helped to address the financial difficulties of combatants through the provision of easy access to credit. Despite the positive role this played economically, membership was restricted to ex-PLA fighters and other Maoist cadres residing in those areas. On the societal level, there was a risk that such closed-membership groups would significantly alienate combatants from the wider society.

These examples of joint micro-enterprises indicated that the war-time legacy of communitarian living persisted for many combatants. The manner in which ex-combatants re-engaged with non-combatant members of the local community through their enterprises and livelihood related economic activities determined their rate of leaving behind the communitarian legacy and developing social bonds with the local communities in the process of their economic reintegration.

However, by no means did all ex-combatants remain within the war-family network, alienated from the community of non-combatant people. A considerable number of combatants detached themselves from the war-family network for various reasons. The Maoists had coerced combatants into recruiting. Hence, many of these ex-combatants, and those whose families wanted them to break away from the Maoists, tended to distance themselves from war-family networks. This category of ex-combatants returned from the war frustrated, preferring to start a new life with a new civilian identity.

A number of ex-combatants were found to have distanced themselves from the war family because of: (a) strong relationships and reconnections with biological families, (b) frustration with the Maoist's leadership for its false promise to integrate them into the national army, and (c) social and moral obligations towards their own families. While war disenchanted many ex-combatants from the rhetoric of the radical Maoist ideology, many were still maintaining relationships with both biological and the war family simultaneously. According to some ex-combatants, a shared past experience, collective identity, sense of security and a safety net provided by the war family, and fraternal relationships between likeminded members of the war-family have encouraged them to perpetuate relationships with other war family members.

Relationship with the Private Sector

The relationship with the private sector (PS) is invaluable for ex-combatant to forge new social capital for two reasons. First, the PS is not only an engine of post-conflict economic growth and development, but it is also the largest job provider in the country (Alexander, Gunduz, & Subedi, 2009). Ex-combatants who sought employment in the market would interact with the PS. Second, even if combatants prefered to engage in micro-enterprises, their businesses would become an inherent part of the value chains and market systems, often dominated by small, medium and large businesses. The term value chain here refers to specific activities and processes that a product undergoes between its production phase and the consumption phase. Thus, because of a value chain system, ex-combatants as entrepreneurs would have to make sure that they re-entered the formal or informal economic and market system. However, significant problems with respect to connecting and benefiting from relationships with the PS was observed.

The relationship of combatants with the PS also carried distrust and suspicion, which is rooted in the history of the armed conflict. In the past, the Maoists categorised the PS as an exploitative capitalist agent, and hence the "class enemy" to be annihilated in the war. As a result, the PS survived the war as a front-line victim with countless incidences of personal security threats, extortion, forced donations, kidnapping and more (Dhakal & Subedi, 2006; Gunduz, Alexander, & Subedi, 2009). In the post-conflict era, because of their political and military background, the business sector is often hesitant to offer ex-combatants employment. A respondent claimed, "they [ex-combatants] could be problematic in the workplace, so that the private sector's willingness to offer ex-combatants employment depends on how they detach from their politicised and militarised mind-set and how they engage in assuming a civilian identity".[23] The way the Maoist parties would redefine their position and views regarding the PS and the economic system would have a tremendous effect on the PS's perception of them.

There were divided opinions on the side of the combatants. For radical combatants, the war legacy of "business as enemy" endured. They continued to see the PS as a "profit making" machine with no concern for the wellbeing of society. Less radical combatants, on the other hand, thought that the Maoist party should redefine and publicise its reformed view on the PS to create an environment for entrepreneur combatants to join business associations and their apex bodies.

Financial Capital

The cash package was the principal source of ex-combatants' financial capital; however, as mentioned earlier, many combatants used it to meet household requirements, leaving only a portion of the cash received available as financial capital. Secondly, as also discussed earlier, some received additional financial support from their biological families.

[23] Interview with a business man in Kathmandu, December 2012.

Beyond these sources, access to financial capital for combatants was extremely difficult. There were two potential ways of accessing credit facilities—through the formal banking system and finance sector, or the informal sector, which involved higher interest rates. All combatants mentioned that it was impossible for them to access credit from banks and finance companies without the required collateral and guarantees. Many combatants have their settlements on government lands, which did not qualify for banking collateral. The formal finance sector would recognise a business registered with a government authority as collateral for loan only if it had existed for a minimum of three years. However, ex-combatants mentioned that they had not yet registered their micro-enterprises, which they had established in the past six months or so. As a result, accessing credit in the formal sector was extremely difficult for combatants.

LIVELIHOOD STRATEGIES AND OUTCOMES

This study has found that even the ex-combatants themselves believed that "money alone cannot provide *aarthik surakshya* (economic security)".[24] One interviewee felt, "giving money is not a heavenly solution in the life of combatants. They should have also been provided with skills and training".[25] Likewise, another female ex-combatant asserted, "I was motivated to fight to liberate the country from feudalism and oppression, not for money. Today, I am economically as vulnerable now as I was several years before joining the PLA".[26] Such testimonies stress the need to shift the focus from examining the uses and misuses of the cash payment towards exploring the extent to which the cash package has actually become beneficial and instrumental in economic reintegration of the PLA ex-combatants into Nepalese society. The findings suggest that livelihood strategies fall into three categories: self-employment or employment, migration, and unemployment.

Self-Employment Versus Employment

Self-employment was the most common form of economic reintegration and livelihood strategy. Out of fifty ex-combatants interviewed, thirty two were self-employed in farm and non-farm based micro-enterprises. Farm-based enterprises included poultry, vegetable, dairy and goat farms.

[24] Interview with ex-combatants, Chitwan, Kathmandu and Banke, February 2013.
[25] Interview with a journalist in Kathmandu, December 2012.
[26] Interview with a female ex-combatant, Kathmandu, December 2012.

Non-farm micro-enterprises included grocery retail shops, tea shops, hotels and restaurants, internet cafés and so on. Ex-combatants generally ran their enterprises in the local areas where the lack of access to low-interest credit facilities in the formal banking and finance sector was a notable constraint. Employment in any formal sense applied only to two out of fifty ex-combatants. This pattern was consistent across the country, demonstrating that combatants were unable to rely on employment in the job market for their reintegration.

The relationship of ex-combatants with their relatives played an important role as social capital, particularly in terms of offering moral and even financial supports to those who were well accepted back into their families. Conversely, social capital generated from ex-combatants' relationships with the war family alienated them from society, although this form of social capital was not inherently harmful, as it offered alternative types and areas of support. Ex-combatants had negative perceptions about the PS and vice versa, and the war legacy affecting personality traits created barriers to finding employment in both the formal and informal economic sectors.

Migration: An Alternative Route to Economic Reintegration

Ex-combatants followed the path of foreign labour migration, a livelihood strategy that is increasingly adopted by the younger generation in Nepal. The history of labour migration started with recruitment of men from the hills to join Ghurkha regiments about 200 years ago (Thieme & Wyss, 2005). More recently, foreign labour migration to the Middle East and Southeast Asia has been growing exponentially (Graner & Gurung, 2003), and is significantly contributing to the national economy through remittances. Remittances increased from 47.22 billion rupees in the fiscal year 2001–2002 to 259.53 billion[27] in 2010–2011, which accounts for nearly 23% of the total GDP (Thagunna & Acharya, 2013).

No actual figure is available to determine the number of PLA fighters in foreign labour employment; however, the fact that five out of fifty interviewees were in the final stages of leaving for foreign employment, and another twelve ex-combatants were either actively seeking foreign employment opportunities or had already made an arrangment

---

[27] This figure accounts for remittance inflow for only the first ten months of the fiscal year, and, therefore, the actual figure for the entire year must certainly be higher.

to migrate to the Gulf countries suggests that this figure was increasing. An ex-combatant in Kathmandu advertised his cyber café for sale, as he was not making enough to survive in the city, and was hence seeking an opportunity for employment abroad.[28]

International labour migration had already been proven attractive to ex-combatants, as some ex-combatants had already left their cantonments for foreign employment.[29] According to a radio journalist in Chitwan, a significant number of ex-combatants who were absent from the regrouping process had reportedly gone abroad for foreign employment.[30] This was also confirmed by the assertions of ex-combatants, civil society and government officials that many ex-combatants, who had already been abroad for foreign employment returned to the cantonments at the time of regrouping to receive their retirement package.

The networks of ex-combatants played a facilitating role in their trajectory of foreign labour migration in two ways. Firstly, some ex-combatants followed their social network to select a destination abroad. Secondly, the network became an source of information for ex-combatants regarding migration. However, human capital became a barrier for some ex-combatants because they lacked skills or experience needed for foreign labour migration. As a result, many of them moved away from Nepal to work as lower paid, unskilled labourers especially in the Gulf countries as well as Malaysia.

Unemployment

Mapping unemployment of ex-combatants was complicated, particularly because of an overlap between unemployment and underemployment. Several ex-combatants stressed that they would consider themselves being in-between unemployment and underemployment, because even if they had started a micro-enterprise, it was hardly possible to earn a living to feed the entire family from such an endeavour. The fact that thirteen

---

[28] Interview with a combatant in Kathmandu, December 2013.

[29] In the past, there were indeed both proposals from civil society and demands from combatants to send the latter to foreign employment as skilled labour as part of their rehabilitation package. Though some sort of skill and vocational training was included in the final rehabilitation option, targeting foreign employment, ironically no combatants became involved.

[30] According to UN report, the VMLRs who were absent at the time of their discharge from cantonments in November–December 2010 are reported to have left the country for foreign employment. This information helps substantiate that foreign employment had already become a popular route for livelihood.

out of fifty ex-combatants were totally unemployed emphasises the difficulties for them in finding employment. Further interviews indicated that some ex-combatants who had started micro-enterprises, had been unsuccessful in their ventures and were likely to join the ranks of the unemployed. This phenomenon points to a potentially alarming situation and raises the question of whether unemployed ex-combatants could, in fact, become a source of destabilisation and a possible security risk.

While limited or lack of access to livelihood assets was a barrier for ex-combatants seeking employment, their personal habits and perceptions towards work were equally important factors. Several years of war had distanced some ex-combatants from the realities and demands of economic activity. Some ex-combatants acknowledged that they were not so used to the practice, behaviour and habits essential for working on a regular basis. Consequently, they faced difficulties in getting used to the demands of labour-intensive jobs. There was also a degree of social stigma associated with this phenomenon, as a few ex-combatants mentioned in interviews that they felt belittled or inferior engaging in commonplace labour intensive jobs and self-employment. A combatant elaborated on this feeling[31]:

> I find it stigmatising to work as an ordinary farmer or shopkeeper after a situation where I had an elevated identity as a PLA fighter – the real, brave agent for social and economic change. This is why I am living in the city, where no-one knows me. Instead of doing any low paid job, I might prefer to go abroad as a worker.

This assertion symbolises the reality that in some cases, unemployment has become a "necessary choice" for ex-combatants to enable them to avoid stigma. A government official asserted that if ex-combatants had chosen a rehabilitation scheme, such stigmas could have been avoided through regular career counselling and mentoring. This bitter reality suggests the need to examine how such feelings of stigma and the situation of being unemployed might have affected ex-combatants in their social reintegration.

The process of reintegration was deeply politicised and lost within the contentious debate of army integration. It is notable here that the number and modality of integration between the PLA and the Nepal Army (NA) dominated the entire process of management of ex-combatants,

---

[31] Interview with a male ex-combatant in Kathmandu, February 2013.

pushing efforts to develop viable and appropriate rehabilitation schemes to the margins. Indeed, ex-combatants had a dream of becoming members of the NA rather than going through the community-based rehabilitation programme. The policy formulation in this regard involved a top-down process with virtually no consultations being carried out with ex-combatants. As a result, the final policy prescription neither garnered support from "below"; nor did it reflect ex-combatants' needs and aspirations.[32]

In the meantime, after more than five years in cantonments, ex-combatants were desperate to experience rapid and tangible changes in their lives. Indeed, a significant number of ex-combatants had already planned their reintegration on their own. For instance, many ex-combatants resettled their families near cantonment sites and assisted them in household activities regularly.[33] The Maoists themselves eventually preferred cash to a reintegration package because (a) there was a possibility of manipulating the cash as several ex-combatants were absent from cantonments and (b) many ex-combatants who had retired with cash could still work as Maoist cadres on the ground. In some cantonments, including Chulachuili (Ilam), Dahaban (Rolpa), and Chisapani (Kailali), a commander and local Maoist leaders discouraged ex-combatants from opting to receive a rehabilitation package. In this situation, ex-combatants would obviously prefer cash because of their dire economic situations and the urgency to fulfil the household needs of their families.

Interviews with ex-combatants, however, revealed that many of them were frustrated with the cash because they saw it as "blood money", a perception which was widely reflected in the interviews with non-combatant respondents. The frustration increased also because the cash did not bring with it any remarkable transformation, particularly in terms of ex-combatants' livelihood development, although several of them have secured a house and/or household materials, which are positives.

The long-term implications of a cash-based scheme, in terms of violence, were felt at societal levels across the country of Nepal. The police arrested several ex-combatants with small arms and guns in their possession, while various interest groups of ex-combatants are increasingly

---

[32] Interview with ex-combatants, Dang, Banke and Chitwan districts, January and February 2013.

[33] Interview with an official from Army Integration Special Committee, Kathmandu, March 2013.

involved in crime and violence across the country.[34] If the ex-combatants' livelihood crisis deepens, which is more likely in the current context, a lack of security and violence are quite likely to increase. At the same time, several interviews revealed that many ex-combatants have already been remobilised by the CPNM, its splinter faction the Communist Party of Nepal-Maoists (CPN-M), as well as many other Maoist splinter groups and criminal groups. The possibility of ex-combatant remobilisation into political and criminal violence has become a constant threat—a situation that the reintegration programme could have minimised or even averted if such programmes were designed and implemented as part of the wider post-conflict economic recovery. Yet, this issue has been side-lined in Nepal's peace process.

DISCUSSION: REINTEGRATION AND LIVELIHOODS—CONSTRAINTS AND POSSIBILITIES

As a starting point, any reintegration programme would need to be conceptualised as a transformative rather than a problem-solving process. The cash-based solution that has taken place was a problem-solving approach because the management of ex-combatants was seen as a means of implementing the peace agreement, rather than a process to transform ex-combatants into productive civilians. Cash helped to diffuse the structure of the PLA, but it failed to contribute or induce any tangible changes in the lives of ex-combatants, at least economically. A reintegration programme targeting ex-combatants would require a deeper understanding of why people became violent in the first place; thus, the efforts to reintegrate them could have helped address some of the causes of the preceding conflict.

First, it would require depoliticising reintegration and a vision as to how reintegration could contribute to post-conflict human capital development.[35] Second, it would require technical expertise and skills

---

[34] It was reported in the fieldwork that police has recently held several combatants for being involved in crime and violence. Also see http://www.thehimalayantimes.com/fullNews.php?headline=Ex-Maoist+fighters+behind+crimes+in+Valley%3A+Police&NewsID=382819.

[35] Ironically, the Maoists used the ex-combatants as a means of power bargaining while the opposition political groups particularly the Nepali Congress and the Communist Party of Nepal Maoists United Marxist and Leninist, tended to diffuse the PLA, without recognition of any possible societal and security consequences of a poorly designed reintegration programme.

in designing a reintegration programme. The entire reintegration programme was designed at the political level, without expert consultations. The narratives of ex-combatants as well as non-combatant respondents suggest that the policy to manage ex-combatants should have completely abandoned the cash option. Instead, cash could have been better integrated into a more comprehensive rehabilitation package. The cash option would only be an immediate restitution or reinsertion support, while the rehabilitation package could have been geared towards supporting ex-combatants to address their livelihood capital constraints, as discussed above.

As stressed earlier, reintegration is a long-term transformative process, involving both social and economic dimensions. This means that an effective reintegration scheme should necessarily involve some components of social reintegration such as providing psychosocial support to ex-combatants to help them overcome the stigma, and more importantly, supporting their families, who would have already played an important role in helping ex-combatants to reintegrate economically. Yet, it must be acknowledged that such holistic reintegration takes a long time. In the short term, promoting employment opportunities and enabling ex-combatants "livelihood capitals" could be a minimum target that would at least make ex-combatants economically secure. From a broader perspective, a reintegration programme could have been designed as part of post-conflict recovery, which would then contribute positively to post-conflict human capital development and employment generation. Such an approach would help to transform not only individual ex-combatants, but also their relationships with the community.

By providing cash, the reintegration scheme failed to make tangible contributions to transform the identity of PLA ex-combatants. In a sense, what eventuated was marginalisation and disenfranchisement of ex-combatants, who largely represented individuals from the lower castes and ethnic groups. Many non-combatant interviewees believed that both Maoist factions, the Communist Party of Nepal Maoists (CPNM) and the Communist Party of Nepal-Maoists (CPN-M) are competing to rearticulate grievances for contentious political mobilisation in the changed social and political context. A significant number of ex-combatants concluded that the Maoists had exploited them in the war. Such frustration has already started to minimise the effects of radicalisation of many ex-combatants. Several ex-combatants who seemed frustrated with the CPNM asserted that the it used them in the war and that the indoctrination and radicalisation tactic was just used as a tool to attract youth to the war. The effect of indoctrination and radicalisation was becoming less sever in situation ex-combatants remained economically vulnerable. In such situations, a reintegration policy which could combine some form of cash payment with long-term reintegration support could be effective to de-radicalise and de-indoctrinate the ex-combatants. Taking a maximalist perspective, the resources that were invested in ex-combatants could have been channelled to address the grievances of not only ex-combatants, but also unemployed and frustrated youth, so that they could minimise the resentments of other war-affected people.

From different sources, this study found that between 2007 and 2012, the government spent 20 billion Nepali rupees in the management of the PLA combatants, including expensed made on cantonment management, and annual allowances and ration for verified ex-combatants. This shows that a huge amount of financial resources has been invested in the management of ex-combatants; actually the total amount was more than the defence budget in the fiscal year 2068–2069 B. S (2011–2012).[36] Indeed, there was a vital opportunity to utilise this resources as part of a resource for post-conflict recovery which then could be invested to address the causes that drove the war in the past. But the way management of ex-combatants has been accomplished has lost a vital opportunity to engage with disillusioned and increasingly frustrated ex-combatants, and this in itself would help to transform them into significant (non-communist) human capital.

Conclusions

This chapter demonstrated that an examination of livelihood capitals and analysis of reintegration constraints, possibilities and options provides some pointers that enable an assessment of the trend and immediate outcomes of economic reintegration. The Nepali peace process has provided a test case to examine whether ex-combatants can reintegrate economically, with a cash package, but without any accompanying reintegration program. In this regard, a number of insights are generated in this chapter.

---

[36] Interview with a defence analyst in Kathmandu, February 2013.

First, in situations where a cash-based scheme replaces reintegration, the success or failure of reintegration is often mapped out by examining whether the ex-combatants use or misuse the cash, but still there remains a lack of an established analytical method to understand ex-combatants' economic reintegration under these circumstances. There is a need to shift the debate from a narrow focus on the use of cash, to a broader understanding of reintegration. "Livelihood capitals", which are used in the Sustainable Livelihood Framework, can be employed as an analytical tool to assist in better-understanding the economic reintegration of ex-combatants through a process of focusing on livelihood constraints, strategies and outcomes. However, it is necessary be cautious in adopting the entire sustainable livelihood framework in these circumstances, because this is associated with a highly political issue—the reintegration of ex-combatants. Reintegration, its outcomes and possible options should also be conceptualised and planned, taking into account the conflict-inducing factors of the past as well as the social, political and economic conditions in the war to peace transition processes.

Second, a significant number of the Maoist ex-combatants did not misuse their cash, but this does not necessarily mean that they invested the money wisely to earn a sustainable livelihood. Despite ex-combatants' self-efforts to earn a livelihood, many are still unemployed and their livelihood concerns are alarming. This generates the lesson that using cash can help release ex-combatants from cantonments, but it cannot reintegrate them in any real sense. The use of cash alone is not a prudent policy option; indeed, cash cannot and should not be a substitute for reintegration. This is a major lesson from the Nepal case study, which is discussed in this chapter.

Third, in any war to peace transition, a country faces multiple challenges, including post-conflict economic recovery and development—a process deemed necessary not only to address past grievances that had fuelled the insurgency, but also to minimise grievances of the various groups, which include ex-combatants, unemployed youth from socio-economically marginalised communities and conflict victims. The cash paid to ex-combatants can be alternatively and more effectively utilised in post-conflict recovery and development where ex-combatants are considered important stakeholders. For instance, if a reintegration scheme for ex-combatants enhances human, social, physical and financial capitals, it could obviously also be an investment in the recovery of a post-conflict economy and society. However, it is necessary to be cautious again, because focusing exclusively on ex-combatants and ignoring other vulnerable and deprived groups in the society might create more tensions.

Finally, although the cash-based reintegration scheme has dispersed the PLA, it has only shifted the problem from cantonments to communities. The ex-combatants who have been suffering from dire economic situations and livelihood crises are likely to be remobilised into crime and violence. This suggests that successful economic reintegration of ex-combatants could be a useful means of addressing insecurity and violence in a post-conflict society and, hence, should be taken very seriously. The cash-based approach is not efficient or effective in facilitating the reintegration of ex-combatants, as demonstrated for Nepal where cash was the main reintegration strategy.

It is relevant to re-stress here that reintegration of ex-combatants has both important economic and social dimensions. While economic reintegration illustrates the changes that occur at an individual level in the lives of ex-combatants and how this affects the material wellbeing of concerned individuals as well as their families, social reintegration helps us in understanding the relationships between ex-combatants and their families and communities. The next chapter examines social reintegration.

References

Alexander, L., Gunduz, C., & Subedi, D. B. (2009). *What roles for business in post-conflict economic recovery? Perspectives from Nepal*. London: International Alert.

Carney, D. (1998, July). *Implementing the sustainable livelihood approach*. Paper presented at the sustainable rural livelihoods: What contribution can we make? Department for International Development's Natural Resources Advisers' Conference, London.

Chambers, R., & Conway, G. R. (1991). *Sustainable rural livelihoods: Practical concepts for the 21st century* (IDS Discussion Paper 296). Brighton: Institute of Development Studies.

Dahal, P. (2011, December 6). 73 pc fighters are 'SLC graduates'. *The Kathmandu Post*.

DFID. (1999). *Sustainable livelihoods guidance sheets*. London: Department for International Development (DFID). Retrieved from http://www.ennonline.net/pool/files/ife/dfid-sustainable-livelihoods-guidance-sheet-section1.pdf.

Dhakal, A., & Subedi, J. (2006). The Nepalese private sector: Waking up to conflict. In B. Jessica, N. Killick, & C. Gunduz (Eds.), *Local business, local peace: The peacebuilding potential of the domestic private sector* (pp. 404–431). London: International Alert.

Ellis, F., & Biggs, S. (2001). Evolving themes in rural development 1950s–2000s. *Development Policy Review, 19*(4), 437–448. https://doi.org/10.1111/1467-7679.00143.

Graner, E., & Gurung, G. (2003). Arab ko lahure: Looking at Nepali labour migrants to Arabian countries. *Contributions to Nepalese Studies, 30*(2), 295–325.

Gunduz, C., Alexander, L., & Subedi, D. B. (2009). *Opportunities for linking economic recovery and peacebuilding: Business perceptions from eastern and central terai*. London. Retrieved from http://www.international-alert.org/sites/default/files/Nepal_LinkingEconomicRecoveryPeacebuilding_EN_2009.pdf.

Hanlon, J. (2004). It is possible to just give money to the poor. *Development and Change, 35*(2), 375–383. https://doi.org/10.1111/j.1467-7660.2004.00356.x.

Harvey, P. (2005). *Cash and vouchers in emergencies* (Briefing Paper 25). London: Humanitarian Policy Group. Retrieved from https://www.preparecenter.org/sites/default/files/cash_based_response.pdf.

Harvey, P. (2007). *Cash-based responses in emergencies* (Briefing Paper No. 25). London: Overseas Development Institute (ODI), Humanitarian Policy Group (HPG).

Harvey, P., Slater, R., & Farrington, J. (2005, March). Cash transfers: Mere "Gadaffi Syndrome", or serious potential for rural rehabilitation and development? Natural resources perspectives 97. *Conflict Management and Peace Science*. Overseas Development Institute (ODI). Available from http://www.odi.org.uk/sites/odi.org.uk/files/odi-assets/publications-opinion-files/1662.pdf.

Hazan, J. (2007). *Social integration of ex-combatants after civil war*. Retrieved from http://www.un.org/esa/socdev/sib/egm/paper/JenniferHazen.pdf.

ILO. (2009). *Socio-economic reintegration of ex-combatants: Guidelines*. Geneva: International Labor Organization/Crisis Response and Reconstruction Programme (ILO/CRISIS).

Isima, J. (2004). Cash payments in disarmament, demobilisation and reintegration programmes in Africa. *Journal of Security Sector Management, 2*(3), 1–10.

Krantz, L. (2001). *The sustainable livelihood approach to poverty reduction: An Introduction*. Swidish International Development Cooperation Agency

(SIDA). Retrieved from http://www.forestry.umn.edu/prod/groups/cfans/@pub/@cfans/@forestry/documents/asset/cfans_asset_202603.pdf.

Lundin, I., Chachiua, M., Gaspar, A., Guebuzua, H., & Mbilana, G. (2000). Reducing cost through an expensive excercise. In K. Kees (Ed.), *Demobilization in sub-Saharan Africa: The development and security impacts* (pp. 173–212). Basingstoke and London: Macmillan.

Meikle, S., Ramasut, T., & Walker, J. (2001). *Sustainable urban livelihoods: Concepts and implications for policy*. Available from http://eprints.ucl.ac.uk/35/1/wp112.pdf.

Özerdem, A., Podder, S., O'Callaghan, S., & Pantuliano, S. (2008). *Reinsertion assistance and the reintegration of ex-combatants in war to peace transitions* (Thematic Working Paper 4). Bradford: Center for International Cooperation and Security, Bradford University.

Peppiatt, D., Mitchell, J., & Holzmann, P. (2001). *Cash transfers in emergencies: Evaluating benefits and assessing risks*. London. Retrieved from https://odihpn.org/wp-content/uploads/2001/06/networkpaper035.pdf.

Scoones, I. (2009). Livelihoods perspectives and rural development. *The Journal of Peasant Studies, 36*(1), 171–196. https://doi.org/10.1080/03066150902820503.

Specht, I. (2010). *Socio-economic reintegration of ex-combatants*. London: International Alert.

Specker, L. (2008). *The R-phase of DDR processes: An overview of key lessons learned and practical experiences*. The Hague: Netherlands Institute of International Relations-Conflict Research Unit. Retrieved from http://www.clingendael.nl/sites/default/files/20080900_cru_report_specker.pdf.

Subedi, D. B. (2013). Dealing with ex-combatants in a negotiated peace process: Impacts of transitional politics on the DDR programme in Nepal. *Journal of Asian and African Studies* (onlinefirst article). https://doi.org/10.1177/0021909613507537.

Swarbrick, P. (2007). *Avoiding disarmament failure: The critical Link in DDR—An operational manual for donors, managers and practitioners*. Geneva: Small Arms Survey, Graduate Institute of International Studies. Retrieved from http://www.smallarmssurvey.org/fileadmin/docs/F-Working-papers/SAS-WP5-DDR-Manual.pdf.

Tanner, F. (1996). Consensual versus coercive disarmament. In UNIDIR (Ed.), *Disarmament and conflict resolution project-managing arms in peace processes: The issues* (pp. 169–204). Geneva: United Nations Institute for Disarmament Research (UNIDIR).

Tesfamichael, G., Ball, N., & Nenon, J. (2004). *Peace in Sierra Leone: Evaluating the disarmament, demobilization, and reintegration process*. Washington, DC: Creative Associates International.

Thagunna, K. S., & Acharya, S. (2013). Empirical analysis of remittance inflow: The case of Nepal. *International Journal of Economics and Financial Issues, 3*(2), 337–344.

Thieme, S., & Wyss, S. (2005). Migration patterns and remittance transfer in Nepal: A case study of Sainik Basti in western Nepal. *International Migration, 43*(5), 59–98.

UN. (2010). *The operational guide to the integrated disarmament, demobilization and reintegration standards (IDDRS)*. New York: United Nations, UN Inter-Agency Working Group on Disarmament, Demobilization and Reintegration.

USAID. (2006). *USAID/OFDA uses cash grants to alleviate chronic food insecurity in Ethiopia*. Retrieved from http://transition.usaid.gov/our_work/humanitarian_assistance/disaster_assistance/publications/focus_articles/6_2004_Ethiopia.html.

WFP. (2006). *Cash and food transfers for food security and nutrition: Emerging insights and knowledge gaps from WFP's experience*. Retrieved from http://www.rlc.fao.org/es/prioridades/seguridad/ingreso/pdf/cash.pdf.

WFP. (2012). *Our work: Cash and vouchers*. Retrieved from http://www.wfp.org/cash-and-vouchers.

Willibald, S. (2006). Does money work? Cash transfers to ex-combatants in disarmament, demobilisation and reintegration processes. *Disasters, 30*(3), 316–339. https://doi.org/10.1111/j.0361-3666.2005.00323.x.

Wood, N. (2003, December 14). Swap guns for prizes? Few comply in Mecedonia. *New York Times*. Retrieved from http://www.nytimes.com/2003/12/14/world/swap-guns-for-prizes-few-comply-in-macedonia.html.

CHAPTER 8

Social Reintegration

For more than five years, ex-combatants lived inside cantonments in a closed networks ex-combatants. Having spent several years fighting in the war disintegrated the People's Liberation Army (PLA) ex-combatants from societal life and integrated into a network of war that looked like a "war family". The war family was a closed network of ex-combatants glued together by a common ideology of war as well as physical, moral and emotional connections among those participated in the war either voluntarily or forcefully. The connection formed a distinct social organisation set up by ex-combatants that functioned like an extended family constructed by the network of war, or the war family.

The function of war family emerged at a time when system of the Maoist armed conflict either disintegrated or disconnected ex-combatants from family and social network and integrated them into the war system. The management of ex-combatants following the peace process was expected to reverse the past trend: disintegrate ex-combatants from the network of war or the war family and integrate them back into society. This process, however, would involve profoundly important social dimension of reintegration such as rebuilding relationships and networks between ex-combatants, their families and communities. In this circumstance, social reintegration of the Maoist ex-combatants was a critical concern, as it played an important role in fostering relationships and social harmony in post-conflict Nepal. In other words, social reintegration is ideally intended to rebuild combatant-community relations, which eventually contributes to fostering social capital and enhancing social cohesion—the elements of which are essential to consolidate and

© The Author(s) 2018
D. B. Subedi, *Combatants to Civilians*, Rethinking Peace and Conflict Studies, https://doi.org/10.1057/978-1-137-58672-8_8

sustain peace; this process is considered to be a vital element in post-conflict peacebuilding (Annan & Cutter, 2009; Leff, 2008; Özerdem, 2012).

Although the literature on social reintegration in the context of formal Disarmament, Demobilisation and Reintegration (DDR) programmes is growing (Duthie, 2005; Kaplan & Nussio, 2012; Karame, 2009; Leff, 2008; McKay, 2004; Özerdem, 2012), the study of social reintegration in situations where no formal reintegration programme is implemented to reintegrate ex-combatants is limited. In the case of Nepal, since no formal reintegration programme was in place, ex-combatants applied and adopted informal processes to interact and build relationships with families and communities. It is maintained in this research that ex-combatants constitute a heterogeneous social category. The heterogeneity means that ex-combatants may experience their social reintegration differently in different times and social settings. This assumption encourages us raising some critical questions: How have the Maoist ex-combatants experienced their social reintegration? What formal and informal mechanisms have they applied to rebuilding their relationships with communities? Has the community accepted them? What factors have either constrained or facilitated their social reintegration? What effects can be seen at present in terms of the relationship between social reintegration and peacebuilding? Engaging with these questions, this chapter exclusively examines social reintegration of the Maoist ex-combatants in Nepal.

This chapter explores social reintegration as a collective social process in which community acceptance of ex-combatants is a determinant. However, without denying the role of community acceptance, it also shifts the focus from collectivism to the agency of individual ex-combatants. The proposition is that if social reintegration is examined in the light of collectivism as well as individual agency, it will be possible to better understand "community acceptance" and "community avoidance" as important themes which shape ex-combatants' relationships and interaction with the community where they have returned. It is found that there are both individual and societal-level factors that can explain why community have limited acceptance of ex-combatants while at the same time many ex-combatants also avoided interactions and contacts with the community of their origin.

Accordingly, this study finds that, at the individual level, ex-combatant's personal circumstances such as war time crime and atrocities, personal background before recruitment in the PLA, social stigma and jobs and livelihood have impacts on the ways in which ex-combatants have experienced their social reintegration. Similarly, at the societal level, factors like the post-conflict social and political environment, and transitional justice and reconciliation can have considerable effects on social reintegration. This chapter also examines the relationships between social reintegration of ex-combatants and the formation of social capital, which is essential to build peace in post-conflict period.

Ex-combatant Community Relations and Social Reintegration in the Nepalese Context

This section explores the factors that have shaped the relationships between ex-combatants and their communities. Community is here defined as geographically bounded physical and social settings that involve social actions, inter-personal and inter-group interactions, and include formal and informal social organisations and institutions (Block, 2009).[1]

The narratives and experiences of the PLA ex-combatants as well that of community people collected during the fieldwork for this study found community acceptance to be an important concept in social reintegration. However, nearly one third of ex-combatants have not returned to the communities of their origin means that barrier and challenges to social reintegration of PLA fighters must also be seen in the light of another concept what this study calls "community avoidance". The idea of community avoidance relates to the fact that due to personal as well as social reasons, many combatants have tended to avoid their community of origin for a significant number of ex-combatants have resettled elsewhere in locations other than their villages of origin. This urban and peri-urban resettlement pattern is possibly a strategic means for the ex-combatants to avoid their communities of origin.

Thus, this study maintains that community acceptance and community avoidance are two parallel concepts that need to be taken into account in order to better understand ex-combatants' relationships with each other, their families and communities. The fieldwork further

---

[1] As opposed to the geographically bounded notion, community is also increasingly conceptualised as a network-mediated de-territorial virtual social space which facilitates group interactions and relations in different ways (see Cohen, 1985; Delanty, 2010). The idea of virtual or symbolic community is also used to refer to the community of PLA ex-combatants.

revealed why there is minimal community acceptance of ex-combatants and why some ex-combatants than others have avoided their communities is a phenomena that has been shaped by factors that are related to both individual ex-combatant level and societal level. Therefore, understanding these two concepts, community acceptance and community avoidance, requires an examination of both individual and societal-level factors. This aspect of enquiry helps us to unpack individual combatants' agency as well as collective efforts of community in the formal and informal processes social reintegration of PLA combatants in Nepal.

Individual-Level Factors Affecting Social Reintegration

Four general themes have been identified regarding individual level factors. These are: (a) war-time conduct and atrocities carried out by individual combatants, (b) a combatant's personal character and background, (c) an individual combatant's socialisation skills and capacity, (d) social stigma associated with an individual's record as a combatant and how this is viewed by family and community, and (e) jobs and livelihood issues associated with the identity of combatants.

Records of War Time Conduct and Atrocities

During the armed conflict, the Maoists used the notion of "class enemy" as an instrument of war mobilisation. However, it soon turned out to be an instrument of violence. Operationalisation of the class enemy perception initially started with classifying rural elites and intellectuals, including big landholders, teachers, those associated with the private sector, police and army officials, journalists, and public officials and political leaders of non-Maoist political parties, as enemies of the people's war. The class annihilation campaigns that followed began with physical punishment, including torture and violence targeted against the so-called class enemies. It was this campaign that not only displaced thousands of people but also helped the Maoists to sabotage their political and rural middle class intellectual opponents in places that were subsequently known as the Maoist hinterlands.[2]

In subsequent years of the armed conflict, the PLA fighters and the local Maoist leaders personalised class enemy perceptions to the extent

---

[2] Interview with a male human rights activities in Dhangadi, December 2011, and a lawyer in Ghorahi, Dang, February 2012.

that it was used as an instrument for taking revenge for personal issues. According to a human rights activist, in several instances, it led to "falsification of the enemy". To clarify, he added:

> Not all people labelled as enemy of people (Janata ka Dusman) and the people displaced involuntarily due to Maoists physical threats are what is termed as "Shosak or Samanti" (exploiters or elites). There are many poor people who were coerced, punished and forced to leave just because they had either some personal issues with or a different ideology than the Maoists and their supporters.

In the cases where violence was personalised or used to take revenge on the basis of personal matters, the public generally knew the identity of these offenders. There was a consensus among respondents, especially non-combatant respondents, that ex-combatants who had clearly identifiable records of atrocity were, consequently, experiencing a relatively higher degree of problems associated with social acceptance in their community. Indeed combatants who have committed such "revealed" or "known" atrocities have actually tended to avoid going back to their community. Past atrocities and violence have remained an open source of retaliation for victims. In this sense, not only are ex-combatants a potential source of insecurity in society, but also, because of their troubled past, some ex-combatants face perceived security threats themselves. These two different forms of security risk have dual effects on social reintegration: people in the community have negative perceptions of ex-combatants who have carried out atrocities and violence during the war, while victim—perpetrator relationships make some ex-combatants reluctant to face their villagers because of the fear of retaliation for past violence in which they have been involved and implicated.

Personal Background Before Recruitment

Ex-combatants' pre-recruitment personal backgrounds are another important factor; this aspect also has implications for his/her social acceptance in the community. At the time of recruitment, the Maoists did not take a thorough account of an individual's personal, social, moral and ideological backgrounds. An "all are welcome" type of attitude was prevalent during the armed conflict, partly due to the need to intensify combatant recruitment. As a result, people, including those who had bad police and criminal records and anti-social as well as infamous backgrounds such as a person being a member of a violent youth gang and so on, were recruited as combatants. A combatant who was interviewed explained this very dynamic, "The war needed fighters, no matter who they were and what background they may have had; the PLA welcomed people with all kinds of backgrounds, whether good or bad".[3]

By joining the insurgency, the people with criminal, unsocial or infamous backgrounds acquired a new identity as a combatant, which provided them with protection and safety while the "all is welcome" type of recruitment policy served the PLA's goal to increase the number of combatants. In the eyes of the community, the combatants with known infamous previous backgrounds has not changed drastically in the post-conflict period. As a result, some combatants have faced more difficulties in being accepted back into the community than others.

Individual combatants' education and upbringing as well as social relationships of their family members were reported to be other important factors determining their acceptance into the community. Equally important was the degree of their radicalisation and indoctrination. Indoctrination and radicalisation, which were major recruitment strategies in the war, had varying effects for different ex-combatants. For instance, ex-combatants who had a dedicated Maoist background, those who served as motivators and whole-time (WT) party workers, and those who had frequent interactions with senior leaders of the CPNM were more radicalised and thus had become ideologically more aggressive than others.[4] More radicalised ex-combatants are seen as aggressive opponents of non-Maoist political leaders and supporters; therefore, they have faced more difficulties in adjusting back into communities with people of mixed political ideologies.

Socialisation Skill and Capacity

Both ex-combatants and non-combatant respondents believed that socialisation requires a particular set of competencies such as communication skills, interest and willingness to make new friends who have different political and ideological worldviews, the ability to take leadership roles in social activities and events, and so on. A large number of

---

[3] Interview with a journalist in Kathmandu, December 2012.
[4] Interview with a male civil society leader in Kathmandu, December 2012.

respondents believed that these competencies differ from person to person based on an individual's education, upbringing, and family environment. Having spent several years fighting the war, many ex-combatants lack socialisation skills and capacity, which they would require in working for a living (employment, voluntary or obligatory community activities) and maintaining social relationships. According to a commander[5]:

> Not all combatants are equal in terms of their communication skills and the capacity to accept and recognise different political views and perspectives. Some are more hostile and aggressive than others. These personal differences matter a lot when each combatant has to interact with the wider society.

Limitations of socialisation skills and capacity mean that many ex-combatants are more comfortable socialising and interacting only with their fellow combatants. As a result, in the case of a considerable number of ex-combatants, they have constructed bonded in-group networks with the members of the ex-PLA fighters, while they have tended to remain alienated from out-group members and the community other than the communities of the war family.

Social Stigma

Social stigma is a reason why some combatants have generally avoided social interactions, community activities or returning back to their villages. An overwhelming number of combatants felt that although the war had induced political and civic awareness throughout the country, the CPNM's promises that the war would bring in radical social, political and economic changes through a new discourse of state building based on the revolutionary philosophy of Prachanda Path,[6] have remained either unfulfilled, or at least they do not see the changes would happen as per the revolutionary idea of so-called Prachanda Path. Further, the official division of the Maoist party into two groups left combatants confused, disillusioned and frustrated. In this situation, almost all the combatants who were interviewed said that they have been struggling to find a convincing answer to explain to community people a justification for the violence and revolution associated with the past war. Upon

---

[5] Interview with a male PLA commander, Kathmandu, December 2012.
[6] Interview with a male Battalion vice commander, Chitwan, January 2013.

their release from cantonments with a cash package, many combatants encountered a moral dilemma and confusion, and have no answer to every single question from people that interrogates their achievements during the war. For some ex-combatants, the question of justifying their involvement in the war becomes even more problematic in villages where hundreds of families have lost members because of the war. A male combatant's assertion is helpful to elaborate this point[7]:

> Wherever I go in my village, I am confronted with several questions for which I really don't have any answers. They ask, What did you achieve from the war? Did you kill people and destroy physical infrastructure just to get money? Where is your revolution? What happened to the promise your party made to us? I have no answer, not at all. How can I go back to my village to face such questions?

Another combatant's remark is similar but more touching[8]:

> I feel extremely uncomfortable and depressed because several of my colleagues who joined the war together with me were killed. What answer can I give to the family of the deceased fellows in the village? This feeling is so disturbing.

This moral dilemma is also a source of social stigma. The heroic image of ex-combatants in the past is now gradually eroding and they are increasingly being seen as "agents of destruction".[9] It is interesting to note that even in this situation, community people have not rejected them totally, although a feeling of rejection and animosity was reported when talking to community people and civil society leaders. With some exceptions, no major case of a combatant clashing with their community was reported during my fieldwork. According to a civil society leader, "the community is watching ex-combatants. Community people have silently accepted them but this does not mean that they are fully accepted". Latent tensions exist between combatants and the community due to a lack of reconciliatory efforts. Combatants have different strategies to cope with perceived feelings of rejection, moral dilemmas and social stigma. For instance many who have not returned to villages have decided to settle in groups elsewhere.

[7] Interview with a male combatant, Kathmandu, January 2013.
[8] Interview with brigade commander, Jhapa, November 2011.
[9] Interview with a male lawyer, Ghorahi, February 2013.

Socio-culturally, for some ex-combatants, inter-caste marriage is another source of social stigma. As also noted in the previous chapter, during the war, as well as while in cantonments, a large number of combatants have had inter-caste and inter-ethnic marriages with fellow combatants.[10] This kind of marriage was not only officially recognised by the PLA, but it was also, to a certain extent, encouraged, because it was believed to be a means of transforming caste and ethnic hierarchies and discriminations, though several such marriages were reported to have broken up later.[11] Ex-combatants who had inter-caste marriages have not been well accepted in their in-law families and so they have settled elsewhere. Economic hardship, family rejection and social stigma are consequences in their lives today. In the view of a psychosocial counsellor, "female ex-combatants who were not accepted in families due to inter-caste marriage were found more vulnerable to depression and psychosocial problems", which also affect their social reintegration in the long-run.[12]

When asked why inter-caste marriage is a problem despite the fact that the agenda of the war had sought to eliminate caste and ethnic hierarchies and discriminations, a civil society activist responded, "the Maoists' rhetoric of social transformation has bounced back".[13] He clarified that although the war has changed public perceptions towards caste-based discriminations and hierarchies, to a certain extent, this change in the past was not spontaneous but an outcome of coercive behaviour by the insurgency. This means that the perceptions of many traditional families towards caste and religious puritanism have not transformed permanently. According to respondents, drastic changes in relation to caste hierarchies, untouchability, and religious puritanism, that are central characteristics of Nepali society, are inter-generational matters; these require a whole generation to phase out for the complete changes that are required to soften these hierarchical cultural attributes. Rejection of inter-caste marriage, either openly or silently, by the families of some ex-combatants is an example of how the status quo in cultural and religious terms has been perpetuated in Nepali society.

[10] Interview with a male vice commander in Padampur, Chitwan, January 2013.

[11] Interview with a journalist in Kathmandu, December 2012.

[12] Interview with a male NGO worker who has been working in the field of psychosocial counselling in Kathmandu, January 2013.

[13] Interview with a male NGO worker from a *Dalit* community, Nepalgunj, February 2013.

Jobs and Livelihood

It is important to note that this study has found mutually reinforcing characteristics between economic and social reintegration. An overwhelming number of ex-combatants and non-combatants interviewed agreed that the ex-combatants who have achieved jobs and livelihood security have the chances to experience better social reintegration. Engaging in livelihood related activities such as micro-enterprises or jobs, have offered ex-combatants a means of entering into an arena of frequent social interaction with community people. In other words, jobs and livelihood related activities have facilitated better relationships between the community and economically engaged ex-combatants. However, responses, particularly from ex-combatants, suggest that they have faced silent rejection from community people that has resulted in a low level of social capital development between ex-combatants and the community. This kind of dynamic has considerably constrained ex-combatants from successfully doing business with local communities. Nonetheless, ex-combatants were hopeful to, over the time, carrying out business activities successfully might help them to rebuild better relationships with community members.

A substantial number of ex-combatants also asserted that both jobs and livelihood opportunities create an environment for them to live a dignified life in society. In their view, over time, such dignity can help them create an alternative identity that is more acceptable than being labelled an ex-combatant. For example, being a local businessman, micro-enterpriser, employee of particular organisations, and so on, are far more respectable from a social identity perspective. Although such transformation in an ex-combatant's identity is profoundly time consuming, it can determine how ex-combatants are able to achieve a secure and dignified livelihood, and is one of the determining elements of social reintegration. Such revealing assertions from ex-combatants as well as non-combatant interviewees strongly suggest that achieving social reintegration becomes contingent upon the success of economic reintegration of individual ex-combatants. Yet, the reality is that not all ex-combatants are fortunate in this regard; only a small proportion of ex-combatants have been able to gain jobs and develop a livelihood. This suggests that a reintegration policy must simultaneously include factors and actors that will contribute to both economic and social reintegration in order to achieve better outcomes for the reintegration programmes. In fact, success of reintegration programmes may depend on such factors and the actors being considered, but it may also simultaneously require a programme to engage with society at the community level to bring out the importance of allowing ex-combatants to engage in work at this level, because without community support, reintegration, whether or not livelihood and employment opportunities are made available, is so much more difficult.

SOCIETAL-LEVEL FACTORS AFFECTING SOCIAL REINTEGRATION

A large number of respondents maintained that social reintegration of the Maoist ex-combatants is also contingent upon macro social and political environments in post-conflict society. In this regard, the social and political environment and transitional justice and reconciliation are major themes identified during the fieldwork.

Post-conflict Social and Political Environment

The Maoist armed conflict has had an enormous human cost (see IDMC & NRC, 2012; INSEC, 2010; NRCS & ICRC, 2011; Shrestha & Niroula, 2005), as well as economic costs (see Kumar, 2003; OCHA & WFP, 2007; Sapkota, 2004; Subedi, 2012; Upreti, 2010) from which the society at large has not yet recovered. Further, the armed conflict in Nepal has also had enormous social and political consequences. In this regard, politicisation of identity and spiralling political instability after 2006 is noteworthy. It is this new conflict dynamic that has unprecedentedly divided the Nepali society, both socially and politically.

The Maoists imposed ideological coercion during the armed conflict. The ideological coercion coupled with radicalism sparked heinous political violence. For instance, the Maoists resorted to torture, killing, or displacement of the Maoist political opposition, particularly the workers and cadres of the CPNUML and the Nepali Congress (NC). Over time, the indoctrination and mass political campaigns of Maoists polarised the society, engendering "us" versus "them" feelings between supporters and opponents of the Maoist movement. As discussed earlier, the notion of "class enemy" and politicisation of ethnicity further aggravated the situation.

Political polarisation has become even more pronounced in the post-conflict period. Unpacking this new dynamic requires examining how post-conflict politics has interacted with exclusionary social and cultural realties, leading to proliferation of contentious and divisive identity politics during the post-conflict period.

To begin with, it makes sense to assert that Nepali society is inherently multi-cultural: currently, there are 125 caste/ethnic groups and

123 languages are spoken in a small country with a population of 26.5 million people (CBS, 2012, p. 4). Similarly, there are ten types of religious categories, of which Hinduism is the largest group, being followed by 81% of the population. The other four major religions in descending order are Buddhism (9%), Islam (4%), Kirat (3%), and Christianity (1%) (CBS, 2012). Despite socio-cultural diversity, horizontal inequalities and discriminations between caste and ethnic groups, such as *Madhesi*, *Janajatis*, and *Dalits* has been a source of contention within the exclusionary and centralised state system for a long time. Thus, tapping the contentions and grievances of marginalised caste and ethnic groups, the Maoist conflict shifted its discourse from a purely class-based mobilisation to a typical fusion of caste/ethnic and class based mobilisation.

The CPNM perpetuated and popularised the politicisation of caste and ethnic identity, which they considered as being a reason for armed conflict and social revolution. To clarify, since January 2007, the grievances of socio-economically and socio-politically excluded and marginalised social categories, including *Madhesi, Janajatis, Dalits*, Muslims and other indigenous groups, triggered a new cycle of conflict and violence particularly in the *Terai*,[14] as well as in the eastern hills. At best, if managed well, this new discourse can be expected to promote socio-economic and socio-political inclusion, social justice and pluralism that can address existing horizontal and vertical inequalities. At worst, it has increased inter-group competition, and social tensions and divisions between different social, religious, ethnic, and caste groups. Society is divided between the *Madhesis* (who have origins in the Terai) and *Pahadi* (who have origins in the hills), *Chettri-Bahun* (high caste) and *Janajati*, *dalits* (low caste), resulting in occasionally violent confrontations induced by the current discourse of identity politics and social inclusion.

In the meantime, political division and proliferation of new political actors characterise post-conflict social transition in Nepal. For instance, a number of non-political ethnic and cultural groups have now registered with the Election Commission as political parties pursuing contentious identity-based political agendas. In 2006, the Madhsi Janadhikar Forum, Sadbhawana Party, Sadbhawana Party- Anandi Devi, and Terai Madhesh Democratic Forum (TMDP) were major political parties pursuing the agendas of marginalised Madhesi people from the Terai. By the end of 2012, the number of Madhesh/Terai based political parties have reached

---

[14] Terai refers to the plain land in the south of the country, bordering to India.

seventeen.[15] In 2008, a total of seventy political parties participated in the Constitution Assembly (CA) election, of which thirty three parties were represented in the CA.[16] By contrast, a total of 139 political parties have applied for registration to take part in another round of the CA elections, which was scheduled for November 2013.[17]

The Nepali case demonstrates that post-conflict transition can lead to more divisive and unstable social and political contexts, engendering fiercely competitive political space and networks, what Nan (2009, pp. 177–78) calls "exclusive networks". The exclusive networks have fixed boundaries that reinforce inequalities and divisions between network members and non-members. Given the rise of divisive social and political contexts, social, religious and political tolerance, respect, recognition and peaceful inter-group relationships among various caste and ethnic groups that had typically become accelerators of social capital in the past are now thrown into crisis. A local resident of Ghorahi highlighted how the socially and politically divided society in Nepal has had damaging effects on social relations and trust at the community level[18]:

> Due to the effects of conflict we are now divided politically between "Maaobadi" [the Maoist], "Kangresi" [supporter of the Nepali congress party], "Emale" [supporters of CPNUML], and socially we are divided into Bahun, Chettris, Dalit, Janajati and so on. One group see the other with suspicion and the environment of trust between people has almost disappeared.

The social reintegration of ex-combatants meets with this divided social and political environment. In the meantime, because of their association with the Maoist party, combatants have a politicised personal identity which will take some time to transform. This means that their political identity is less likely to be completely accepted in the current politically

---

[15] Interview with a male civil society leader, Biratnagar, January 2013.

[16] Downloaded from http://www.election.gov.np/EN/downloads/political_parties_list.pdf.

[17] Downloaded from http://www.election.gov.np/EN/downloads/political_parties_list.pdf.

[18] Interview with a male respondent in Ghorahi, Dang, February 2013. It is notable here that the CPNM and the CPNUML formed a joint alliance to contest the election of the Federal Parliament held in December 2017. At the time of finalising the manuscript for this volume, the CPNM and CPNUML have formed a joint government, and the exercise for amalgamation of the two parties is in progress. The unification of CPNM and CPNUML is a new phenomenon, which is not dealt with in this volume. However, it would be certainly interesting to see what impact the unification might have on social reintegration of ex-combatants and social cohesion in the long-run.

divided society that exists in Nepal. Further, since the Maoist party has divided into two groups, the division has vertical effects, splitting party workers and supporters into two camps.

Therefore, for ex-combatants, the problem in building relationships across the political divide starts from within the parties themselves, because of their confronting political relations that have occasionally resulted in violent clashes, as was the case in Narayanghat, Chitwan in June 2013.[19] In the meantime, the fact that the lower ranks of the PLA have a large number of combatants from various ethnic and minority groups means that their social reintegration can be even more complicated because of prevailing ethnic divisions in the society.

The analysis in this section reveals that minimum levels of social and political stability and harmony are required for combatants to be accepted into their communities. However, despite this reality, offering a voluntary retirement package to ex-combatants seemed to have mired with the unscrupulous policy response which has pushed ex-combatants to struggle for their reintegration into a society that is deeply divided. The Assertion of a respondent working in a peacebuilding Non-Governmental Organisation (NGO) in Kathmandu is worth mentioning here to amplify this point further[20]:

> The political actors involved in the management of ex-combatants were overtly pre-occupied with the notion that releasing combatants from cantonments would fix all the remaining sticking points in the peace process. Releasing ex-combatants would not necessarily make peace; it is only one element of the entire peace process. Minimum levels of stability would enable former PLA fighters to better adjust in society.

This assertion implies that reintegration of ex-combatants has taken place in isolation from other frontiers of the peace process. On this point, it is suggested if ex-combatants were released from cantonments in a situation where significant progress was made simultaneously at least in one or more domains of the peace process such as the formation of the Truth and Reconciliation Commission (TRC), it would have helped to reduce social and political tensions and divisions in the community at large. However, this was not the reality that eventuated because ex-combatants

---

[19] Interview with male FM radio journalist, Chitwan, January 2013.
[20] Interview with a male peacebuilding worker, Kathmandu, December 2012.

faced a relatively challenging environment when they were seeking to reintegrate into society and their various communities. The other domains of the peace process include issues relating to but not limited to addressing grievances of marginalised groups, expanding socio-political inclusion and socio-economic opportunities for ethnic and indigenous groups, including the *Madhesi* and *Dalits* through a new constitution designed to accelerate post-conflict economic recovery and development processes. Of these various elements of the peace process, issues of transitional justice and social reconciliation were repeated frequently during interviews held with ex-combatants; therefore, this complex theme of "reconciliation" deserves further elaboration and analysis, which follows here.

Transitional Justice and Social Reconciliation

Given that post-conflict Nepali society is deeply divided due to conflict and its legacy, there is a widely felt need to address transitional justice to promote inter-group relations and harmony. The peace process has recognised this need; therefore, it has stipulated a provision for a Truth and Reconciliation Commission (TRC), although the TRC was not formalised as of early 2014. Political disputes over the process and function of the TRC have placed its future in limbo. An example of such a dispute is the provision of a "blanket amnesty" for the perpetrators associated with various atrocities or acts against humanity during the war; this was an idea the CPNM pushed but it was rejected by opponents, namely the NC and CPNUML, as well as human rights activists and civil society organisations. Delaying in formalising the TRC means that horizontal animosity between victims and perpetrators, and vertical resentments towards the state's inability to deliver justice and reconciliation has been growing exponentially, dividing society even more and pushing state–society relations into crisis. In this regard, an assertion of a female conflict victim is noteworthy. She said "victims and perpetrators of the war have been living in the same community without any attempt at reconciliation; mistrust, suspicions and security threats dominate their everyday life".[21]

---

[21] Interview with a female conflict victim and a male NGO worker in Nepalgunj, January 2013. It is notable here that in 2014, the Parliament ultimately passed the TRC Act. Accordingly, the government formed the Commission on Investigation of Disappeared Persons and the Truth and Reconciliation Commission. However, the two years term of these two Commissions have passed but the progress on transitional justice including finding truth and initiating reconciliation is still incomplete.

In the meantime, the frustrations and grievances of conflict victims have not been addressed in the current peace process. In the Nepali context, conflict victims can be broadly classified into several categories: Internally Displaced Persons (IDPs); individuals and families who have lost their family members during the war; those whose family members have disappeared; those who have become disabled during the Maoist conflict and Madhesh movement; war widows; and those whose land and property were seized by the Maoists but where these have not been returned. Although the government delivered an interim relief programme to conflict victims, their needs and basic requirements have not been properly addressed, even within the past seven years.[22]

For instance, only around 25,000 out of the 78,000 officially registered IDPs have returned home with support and assistance from the Ministry of Peace and Reconstruction (MoPR) (IDMC & NRC, 2012). No progress has been made in returning the lands confiscated by the Maoists during and even after the war. Although there is no accurate figure available on how much land has been confiscated by Maoists across the country, a human rights activist estimated that the Maoists have not returned more than 1600 hectares of land in the mid-west and far-west regions alone[23]; this figure more or less matches an estimation made by a non-government organisation, Informal Sector Service Centre (INSEC) (see IRIN, 2012).

A growing need for transitional justice has been felt across the country, and in some places it has resulted in confrontations, disputes and public backlash. One useful example comes from the Dailekh district headquarters where police opened a file on Maoist war crimes, arrested the offenders and began an investigation in January 2013. This process, however, was obstructed by direct intervention from the Maoist Prime Minister and Attorney General, stating that war-time crimes cannot be dealt outside the TRC structure. This erupted as a national and international issue, resulting in clashes between Maoist supporters and non-Maoist groups, including local civil society. This event indicates the severity of the need to deliver transitional justice. It also suggests the likelihood of difficulties and the possibility of political differences on dealing with war crimes. According to an interviewee, this event

---

[22] Interview with a human rights activist from Nepalgunj, January 2013.
[23] Interview with an NGO worker, Nepalgunj, Banke, January 2013.

suddenly made the war-time offenders suspicious about their safety and security.[24]

The need for social reconciliation and its potential to complement ex-combatants' acceptance into post-conflict society is vital for successful peacebuilding. Theory suggests that while post-conflict reconciliation ideally prevents the use of the past as a seed for renewed conflict and that helps victims and perpetrators to break away from a bitter past to inculcate a shared future (Bloomfield et al., 2003), reintegration of ex-combatants, on the other hand, is one of many means of preventing states and societies from slipping back into instability and ultimately violent conflict or war (Kingma & Muggah, 2009; Ngoma, 2004). Reintegration and reconciliation programmes have shared objectives, as both post-conflict initiatives are generally geared towards the transformation of conflict and the fostering and rebuilding of new non-violent personal and social relationships.

A number of interviewees, however, perceived reconciliation as a being formal political process. Based on their narratives, political reconciliation can be explained as a formal process of truth and reconciliation that is organised with formal structures and mechanisms; hence, they referred to the Truth and Reconciliation Commission (TRC) in this context. Because of the political wrangling and debates surrounding the TRC, optimism regarding the process and outcomes of the TRC even more than two years after its formation is declining on the ground. A conflict victim showed his scepticism stating that, "the TRC is certainly necessary but I fear its outcome might be too little, too political or too late".[25]

Given that the TRC is unlikely to accomplish its task within its mandated period due to the lack of political commitments by key political actors as well as the government, some respondents pointed towards a reconciliation process which could be entirely non-political and happening at the community level as a locally driven effort that the respondents called *Samajik Melmilap* (social reconciliation). Many respondents mentioned that Nepali society has a discrete tradition of reconciling bitter events and relations through festivals like *Dashain, Fagu Purnima* and so on. Other respondents from a NGO background have suggested that social reconciliation could be accomplished by bringing adversary groups into contact

---

[24] Interview with a journalist, Ghorahi, Dang, February 2013.
[25] Interview with a male conflict victim, Kathmandu, January 2013.

with each other and to facilitate interactions through various means, such as development works, social dialogue, sports and arts. Others suggested that formal and politically driven reconciliation might not have a substantial effect at the community level due to prevailing political and ethnic divisions that exist. It might take some time before people are ready to accept the co-existence and identity of perpetrators. In such situations social reconciliation might fill the gap. A respondent was specific in providing examples of social reintegration, "cultural tools such as street theatre, cultural festivals, community events, arts competitions among school students and so on so can be applied to help people overcome their difficult relations".[26]

Some non-state actors have already begun helping people to reconcile in one way or another. For instance, it was learned that some NGOs as well as the United Nations Development Programme (UNDP) in Nepal, have been helping to mediate between divided communities through local mediation, collaborative dialogue and social reconciliation, sports, and radio programmes. Although respondents are optimistic about such programmes, they suggest that there have to be efforts made to include ex-combatants. Some respondents mentioned that Nepali society has a typical social resilience capacity. A respondent from Biratnagar said that it is due to a quality of resilience that Nepali society has so far avoided disastrous bloodshed, even in such an ethnically, socially and politically divided context. There are, therefore, suggestions to identify the bases of such a resilience capacity and to promote them, not only for social reintegration, but also for social harmony and cohesion in the long run. Promoting social reconciliation at the community level will not only fill the absence of a formal reconciliation process, but it might also make combatant—community relations smoother and healthier. The harmonious social environment that social reconciliation efforts could create might also help ex-combatants to mitigate the avoidance problem of running away and hiding in seclusion, which is hampering their interaction and engagement in social and civic activities.

Discussion: Social Reintegration, Bonded Social Capital and Peacebuilding

As seen above, the Maoist ex-combatants are a constituency of heterogeneous members who have varying degrees of personal differences with respect to their records of war-time conduct and atrocities, socialisation

[26] Interview with a male NGO worker, Nepalgunj, January 2013.

skills, personal background and social stigma. All of these individual-level factors have affected individual ex-combatants in many ways, meaning that different ex-combatants have experienced their relationship with the community in different ways. Contrary to the conventional belief that community acceptance is a marker of social reintegration, it was found that in the case of the Maoist ex-combatants, they had rejected or avoided facing the community for various personal/individual-level reasons discussed above. In the meantime, the social and political environment is not favourable, particularly with regard to fostering networking, relationships and interactions between ex-combatants and community people. As such, the entire Nepali society has been fractured and divided as direct effects of the ethnic, caste and class-related issues that emerged due to the war. The discourse of identity politics has further polarised the society, resulting in low-level social cohesion in post-conflict Nepal.

In this kind of situation, it is obvious that ex-combatants are bound to experience several difficulties in adjusting to living back in their respective communities and villages or suburbs in cities. As has been seen from the findings of this research project, ex-combatants have become polarised and alienated from communities and have tended to form their own closed networks and interactions with various groups. This reveals that, currently, such polarisation has led to the formation of "bonded social capital", which is fragmentary and prone to widen cleavages between ex-combatants and several other social categories, such as war victims and IDPs. Formation of bonded capital further indicates a situation where community relationships have become stranded, requiring some form of facilitation to bring adversaries into interacting with each other and engaging in a process of dialogue.

Peacebuilding in Nepal has not effectively dealt with social and psychosocial effects of the Maoists' armed conflict. As explained above, this is particularly the case with the Maoist ex-combatants who are marked by social stigma and face rejection in their everyday lives due to their association with armed violence and Maoism, as well as the atrocities in which they may or may not have been involved. The lengthy politicised process involved in the management of ex-combatants has failed to recognise the need to address social, psychosocial and emotional needs of ex-combatants. As a result, while some ex-combatants have done well in terms of their social reintegration using their personal capacities and networks, the rest have no other options but to rebuild and re-strengthen their wartime networks. In the long run, this will only increase existing chasms between ex-combatants and communities, which is, in turn, harmful for building peace in post-war Nepal.

Conclusions

This chapter has examined social reintegration of ex-combatants in Nepal, where no formal programme was implemented to reintegrate the Maoist ex-combatants. As in formal DDR programmes, combatant–community relations and the former's acceptance by the latter remains central to social reintegration in a context like post-war Nepal, with its distinct social and cultural context. However, in such situations, social reintegration involves complex informal processes and the fluidity of informality makes the entire process even more complicated.

Social reintegration of the Maoist ex-combatants is as much an individual process as it is a collective societal process. This finding establishes the agency for individual combatants in their experience of socially reintegrating back into society and the community without rejecting the significance of macro-societal processes that might affect an individual's agency, either positively or negatively. Drawing on the analysis in this chapter, it can be concluded that the way in which ex-combatants might see their own social reintegration could be quite different from how non-combatants may perceive it; these are important differences in perspectives. This is perhaps one of the most unassuming facts about social reintegration that would need to be taken into account seriously when researching reintegration or making social reintegration policies, because it does not appear to be obvious. Investigating individual and societal level factors may help, to a certain extent, in addressing this challenge, particularly in a context where no formal reintegration programme is in place at the national level. Reminding us to recognise the heterogeneity that exists among the ex-combatants, this chapter provides suggestions that we should examine ex-combatants' personal circumstances, as well as their macro socio-political context, in the process of analysing their circumstances in any study of social reintegration, and particularly in Nepal.

As an individual process, the experience and outcomes of one's social reintegration depends on one's personal background, war-time crime record, psychosocial problems experienced, education, jobs and livelihood opportunities. This chapter has also explored mutually reinforcing character of economic and social reintegration. The analysis also reveals that in addition to community acceptance, community avoidance is an equally pertinent concept of social reintegration, particularly in the post-war socio-political, socio-cultural and socio-economic environment, which is divided and unstable for all concerned.

Analysing societal-level factors has suggested that macro socio-political environment can directly and indirectly impact on social reintegration. In the Nepali context, post-conflict society is divided as never before and this division has severed inter-group social relations, with implications for the way ex-combatants are generally seen and received in communities. An analysis of societal-level factors also encourages us to recognise that reintegrating ex-combatants require a minimal level of social and political stability and harmony. In practical terms, this conclusion suggests the need to organise reintegration of ex-combatants in tandem with other aspects of the peace process. In this regard, a symbiotic relationship between post-conflict reconciliation and social reintegration of ex-combatants is clear. While reconciliation might create a favourable environment for social reintegration of Maoist ex-combatants in Nepal, social reintegration, in turn, can also complement post-conflict reconciliation.

Assisting ex-combatants in their social reintegration would have the potential to contribute to the improvement of relational-level changes, particularly between ex-combatants and communities. Such changes would be highly essential to foster better relationships, trust and networks between ex-combatants and community, which, in turn, could help rebuild social capital that was damaged during the war. However, as has been shown in this chapter, not all ex-combatants have favourable personal circumstances to enable them to be readily accepted into communities. There has also been a discussion of societal level factors that have constrained social reintegration, and thereby limited the possibilities of creating bridging social capital.

In this and preceding chapters, this volume has discussed economic and social reintegration of ex-combatants from different perspectives. When arriving at this stage of analysis, a pertinent question that arises is: What are the immediate consequences of social and economic rehabilitation of ex-combatants to peacebuilding, particularly if we look at peace from the perspective of security and violence? The next chapter will focus on this issue, with particular emphasis on ex-combatants' remobilisation and ex-combatant-led post-conflict violence, and its potential impact on building sustainable peace.

References

Annan, J., & Cutter, A. (2009). *Critical issues and lessons in social reintegration: Balancing justice psychological wellbeing and community reconciliation.* Retrieved from http://cartagenaddr.org/literature_press/ART_21.pdf.

Block, P. (2009). *Community: The structure of belonging.* San Francisco: Berrett-Koehler.

Bloomfield, D., Barnes, T., & Huyse, L. (Eds.). (2003). *Reconciliation after violent conflict: A Handbook.* Stockholm: International IDEA.

CBS. (2012). *National Population and Housing Census 2011: National Report.* Kathmandu. Retrieved from http://cbs.gov.np/wp-content/uploads/2012/11/NationalReport.pdf.

Cohen, A. P. (1985). *The symbolic construction of community.* London and New York: Tavistock Publications.

Delanty, G. (2010). *Community* (2nd ed.). London and New York: Routledge.

Duthie, R. (2005). Transitional justice and social reintegration. In *Stockholm: Stockholm Initiative on Disarmament, Demobilisation and Reintegration (SIDDR)*, Ministry of Foreign Affairs, Sweden. Available from http://www.regeringen.se/content/1/c6/06/54/02/7545e870.pdf.

IDMC, & NRC. (2012). *Global Overview 2011: People internally displaced by conflict and violence.* Geneva. Retrieved from http://www.internal-displacement.org/publications/global-overview-2011.pdf.

INSEC. (2010). *Conflict Victim's Profile.* Kathmandu. Retrieved from http://www.insec.org.np/victim/reports/total.pdf.

IRIN. (2012). *NEPAL: Land could sow "seeds of serious discontent".* Retrieved from http://www.irinnews.org/report/96067/NEPAL-Land-could-sow-seeds-of-serious-discontent.

Kaplan, O., & Nussio, E. (2012, August 30–September 2). *Community counts: The social reintegration of ex-combatants in colombia.* Paper presented at the The 2012 Annual Meeting of the American Political Science Association, New Oreleans, LA. Available from http://papers.ssrn.com/sol3/papers.cfm?abstract_id=2138188.

Karame, K. (2009). Reintegration and relevance of social relations: The case of lebanon. *Conflict, Security and Development, 9*(4), 495–514.

Kingma, K., & Muggah, R. (2009). *Critical issues in DDR: Context, indicators, targeting, and challenges.* Cartagena: Center for International Disarmament Demobilization and Reintegration.

Kumar, D. (2003). Consequences of the militarized conflict and the cost of violence in Nepal. *Contributions to Nepalese Studies, 30*(2), 167–216.

Leff, J. (2008). The nexus between social capital and reintegration of ex-combatants: A case for Sierra Leone. *African Journal on Conflict Resolution, 8*(1), 9–38. http://dx.doi.org/10.4314%2Fajcr.v8i1.39419.

McKay, S. (2004). Reconstructing fragile lives: Girls' social reintegration in northern Uganda and Sierra Leone. *Gender & Development, 12*(3), 19–30.

Nan, S. A. (2009). Social capital and exclusive and inclusive networks: Satisfying human needs through conflict and conflict transformation. In M. Cox (Ed.), *Social capital and peace-building: Creating and resolving conflict with trust and social networks* (pp. 172–185). London and New York: Routledge.

Ngoma, N. (2004). Disarmament, demobilization and reintegration: A conceptual discourse. In G. Chileshe (Ed.), *Civil military relation in zambia: A review of zambia's contemporary civil military relation and challenges to DDR* (pp. 79–89). South Africa: Institute for Security Studies (ISS).

NRCS, & ICRC. (2011). *Missing persons in Nepal: The right to know*. Kathamandu. Retrieved from https://www.icrc.org/eng/assets/files/reports/missing-persons-nepal-2011-en.pdf.

OCHA, & WFP. (2007). *Impact of conflict and priorities for assistance*. Kathmandu: Office of Coordination of Humanitarian Affairs (OCHA) and World Food Programme (WFP).

Özerdem, A. (2012). A re-conceptualisation of ex-combatant reintegration: 'Social reintegration' approach. *Conflict, Security & Development, 12*(1), 51–73. https://doi.org/10.1080/14678802.2012.667661.

Sapkota, B. (Ed.). (2004). *The cost of war in Nepal*. Kathmandu: National Peace Campaign.

Shrestha, B., & Niroula, S. (2005). Internally displaced persons in Nepal. *Peace and Democracy in South Asia, 1*(2), 44–55.

Subedi, D. B. (2012). Economic dimension of peacebuilding: Insights into post-conflict economic recovery and development in Nepal. *South Asia Economic Journal, 13*(2), 313–332. https://doi.org/10.1177/1391561412459387.

Upreti, B. R. (2010). Reconstruction and development in post-conflict Nepal. In B. R. Upreti, S. R. Sharma, K. N. Pyakuryal, & S. Ghimire (Eds.), *The remake of a state: Post-conflict challenges and state building in Nepal* (pp. 129–150). Kathmandu: NCCR North-South and Kathmandu University.

CHAPTER 9

DDR and Peacebuilding: Implications for Peace and Security

States experiencing a war to peace transition are confronted with insecurity and violence, and in some cases, the scale and intensity of violence is worse than it would be during the conflict period (Steenkamp, 2005; Suhrke & Berdal, 2012), often making the distinction between conflict and post-conflict periods somewhat unclear. The source of insecurity and violence in a post-conflict society may vary from context to context. However, there is general agreement about what to expect in post-conflict society that receives ex-combatants who are unemployed and lack marketable skills. The general consensus is that in such situations, the society is more likely to experience ex-combatant-led insecurity and violence (Colletta, Kostner, & Wiederhofer, 1996; Knight & Özerdem, 2004). The existing literature, however, frames ex-combatants as a homogeneous social category, and there are biases towards accepting only those ex-combatants who are non-violent and gradually immerse into civilian life. Furthermore, why some post-conflict societies rather than others see more ex-combatant-led insecurity and violence is a critical question that is relatively under-theorised in the literature (Suhrke, 2012; Themnér, 2011).

It is notable that once the Maoists ex-combatants have returned to their communities, a concern regarding security threats by these ex-combatants seized the attention of policy makers and researchers alike. Similar to how ex-combatants are treated elsewhere, the Maoist ex-combatants in Nepal are seen as a homogeneous category and an actor of insecurity and violence. In this regard, a number of critical questions arise: How do ex-combatants themselves see violence and peace? What evidence is

© The Author(s) 2018
D. B. Subedi, *Combatants to Civilians*, Rethinking Peace and Conflict Studies, https://doi.org/10.1057/978-1-137-58672-8_9

there to suggest that ex-combatant-led insecurity, crime and violence will take place at present or in future? How and why do some ex-combatants engage in violence while others do not? What are the possibilities of ex-combatants' remobilisation and who are the key potential mobilising actors? These questions are addressed in this chapter to explore immediate consequences of reintegration on peace.

For the purpose this volume, remobilisation is defined as a formal or informal process through which ex-combatants are motivated or coerced into participating in violence, contentious politics, criminal activities or socially and legally unacceptable disruptive activities. Remobilisation vulnerability refers to conditions that facilitate remobilisation including a possibility of remobilisation in future. In this chapter, such conditions are the socio-economic vulnerability of ex-combatants, stereotyping and negative perceptions with respect to their identity, and other societal conditions, including culture of youth militarisation and the way these factors motivate ex-combatants to engage in crime and violent behaviour in post-conflict Nepal.

This chapter argues that the Maoist ex-combatants should be viewed as a heterogeneous group in which different sub-groups respond in very different ways to insecurity and violence. Exploring the interface between various categories into which ex-combatants fall, their remobilisation vulnerability and the position of remobilising actors, it can be better predicted how and by what means ex-combatants are likely to be mobilised into violence. This chapter expands on the findings on how ex-combatant-led insecurity and direct violence, including petty crimes, have occurred increasingly at the micro-level. The macro-level threats across the Nepalese landscape at present are, however, limited to confrontational, disruptive and violent political actions rather than remobilisation of ex-combatants in another insurgency.

Defining Violence

Conceptualisation of violence is deeply contested in Social Sciences. Based on how violence is expressed, several concepts have been developed. The concept of direct violence refers to "targeted physical violence and terror administered by official authorities and those opposing it, such as military repression, police torture and armed resistance" (Bourgois, 2001, p. 8). Johan Galtung (1969, 1990) has developed the concept of direct/personal violence, structural violence and cultural violence. According to Galtung, personal or direct violence occurs physically; it is visible and an actor of violence is identifiable. Structural violence can be understood as a form of indirect violence which is induced by political and economic systems and structures that are exclusionary, exploitative and coercive (Galtung, 1969). Galtung has argued that absence of all forms of violence is essential for peace, especially for positive peace to flourish and sustain. Political violence is another concept of violence that refers to violent behaviour driven directly and purposefully by political ideology, political movements or armed struggle against a regime (Bourgois, 2001, p. 7). Similarly, if material motivation and incentives drive violence, it can be classified as economic violence (Moser & McIlwaine, 1999). Street crime, a civil war driven by greed, a network of organised crime, low-level crime such as theft and burglary, kidnapping for ransom and so on are some of the examples of economic violence. The violence driven by economic inequality, urban poverty, and structural conditions can also be categorised as economic violence (Fajnzylber, Lederman, & Loayza, 2002).

Drawing on these different concepts and manifestations, the operational definition of violence for the purpose of this study is as follows: violence is the intentional use of physical force to harm others. It occurs collectively as well as at an individual level. Its form and expression can be personal, political, or both, and has the capacity to inflict physical and mental damage on victims. It can destabilise society and create terror. The next section further elaborates typologies of violence with particular reference to violence taking place in post-conflict societies.

Understanding Post-conflict Insecurity and Violence

Contrary to a general anticipation that a country entering into the post-conflict period should experience less violence, evidence from Kosovo (Hughes & Pupavac, 2005), El Salvador (Call, 2007, pp. 29–67), Timor Leste (Babo-Soares, 2012), Iraq (Burnham, Lafta, Doocy, & Roberts, 2006) and Guatemala (UNDP, 2007; Torres, 2008), among other places, amply demonstrates that countries in war to peace continuum are also likely to encounter increased rates of crime, insecurity and violence. For the purpose of this article, the term post-conflict refers to a period that follows the cessation of armed violence. Such a situation may be depicted by peace negotiations, as in Nepal; a one-sided military victory, as in Sri Lanka; or as a result of external intervention, as in Iraq and Afghanistan.

This chapter assumes that violence is an outcome of dynamic interactions between victims and perpetrators. Perpetrators have different goals and motivations for participating in violence. If material motivations and incentives drive violence, it can be classified as a form of economic violence (Moser & McIlwaine, 1999), as is violence motivated by inequity and poverty and structural conditions (Fajnzylber et al., 2002). If, on the other hand, violence is driven by political motivations, such as the use of force by the state, ethnic insurgency or expression of discontent on the streets, it can be classified as political violence (Winton, 2004). If violence occurs as a result of social elements, such as social exclusion or social relationships and networks between perpetrators, it can be termed social violence. Winton (2004), however, contends that in certain given contexts, social violence co-exists with economic and/or political violence. For instance, a street gang formed from networks of unemployed youth can have economic motivations and also political motivations to bring about a transformation of the political system with a view of gaining employment under a different system. Thus, for the purpose of this chapter, the idea of violence especially taking place in a post-conflict society, is defined as a condition where "deliberate physical harm is inflicted on people and property" (Berdal, 2012, p. 309). More specifically, the term post-conflict violence refers to political, economic or social violence that has occurred during transition from armed conflict to peace.

Ex-combatants in Post-conflict Violence

Empirical evidence supports the view that ex-combatants are one of the principal actors of insecurity and post-conflict violence (Maringira & Brankovic, 2013; Nilsson, 2008; Suhrke & Berdal, 2012). In the literature, ex-combatants are treated as a homogeneous group where individuals are prone to engage or re-engage in generating or perpetuating violence. Homogenisation of ex-combatants, however, can be misleading because all ex-combatants are not necessarily actors involved in post-conflict violence. This study assumes that failure to see ex-combatants as a heterogeneous group can obscure some ex-combatants' efforts to transition into civilian life peacefully.

In the literature, several theoretical approaches are adopted to explain ex-combatant-led violence in the post-conflict period. Firstly, the institutional approach maintains that fragile security and violence that follows settlement of an armed conflict is due to weak and incompetent state institutions and mechanisms. Weak security institutions weaken the state's capacity to maintain its legitimate control over violence, leading to proliferation of war-lords, criminal rackets, and petty crimes by militias, ex-combatants and criminal gangs (Ebo, 2005; Hanggi, 2005; Suhrke, 2012). Because post-conflict states are fragile and at a times less efficient in placing security delivery mechanisms in place (although this was not the case in post-conflict Nepal), it is possible that ex-combatants reorganise themselves in ways in which they can substantially challenge the state and, in the worst case scenario, renewed insurgency may occur (Kingma, 1997; Spear, 2002).

Effective Disarmament, Demobilisation and Reintegration (DDR) programmes contribute as another major institutional factor to determine how and to what extent ex-combatants can generate violence and insecurity in a post-conflict society. Empirical evidence from different post-conflict contexts supports this theoretical proposition. For instance, badly sequenced and rapid demobilisation that failed to recognise local realities resulted in catastrophic destabilisation and violence in Iraq and El Salvador in 2003–2004 (Berdal, 2012, p. 316). Incomplete disarmament in Mozambique contributed to the proliferation of weapons not only throughout the country, but also in neighbouring South Africa, Zambia and Malawi (Knight, 2008, p. 4). At some point, poorly organised disarmament led to Mozambique constituting the single largest source of small arms to the South African domestic market by 1998 (UNIDIR, 1999, cited in Knight & Özerdem, 2004, p. 501). Babo-Soares highlights how the failure of government institutions to meet the expectations of ex-combatants resulted in the violence and riots in East Timor in December 2006 (Babo-Soares, 2012).

Secondly, many studies have taken what is called for in this chapter the socio-economic approach. Placing greater emphasis on the economic and livelihood conditions of ex-combatants has shown that under circumstances where ex-combatants are not provided with viable and peaceful economic opportunities and alternatives, their chances of re-engaging in economic and political violence remains high (Colletta et al., 1996; Collier, 1994; Knight & Özerdem, 2004). The role of the economic opportunities available to ex-combatants and their livelihoods are important factors in tackling post-conflict security because ex-combatants fall into a special social category of people who are deprived economically, as they are seen to hardly possess adequate skills to earn a living in competitive job markets. Thus, economically deprived ex-combatants may re-organise to engage in economic violence or they can be remobilised by other criminal and armed outfits. Recognising the security challenges emerging from ex-combatants, the DDR programme in the 1980s and 1990s remained security-focused in nature (Muggah, 2005).

Concentrating exclusively on ex-combatants who are thought to be the spoilers of peace, reintegration programmes in this period were ex-combatant focused in order to motivate them to comply with the peace process, that means reintegration programmes were heavily securitised.

As a result, DDR programmes in the 1980s and 1990s remained preoccupied with measuring the success of reintegration by putting security outcomes at the centre. This means that success was mapped out in terms of the number of weapons collected and disposed, the number of ex-combatants who received vocational trainings, and the diminished recurrence of the violence, rather than the "extent to which DDR has demonstrably improved safety or security, much less human development or addressed elements of the Millennium Goals" (Muggah, 2005, p. 246). While the socio-economic approach provides a useful analytical lens for studying ex-combatant-led violence, it does not sufficiently recognise the role of non-economic factors, such as ex-combatants' networks and their militarised identities, which are also found to be equally important in generating ex-combatant-led violence (see Maringira & Brankovic, 2013).

Thirdly, the socio-cultural approach to security and violence posits that war and armed conflict disintegrates society and creates a special condition that legitimises violence in the everyday life of people (Suhrke, 2012, p. 2). Seeing violence as a legacy of war, it is argued that conflict creates a "culture of violence", which produces a socially permissive environment within which the use of violence continues, even though violent politics would have officially ended (Steenkamp, 2005, p. 254). In other words, violence is normalised to a certain extent by a culture of terror and impunity. Nevertheless, it may not be possible to understand the depth and breadth of the normalisation of violence in a society unless we speak to the people from war zones and understand their everyday lives by listening to what they have to say about these matters.

A plethora of the literature further covers the idea of "a culture of violence" (Bourgois, 2001; Curle, 1999; Hamber, 1999; Matthew, Bankston, Hayes, & Thomas, 2007; Rupesinghe & Marcial, 1994; Shah & Pettigrew, 2009). Ex-combatant-led violence is, to a certain degree, embedded in social and cultural norms of war and how such norms affect social relationships in the post-conflict period. For instance, ex-combatants' relationships with the community are shaped by the perceptions rooted in the dynamics and history of the preceding armed conflict. As war ends, violence between combatants and the community can occur when ex-combatants who had committed crimes and atrocities in the past now return back to their community, but often in the absence of any reconciliation programme (Annan & Cutter, 2009). It is likely under such circumstances that tensions can escalate when a rapidly increasing sense of injustice among victims of the preceding conflict coincides with no one else but the ex-combatants who are observed to be benefiting economically from reintegration programmes (Annan & Cutter, 2009; Kingma & Muggah, 2009). In the case of South Africa, Maringira and Brankovic (2013, p. 7) show that ex-combatants' military identity not only normalised the violence generated by ex-combatants but the community also perceived ex-combatants as protectors; therefore, the latter situation itself encouraged ex-combatants to engage in what they called "violence against violence". While the socio-cultural approach is recently growing as an alternative lens for understanding ex-combatant-led violence, more evidence-based studies along these lines are needed in order to understand the causes, dynamics and functions of violence associated with these situations (Steenkamp, 2005).

In addition to the above mentioned approaches, Suhrke and Berdal (2012) contend that post-conflict violence is contingent upon the history and context of the war. They argue that it is the condition of the peace process, and the security environment it produces that determines post-war violence. Themnér (2011), however, emphasises the agency and relational aspects—it is the relationship between perpetrators and their mobilisers and the way the former has access to the latter that can determine how remobilisation is either sustained or fails to occur.

The analytical framework of this article draws on the various approaches discussed above. However, based on major themes identified from the fieldwork, particular emphasis has been put on three different dimensions of analysis, which include the categories into which ex-combatants fall, the socio-economic vulnerability context and the position of mobilisers (see Fig. 9.1).

To clarify the framework illustrated in the figure, a closer examination of the social and economic life of ex-combatants helps to recognise various categories of ex-combatants who respond to insecurity and violence differently. As mentioned earlier, remobilisation vulnerability involves an overarching motivating or coercing set of conditions. Another important facet of analysis is how ex-combatants access relationships with their wartime mobilisers, also what mobilising strategies they use and the positions they work from or hold are equally important to understanding ex-combatant-led post-conflict violence.

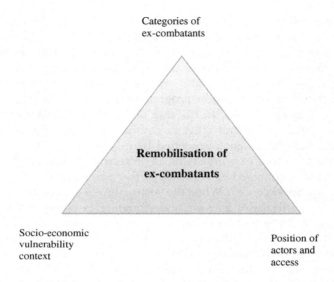

Fig. 9.1 Analytical framework for ex-combatant-led violence (*Source* Designed by the author 2013)

Three Categories the Retired Ex-combatants

Several ex-combatants have adopted different strategies to cope with their present or post-cantonment condition. For instance, in the Dang district, a number of ex-combatants have jointly started micro-enterprises while others have chosen to actively participate in Maoists politics. In several locations including in Kathmandu, Dhangadi and Biratnagar, ex-combatants lived in small groups. The everyday life of ex-combatants that was observed in Chitwan, Dang, Banke and Kathmandu districts revealed that heterogeneous categories of ex-combatants have gradually emerged among them; they do not fall into just one category, other than the undeniable fact that all of them are obviously ex-combatants. These categories become even more apparent if they are seen in terms of how these relate to their current economic life (their means of earning a living), social life (the way they interact with people in their community), and political life (how or the way in which they participate in Maoists politics). Overall, the ex-combatants' narratives and perceptions about war and peace further reveal that there are different types and categories of ex-combatants.

When personal observations in the field were combined with the ex-combatants' narratives, as well as the narratives of non-combatant respondents, it was concluded that the Maoist ex-combatants could be categorised into at least three distinct, but to a certain extent overlapping, categories, as discussed below.

Socially and Economically Engaged Group

Upon their retirement from the People's Liberation Army (PLA), a significant number of ex-combatants resettled in urban and semi-urban areas in Sunsari, Chitwan, Sindhuli, Nawalparasi, Dang, Banke, Kailali, Surkhet and Bardia districts. A large number of ex-combatants have also ended up living in the Kathmandu valley.[1] While a small number of ex-combatants have engaged in farm and non-farm related micro-enterprises, an overwhelming number of ex-combatants were still unemployed and idle. As noted in Chapter 7 in detail, the cash paid as part of the retirement package was spent mostly on household consumption, as well as on purchasing land (for residences) and building houses. Livelihood was still a major challenge for most of them.

Nonetheless, a small group of ex-combatants have engaged in enterprising work, both socially and economically. Economically, the ex-combatants who could be identified in this group started some form of farm and/or non-farm based micro-enterprises such as poultry production and vegetable farming, raising cows for milk production, also opening grocery shops, vegetable shops, stationary shops, mobile phone repairing centres, a beauty parlour and an internet cyber café. With a few exceptions, the majority of ex-combatants in this category have a profound sense of social, moral and economic obligation towards their families. It is this sense of moral as well as responsibility and obligation that has motivated them to accept the peaceful livelihood options. In the words of an ex-combatant, "several ex-combatants have now engaged in looking after their families and want a new beginning".[2]

The ex-combatants from this category seemed politically less active; many of them did not have strong connections with their wartime mobilisers, although they were in regular contact with fellow

---

[1] The Kathmandu valley includes urban and semi-urban areas of three districts: Kathmandu, Lalitpur and Bhaktapur.

[2] Interview with a male ex-combatant, Kathmandu, 2013.

ex-combatants. The narratives of ex-combatants revealed that many of them possessed a degree of war fatigue. They looked frustrated, partly because of their high expectations of what the war could achieve for them and the country but did not deliver, and partly due to their current impoverished situation. When asked about their expectations of the war, a group of ex-combatants interviewed in Dang said that their main expectation was a total transformation of the state, economically, politically and socially, but more importantly they were also very hopeful to become a member of a national army. Moreover, the ideological rift between the CPNM and its splinter, the Communist Party of Nepal-Maoists (CPN-M), has made many ex-combatants even more confused and disoriented. As a result, they expressed cynicism towards the Maoist leadership, as a female ex-combatant's statement illustrates[3]:

> I sacrificed my youth in the war, but my dream has remained unfulfilled because I did not fight to get money. We were promised by the CPNM a dream to become a member of the national army and to achieve a total transformation of the state. I feel now that I have wasted my time.

Many ex-combatants who belong in this category believed that the emotion, ideology and collectivism that once united the PLA and fostered altruism have gradually deteriorated. The frustration of ex-combatants has been partly exacerbated by the revelation that some PLA commanders and CPNM leaders have accumulated massive wealth by misappropriating the PLA funds, while the majority of the ex-combatants were languishing with negative social stigma, social rejection and poverty.[4] Nonetheless, with a few exceptions, where they have reacted towards the leadership violently,[5] socially and economically engaged ex-combatants seemed somewhat detached from the active Maoist politics and

---

[3] Interview with a female combatant in Kathmandu, December 2012.

[4] Interviews with ex-combatants in Chitwan and Dang in January 2013 and February 2013 respectively.

[5] A former PLA member, Padam Kunwar, slapped the CPNM Chairman Prachand in a public programme in November 2012 in Kathmandu. An ex-combatant in Kohalpur, Banke said that it was a symbolic expression of the deep frustration and depression of ex-combatants. He further said a group of deeply frustrated ex-combatants allegedly attempted to kill the Maoist leader, Pushpa Kamal Dahal, on his way to Bardia to attend a programme in September 2012.

did not support the idea of violence and its use for social change and transformation.

(In)formal Interest Groups

A considerable number of ex-combatants had a tendency to reorganise themselves into small formal and informal groups based on their shared interests, reciprocal relationships and a common purpose that brings them together. As a result, several (in)formal interest groups of ex-combatants emerged in different localities. These interest groups had both formal/organisational and informal characteristics.

Informal interest groups were based on loose networks. It is this informal character which made this group difficult to recognise. An ex-combatant referred to these as a "friendship group" and acknowledged that such groups exist throughout the country.[6] Membership was either voluntary or driven by peer pressure. It also kept on changing, defusing and reforming according to the shifting interests of group members. Residential proximity, shared background of serving in the same battalion in the PLA, sharing a common geographic origin, age, caste and ethnicity, all of which brought them together to form various informal interest groups that are largely opportunistic in nature. With both economic and political motivation, they formed a high-risk group from a remobilisation point of view.

By contrast, formal interest groups were also observed. For instance, the Verified Minors and Late Recruits (VMLRs) who were released from the cantonments in 2010 with a rehabilitation package have now formed a National Struggle Committee. With collective bargaining with the government and the CPNM, the committee has been demanding equality of benefits on par with their colleagues, the verified ex-combatants and their struggle has continued even today at the time of finalising the manuscript by the end of 2017. Similarly, a group of ex-combatants formed an organisation called *Jana Yuddha Rakshya Front* (People's War Protection Front).[7] The interviewee further mentioned that although no actual number of members was available for this organisation, it was reported as being active in west and far-west regions of Nepal. Some

---

[6] Interview with an ex-combatant, Chitwan, 2013.
[7] Interview with a journalist in Kohalpur, Banke, February 2013.

politically active ex-combatants, being frustrated with the political behaviour of the CPNM, formed this particular organisation, which has not yet been involved in any violent activities.

Similarly, the returnee ex-combatants in Dang, Chitwan and Banke districts have associational life through the formation of savings and credit groups, and cooperatives. In the Banke district, some 100 ex-combatants have organised and jointly invested in a real estate business (that is selling residential lands). A group of former commanders and Young Communist League leaders have started a private security company in Koteshwor, which suggests that the boundary of such formal interest groups is extensive, and perhaps beyond the ex-PAL community. Furthermore, the CPNM leader, the former Constitution Assembly (CA) member Chandra Bahadur Thapa (Sagar), formed the Unemployed Youth Association, which brings in members from among ex-combatants and also the Yung Communist League (YCL), as well as many other unemployed youth groups around the nation.[8] In the past, a group of people formed an opportunistic and crime-oriented outfit called the People's Liberation Army Former Soldiers' Unity Organisation, which was reported to have engaged in criminal activities in the eastern region of Nepal.[9]

Politically Active Ex-combatants: Political Reintegration?

One of the major outcomes of the peace process in Nepal was to transform CPNM into a mainstream political party. The way the formal rebel group has transformed into a political party in the democratic system itself point to the phenomena that many CPNM leaders as well as many leaders of the PLA have turned to be politicians. Therefore, it is unsurprising to observe that those leaders who played a dual role in the Comprehensive Peace Agreement (CPA) and in the PLA such as Pushpa Kamal Dahal (Prachanda), Ram Bahadur Thapa Badal, Barsaman Pun, Janardan Sharma (Prabhakar), to name a few of them, are now well known political leaders in the country. What is, however, more

---

[8] Interview with an ex-PLA commander, Madan Chowk, Banke, 2013.

[9] Interview with a journalist, Biratnagar, 2011. Similar information was reported in http://www.ekantipur.com/the-kathmandu-post/2011/01/09/nation/ex-combatants-into-crime-say-police/217045/.

interesting to observe is that a large number of former combatants from national to local levels have eventually engaged in politics actively. The scale and depth of the phenomenon is clearly suggests that the way the DDR process include cash option created an enabling environment for several ex-combatants to return to the politics. In other words, DDR facilitated political reintegration of ex-combatants rather than their social and economic reintegration.

Some ex-combatants are more politically active than others for various reasons. Firstly, ex-combatants' access to former rebel leaders and high ranking PLA commanders have provided some of them with the privileges of power and position in the Maoist party and its sister organisations. The CPNM had provided several ex-combatants who had returned to their villages with particular influential positions (ranks, leadership roles) in the party as well as in the YCL.[10] The CPNM's decision made in 2012 to offer ex-combatants the responsibility of mobilising the youth in several districts such as Khotang district, suggests that there is a likelihood of many young ex-combatants being remobilised into Maoist politics, especially if they are not satisfied with their lives and status in the community. Other ex-combatants who were interviewed mentioned that the CPNM and the CPN-M have repeatedly expressed their keen interest to mobilise ex-combatants to participate actively in their political agendas at the grass-root levels.

The Maoists parties are essentially hierarchical, with the power centralised at the top. There is a culture of patronage politics within the Maoist hierarchy that requires ex-combatants to access the high-level leadership if one aspires to hold an important position. This can be further explained by an ex-combatant's assertion[11]:

> The Maoist party has a highly centralised power structure and distribution of positions within the party is governed by nepotism and favouritism. This means only selected PLA leaders have so far been able to hold important positions from central to local level.

The motivation behind this category of ex-combatants is both political and economic. Politically active ex-combatants seek to increase their political and economic opportunities through the use and misuse of

---

[10] Interview with an ex-combatant, Kohalpur, 2013.
[11] Interview with a male ex-combatant, Padampur, Chitwan, 2013.

power. "If one is an active member of the Maoists parties, the membership can insulate him/her from any possible action by police".[12] Some frustrated ex-combatants mentioned that many politically active ex-combatants co-opted and even in some cases collaborated with local business people who are known to have been involved in shadow economic activities. The former provides political protection to the latter, whereas the latter share economic benefits with the former. This reciprocal relationship is being sustained in a typical shadow economy after the 2006 peace process.

Some form of commonality, as well as differences, exist between the three groups: socio-economically engaged ex-combatants, (in)formal interest groups and politically active ex-combatants. For instance, war fatigue is clearly observed in all three groups, though the degree of severity might be different but difficult to gauge in an interview setting. Socially and economically engaged ex-combatants seemed to reveal a relatively higher degree of war fatigue. Though those ex-combatants in the other two categories did also mention war fatigue, they also expressed, albeit ambiguously, a willingness to fight if a situation demands such action. In this regard, it will not be out of context to note that since the war-time belligerence has not withered away amongst those in this category of ex-combatants. If incentives were created in support of insurgency and violence and where these were perceived as being higher than those of peaceful livelihood options, the combatants from these two categories are more likely to re-engage in violent activities or in other words, be willing to remobilise. However, before making a definite claim in this regard, what the ex-combatants themselves say about violence and peace was explored. This exploration is particularly useful as a starting point if post-conflict violence and security is examined by putting ex-combatants at the centre.

Violence and Peace: What Ex-combatants Say?

When it is aimed to understand violence as well as peace, the analysis would be better benefited by listening to the conflict actors themselves than depending on preconceived ideas (Graham, 2007). Hence, it is indispensable to collect the perceptions and narratives of the Maoist

---

[12] Interview with an analyst in Kathmandu, 2013.

ex-combatants themselves to assess violence and peace in the aftermath of a conflict.

When talking about violence, the majority of ex-combatants understand it as direct violence and political violence. The ex-combatants were divided on the question of whether the political and direct violence occurred during the war was necessary for bringing about the changes for which the Maoists had advocated was part and parcel of revolution. Ex-combatants who seemed socially and economically engaged thought that the war-time violence was unjustifiable, particularly given the level of social, political and economic change it has driven thus far, although a small number of ex-combatants were hopeful that if a new constitution is drafted, significant social, political and economic transformation is possible in new Nepal. An ex-combatant said, "eventually we have come to a peaceful solution, the revolution could not yield any revolutionary change, politically. If you need to find a solution through politics, why do you need bloodshed?"[13] Many others repeated her message in one form or another, and confirmed that the *Jana Andolan II* was more powerful than a decade of war, as it was a peaceful struggle that eventually forced king Gyanendra to step down. The ex-combatants who expressed this view have increasingly tended to believe in non-violence as a means of bringing about social and political change, rather than a violent revolution, which only led to catastrophic losses of social, physical and human capitals. The ex-combatants who fit into the first category clearly rejected the possibility of re-engaging in political violence, let alone insurgency.

By contrast, politically active ex-combatants are convinced that the violence is necessary for transformation. They believed that the violence in which they had participated in the past is justifiable because it has induced so many social, economic and political transformations, including the elimination of the monarchical system in Nepal. "If you want to make a *challang* (big leap), you need to use violence together with other tactics, the change will then be revolutionary", said a vice commander interviewed in Kohalpur in February 2013. In their view, violence also occurs as a counter action, meaning that the political violence in the war was not only related to Maoist ideology, but also something that was driven as a counter-action to pacify state-led violence. The ex-combatants

[13] Interview with a female ex-combatant in Kathmandu, January 2013.

who would better fit into the politically active category were still in favour of violence, as or when it is necessary. They saw a possibility of another insurgency if the Maoists are pushed to the margins in the current political and statebuilding process.

The informal interest group is opportunistic, seeking economic and political opportunities whether peacefully or violently; therefore, their understating of violence is somewhat mixed, although many of them thought that the war-time violence was necessary to fight and change the conservative society and corrupt political system.

As can be seen from the discussion above, ex-combatants have very little understanding of the violence embedded in exclusionary systems and structures, hence forms of structural violence. Nonetheless, some interviewees implied that direct violence in the past was targeted to change and transform structural inequalities, meaning that there was a degree of causality between direct violence and structural violence. In other words, ex-combatants believed that structural violence persisted in society and hence, propagated direct violence as a means of changing violent and oppressive social and political structures. This means that averting further direct violence at present or in the future will depend on the extent to which the peace process can reduce structural inequalities and promote a more equal and egalitarian society in Nepal. Even non-combatant respondents commonly believed that after *Jana Andolan II*, Nepal has entered into a new discourse of social justice. Therefore, peacebuilding should focus on social justice and address inequalities in order to build a more cohesive and harmonious society.

Regardless of the different categories, ex-combatants who were interviewed have more or less a common understanding of peace. They see peace at an individual level as well as a societal level. At the individual level, ex-combatants who would belong to all the three categories are concerned about their economic wellbeing, and dignity and quality of life. The idea that economic freedom brings happiness and peace in one's life seems very much a reality in the views of ex-combatants. Individual-level change in terms of economic wellbeing, according to an interviewee, is "a foundation for other changes such as skill, health, and relationship with others".[14] Economic insecurity, it seems, makes people vulnerable and motivates them to work positively to improve

---

[14] Interview with a male ex-combatant, Madanpur, Banke, February 2013.

their circumstances. The question is whether vulnerability is enough to get people involved in non-violent economic and livelihood activities, which enhance other positive changes in their lives to essentially live as dignified members of society? To clarify, he added: "If I am economically secure, I also earn respect and dignity in my society". From this and similar responses from other interviewees, it is clear that ex-combatants place high priorities on their own and their household's economic wellbeing, as this is an important source of respect, dignity and peaceful social relations.

Ex-combatants were, however, equally vocal in terms of talking peace from macro perspectives. Their views expressed the message that a peaceful society is one where all people feel and enjoy equality and wellbeing, where there is no discriminations against one's caste, race, religion and gender, and where wealth is distributed among people proportionately. Some ex-combatants also mentioned that horizontal inequalities perpetuated by caste and ethnic exclusion should be one of the major priorities to end structural violence and create a more just and equitable society. Similarly, social justice and socio-economic equality, in the views of ex-combatants, is a key condition for peace at the societal level. For some ex-combatants, though, peace will be possible when the society overcomes the trauma of the past and moves away with renewed relationships between people with different political and social background. Interestingly, the concept of amnesty recurred in interviews in which many interviewees, mostly ex-combatants, stressed that peace at the societal level will be almost impossible if the ex-combatants and the Maoists leaders are not provided amnesty for the violence and crimes they have committed in the past. Non-combatant respondents had a counter view to the preceding argument; they tended to think from the perspective of the victims that peace is impossible unless the Maoists and PLA leaders as well as relevant political leaders, government officials and security personnels are held accountable for the violence and atrocities they have committed in the past.

From the narratives of ex-combatants, peace can be built and violence can be avoided if there are serious efforts made to address enduring structural inequalities in the Nepalese society. While they clearly emphasised a need for societal level changes as preconditions for peace, ex-combatants tended to focus more on amnesty rather than efforts to address reconciliation. They are clearly concerned about better social relationships, which is something that can also be called social capital, as a foundation for consolidating peace in society. However, what seemed problematic is their biasness towards politically driven reconciliation augmented by amnesty, which may increase tensions rather than diffuse existing problems that are related to structural and perhaps also cultural inequalities within Nepal.

REMOBILISATION VULNERABILITY CONDITIONS

Socio-economic Vulnerability

With few exceptions, the cash paid as part of the voluntary retirement package has not contributed to addressing ex-combatants' economic challenges and livelihood insecurity. Lack of entrepreneurial skills and life skills, the poor economic environment, lack of access to credit, the unpredictability and volatility of the markets, lack of jobs, and the lack of confidence of business people in hiring ex-combatants are some of the major factors which have considerable implications for ex-combatant livelihood challenges. That a large number of ex-combatants are unemployed and frustrated is a disturbing fact.

If the focus is expanded from individual ex-combatants at their household level to macroeconomic conditions, the picture is even grimmer. As discussed in detail in Chapter 2, in the past, socio-economic inequalities, lack of economic opportunities and marginalisation of certain caste and ethnic groups, which can be labelled as enduring cultural inequalities, provided the CPNM with an opportunity to indoctrinate and radicalise masses of rural poor and disenfranchised youth (Subedi, 2013). Even seven years after the signing of the peace agreement, the social and economic vulnerability conditions continue unabated, leaving the possibility for different forms of radicalisation and extremism open.

In macroeconomic terms, hopes and despairs exist simultaneously. The post-conflict economy is mired in slow economic growth. Though the United Nations Development Programme (UNDP) Human Development Reports show that although Nepal has made some progress in the Human Development Index (0.428 in 2010, 0.458 in 2011, and 0.463 in 2012), it has fallen behind in the human development ranking from 138th (out of 169 countries) in 2010 to the 157th position in the years 2011 and 2012 (UNDP, 2013).

The country's Gross Domestic Product (GDP) growth-rate, which rested at 2.75% in the year 2006–2007 (the year when the peace agreement was signed), has grown slowly in the last several years. In the fiscal year 2011–2012 the GDP growth rate was 4.6% (ADB, 2013), which slowed down to 3.5% in the year 2012–2013 (IMF, 2012, p. 195). By the first half of the fiscal year 2012–2013, the inflation rate was 9.8% compared with 6.8% being the figure in the previous year. According to a recent report by the Central Bureau of Statistics (CBS), the population living below the poverty line has declined to 25.16% in the year 2010–2011 (CBS, 2011), compared to 41.76 and 30.85% in 1995–1996 and 2003–2004 respectively.[15] Despite these encouraging changes, horizontal inequalities and regional disparities still continue. For instance, the poverty level is the lowest among the Hill-origin *Brahmins* and *Newars*, whereas the Hill-origin *Dalits* and Terai *Dalits* have the highest level of poverty (CBS, 2011). Similarly, going by the regions, the eastern region has the lowest poverty level (21.44%), whereas 46% of the population in the far-west region are below the poverty line (CBS, 2011).

Although the poverty level has decreased, it nonetheless coincides with a lack of sustained GDP, which has been running below 4% for more than one decade. This is a profound contradiction in the current economy that does not provide much hope for the poor households and younger the generation. The result, among other things, is a massive out-migration of young people.

Unemployment and poverty have become a push factor that has encouraged many young people to join armed groups and gangs, especially in the Terai Region and eastern hills (Subedi, 2012b). It is in this grim situation that Nepal has not fully recovered from the economic and social damages it suffered during the armed conflict (see Subedi, 2012a; Upreti, 2010). Many believed that if a reintegration programme was designed as part of a wider post-conflict economic recovery scheme, it could have contributed to post-conflict social development and redressed socio-economic inequalities. Contextualising the livelihood crisis and economic vulnerability ex-combatants face, many respondents acknowledged that particularly for those who form opportunistic informal interest groups with their past connections to the war ideology or crime

---

[15] The last two figures are based on the First and Second Nepal Living Standards Surveys (NLSS) conducted by the CBS. In the NLSS, the CBS uses 2200 calorie consumption per person per day and access to essential non-food items as the index to measure poverty.

networks, these people run a high risk of being remobilised for political violence and criminality. Therefore, by contextualising the ex-combatants' livelihood crisis and economic vulnerability in the slow pace of post-conflict development in the dire current economic climate in Nepal, it was acknowledged in the fieldwork that ex-combatants who linked to informal interest groups related to the Maoist cause, run a high risk of being remobilised for political violence against the state. There is also some evidence to suggest that some ex-combatants have been involved in crime and violence (elaborated later in the chapter).

Identity Trap

Identity in this study is defined as "mutually constructed and evolving images of self and other" (Katzenstein, 1996, p. 59). The images of self and others render two important dimensions to identity: personal/individual and social/collective. Personal/individual identity can be defined as relatively stable role-specific understanding and expectations about self (Wendt, 1992, p. 397), whereas social identity is collective and is constructed based on similarity and differences between groups of people (Lawler, 2008).

Identity has particular significance to ex-combatants' acceptance in the community, hence social reintegration. It is due to this significance that reintegration and rehabilitation programmes are intended to support ex-combatants in ways that help to transform their personal and social identity into a new civilian identity (Muggah, 2010). However, identity transformation takes a profoundly long time before the society fully accepts ex-combatants as civilians. A study by Maringira and Brankovic (2013) has shown that ex-combatants' militarised identity has not changed in South Africa even after nearly twenty years, and the militarised identity of ex-combatants has remained a source of violence.

In the present case, it is observed that because of their long association with the insurgency, ex-combatants' collective/social identity has taken precedence over their individual identity. In the public perception, an ex-combatant's identity is labelled as either *Maobaadi* (the Maoists) or *Purba Ladaku* (ex-combatants). Politically active ex-combatants who have frequent involvement and association with the YCL activities are gradually being identified as YCL rather than ex-combatant. Ex-combatants' identity has been embedded in the structure and culture of the war. Therefore, their identity is shaped by the identity of their war mobilisers. A respondent's assertion further elaborates on this point[16]:

> People identify them as Maoists or YCL rather than former PLA fighters. Their [ex-combatants] identity and the way people behave with and perceive them depend on the political performance of CPNM and CPN-M and to a certain extent the level of violence that the YCL creates.

Given that ex-combatants' individual identity is subsumed into the collective identity of the Maoists, the ex-combatants are entangled in a situation that this study calls an "identity trap". It is a situation where individual identity is increasingly taking a collective character and this plays an instrumental role in reconnecting ex-combatants with the remnants of the structure and institution of the preceding war.

Overcoming the identity trap hinges on the extent to which the Maoist parties become accustomed to democratic political culture, and also the extent to which the YCL-led violence is diffused permanently.[17] Many others believe that changes in the identity of ex-combatants may be possible only if ex-combatants acquire some form of social roles or employment that provide them with social dignity and a space for healthy interactions between ex-combatants and the people from the community. However, this cannot happen in isolation from post-conflict reconciliation, which is a need that has been felt widely but pushed to the margins in the current peace process.

Youth Militarisation and Radicalisation

The definition of youth is ambiguous in Nepal. In the Three Years of the Interim Plan 2007–2010, the government defined youth as people between 15 and 29 years of age. The National Youth Policy 2010 defines youth as persons between 16 and 40 years of age. Contrarily, non-government organisations (NGOs) such as the Association of Youth Organisations Nepal (AYON), define youth generally as persons between 16 and 35 years.[18] Using any of these definitions of youth, almost all ex-combatants at the time of the fieldwork could be recognised as youth.

---

[16] Interview with a journalist, Chitwan, 2013.
[17] Interview with a NGO worker, Chitwan, 2013.
[18] Interview, Kathmandu, 2013.

Given various competing definitions of youth, the actual population of youth has always remained controversial. Nonetheless, according to the recent data, young people between 10 and 24 years make up almost 33% of the total population (MoHP, 2011, p. 18). According to the Ministry of Youth and Sports (MoYS), the population aged between 16 and 40 accounts for 38.8% of the total population.[19] Similarly, among women, about 49% are in a reproductive age-group (MoHP, 2011, p. 18). As these figures suggest, Nepal's demography is characterised as moving towards a "youth bulge". "Youth bulge" is a demographic condition containing exceptionally large youth cohorts (Urdal, 2006). The theory that deals with "youth bulge and political violence" stresses that if large youth cohorts face institutional bottlenecks, unemployment and the lack of political openness, the rise in cultural pluralism, self-determination and political activity, the risk of political violence is high (Braungart & Braungart, 1990; Goldstone, 1991). It is also argued that a country with a condition of a "youth bulge" is likely to breed armed conflict (Goldstone, 2002; Urdal, 2004). This proposition has significance in the Nepali context because of the fact that youth have played an important role in the escalation of the Maoist armed conflict. Even success of the democratic change in 1990 is ascribed to the central role played by youth and young university students.[20] Because of the potency of youth acting as agents of change, political parties in Nepal have an established tradition of engaging youth in violent as well as non-violent politics and social movements. This is often accomplished through formation of youth wings or student youth wings. In recent times, the culture of mobilising youth in various forms of protests, social movements and revolutions, involving activities ranging from armed violence to contentious politics, violent political street movements, demonstrations over ethno-political conflicts and identity group differences, has grown exponentially. In other words, democratic political space has been unprecedentedly tainted by a growing culture of militarising and radicalising youths.[21] Most

---

[19] http://www.moys.gov.np/policy-12-en.html.

[20] Interview with an analyst in Kathmandu, 2013.

[21] In this volume, I have borrowed the definition of militerisation from Geyer who defined it as "the contradictory and tense social process in which civil society organises itself for the production of violence" (Geyer, 1989).

political parties and ethno-political identity groups have mobilised youth thorough the formation of youth wings.

Amongst various groups, the YCL and Youth Force (YF) are politically more active than others and are reported to have violent confrontations in different parts of the country (Carter Centre, 2011). The YCL, in which a significant number of ex-combatants have membership, is criticised for operating as a paramilitary group (Carter Centre, 2011). Militarising ex-combatants in such an environment in Nepal is likely to lead to further violence for several reasons. Firstly, because ex-combatants are trained to fight, they qualify to be the most sought after youth group to be mobilised in contentious political activities. Secondly, both Maoist parties, the CPNM and the CPN-M, have offered responsibilities to politically active ex-combatants to mobilise youth. Hence, it is likely that politically active ex-combatants can convince a large cohort of their fellows into joining disruptive political actions.

Thirdly and more importantly, YCL and the community of ex-combatants share a fraternal relationship. In the past the Maoists prevented a large number of ex-combatants from going through the combatant verification process in order to send them off to take up political roles and positions in the YCL. As mentioned earlier, several formal and informal groups bring both categories of ex-combatants to a unique functional alliance. In this situation, it is obvious that the YCL's militant culture is likely to contaminate a significant number of ex-combatants, particularly those from the two categories, (in)formal interest groups and politically active ex-combatants, as discussed above.

REMOBILISATION ACTORS AND THEIR POSITION AND INTEREST

The following section examines different actual and potential actors and access for remobilisation of the Maoist ex-combatants.

The CPNM

Amongst various political parties active in the country, the CPNM is thought to be more organised, tactical and strategic in radicalising youth with revolutionary political slogans and rhetoric.[22] The Carter Centre

---

[22] Interviews with non-combatants category of respondents, Kathmandu, Biratnagar and Nepalgunj, 2013.

(2011) estimates that the vast structure of the YCL mobilises around one million cadres who are involved in advocating Maoist political ideology and setting agendas. The political landscape of the CPNM has, however, changed following its official division. As a result, its monopoly and control over Maoist supporters and ex-combatants has weakened. A pertinent effect of this change is that it has eroded the CPNM's monopoly over mobilisation of youth and ex-combatants who have been clearly divided into two groups.[23] While no accurate figure was available on how many combatants exist in each faction, a respondent estimated that approximately 6000 out of 13,000 retired combatants actively support the radical breakaway faction, the CPN-M.[24] Others, however, think that an accurate estimation might be almost impossible at this stage because some ex-combatants are in a "wait and see" mode and can switch sides depending on how the CPNM and the CPN-M perform in the future. What is less debatable, though, is that the CPNM has recently been under mounting pressure to find new and attractive strategies and tactics to remobilise youth, including youth from among the ranks of the ex-combatants.

The CPNM has responded to this challenge in many ways. It has taken an initiative to re-institutionalise the community of ex-combatants. Under the leadership of Nanda Kishor Pun "Pasang", the former head of the PLA, the Ex-People's Liberation Army Association was formed in April 2012. Although the objective of the association was said to recognise the historical contribution of combatants and keep them united, the public perceived this association as being one of the CPNM's tactics to perpetuate the war-time command control structures in one way or another.[25] In reference to the three categories of ex-combatants that have been described and discussed above, the ex-combatants from the (in)formal interest groups and politically active ex-combatants are relatively more united through this association. However, some of the ex-combatants who fall into the socially and economically engaged category also reported that they had become members of the association. According to an ex-combatant who had obtained membership of the

---

[23] Interview with a PLA ex-commander, Chitwan, 2013.

[24] Interview with a journalist, Kathmandu, 2013.

[25] Interviews in Ghorahi and Nepalgunj, 2013.

association, individuals join "hoping that the membership might provide emotional and psychological support, as well as safety and security".[26]

In this changed context, the CPNM replaced its political ideology with a socio-economic slogan, which they are applying strategically as a new instrument for mobilisation. In its Seventh General Convention held in Hetauda in February 2013, the CPNM endorsed the idea of formulating the Production Brigade (PB) (Subedi, 2014). The aim of the PB was reportedly to engage the Maoist cadres in contributing to production growth and development works, but it is not clear whether it will take place in the private or public sector. Nonetheless, the first PB was launched in Pokhara in August 2013.[27] While the Maoists claimed that the PB was essential for economic revolution in the country, analysts believe that this is a new tactic to mobilise youth for political activities, especially the YCL and ex-combatants. Other respondents believed that establishment of the PB indicates that the CPNM has shifted from political ideology to using economic incentives as an instrument of political mobilisation. Regardless of the motives behind the PB, it is possible that this new economic slogan could possibly attract many young people, particularly ex-combatants and especially unemployed youth.

Although the PB was endorsed as the CPNM's new commitment to economic revolution, presently and into the future, this new strategy has lost its momentum when CPNM went through massive intra-organisational conflicts and reorganisation. Between 2014 and 2016, CPNM had unprecedented setback when one of its influential leader Dr. Baburam Bhattrai quit and established his own party called "Naya Shakti". The ideological rift between CPNM and Naya Shakti parties has also resulted in a sharp division of ideological support to these parties by former ex-combatants. But what is important to note is that the fragmentation of Maoists parties has not only stimulated ideological debates as to what should a Maoist party look like in twenty-first century, but the fragmentation has also created more spaces for politically active combatants to take up new roles in politics.

---

[26] Interview, a male ex-combatant, Kathmandu, 2013.
[27] See http://www.ekantipur.com/the-kathmandu-post/2013/08/23/nation/ucpn-maoist-launches-production-brigade/252739.html.

The CPN-M

The CPN-M has emerged as a powerful rival of the CPNM and has purported to mobilise people, including ex-combatants, in several ways. For instance, by expanding the newly formed structure of the party, the CPN-M has strategically divided the entire geography of Nepal into three commands, East Command, Mid Command and the West Command, and it has already declared State Committees in each region. Interviewees reported that several ex-combatants have been accommodated with some political roles in the newly formed organisational structure of the party.[28]

In April 2012, the CPN-M reactivated the People's Volunteers Bureau (PVB), reportedly incorporating a significant number of ex-combatants as members.[29] Although the objective of the bureau is still dubious, it was allegedly reported that the bureau was to develop into a new PLA (Pun, 2012). Whether the CPN-M will develop a PLA out of the bureau may largely hinge on several political, geopolitical and economic factors, and this cannot be clearly predicted at this stage. Nonetheless, the bureau sought to facilitate associational life and networks among frustrated ex-combatants, and the CPN-M involved youth, including ex-combatants, in disruptive political activities, including violent disruptions targeting the activities of the constitutional assembly election in November 2013 (Subedi, 2014).

The revolutionary agendas of change and reform that the CPN-M has pursued appears to be a continuation of those revolutionary demands that the Maoists wanted the government to address before they initiated the armed conflict in 1996. In other words, the revolutionary and radical ideology and aspiration of waging a war against the state that motivated hundreds of youth to join the armed conflict in the past constitute the political and revolutionary position of CPN-M.

The CPN-M accuses CPNM for being a "neo-revisionist" which exchanged the so-called "unfinished" revolution with power and luxury in the mainstream politics. CPN-M contends that the country is in semi-colonial, semi-feudal and neo-colonial situation that require a new struggle to end oppression and bring emancipation to the poor and

---

[28] Interviews, Kohalpur and Dang, 2013.

[29] The PVB was formed during the insurgency, but dissolved before the CPNM entered the peace process.

oppressed people. CPN-M also continue to advocate the key demands of the past that reflect anti-Indian sentiment, profiling India as an enemy in the so-called "new struggle". Thus, by professing new nationalism driven by an anti-Indian sentiment, the CPN-M has capacity to mobilise those frustrate and disgruntled ex-combatants who think they were betrayed by the CPNM as well as the government in the peace process.

The Biplav-led CPN-Maoist

In November 2014, the CPN-M party, led by Mohan Baidya Kiran was officially divided. The party's secretary, Netra Bikram Chand, announced that he quit the CPN-M and reorganised its own party—Biplav-led CPN-M. The Biplav-led faction is of the view that failure of the previous Maoist insurgency to end imperialism, capitalist hegemony and social and political oppression has called for another round of insurgency in the country.

Of the various Maoists factions formed between 2012 on ward, Biplav-led CPN-M seems to have taken the most radical political ideology and accordingly a virulent political force that has countered the mainstream democratic parliament politics. Its aims are to dislodge the federal parliamentarian political system put in place after 2006 and establish People's Republic with a new economic and political order.

I deliberately refrain from engaging in an elaborate discussion of the Biplav-led CPN-M's political ideology, that may be a subject to a separate volume. However, what is worth noting here is that recently, Biplav's CPN-M has been the most furious actor of disruptive political actions and violence in the country. Although no actual data is available about the number of ex-combatants that Biplav has mobilised, triangulating information from different sources suggest that a large of frustrated ex-combatants including those opportunists and with criminal orientations are involved in the activities of this group. Biplav-led CPN-M has boycotted the elections of local bodies, state parliament and federal parliament held in 2017. However, the cadres and members of Biplav-led CPN-M are found heavily involved in election violence, forced donations, petty crimes, land grabbing, and so on.

Table 9.1 The groups splintered from the CPNM (*Source* Compiled by the author)

S. No.	Party/Group	Leader
1	The Communist Party of Nepal-Maoists (CPN-M)	Kiran Vaidya
2	The Biplav-led CPN-Maoist	Netra Bikram Chand (Biplav)
3	The Communist Revolutionary Party (CRP)	Mani Thapa
4	Nepal Communist Party of Maoists (Matrika group)	Matrika Yadav
5	Hamro Nepal Party	Kumar Humagai
6	Samjbaadi Jana Ekata Party	Janak Adhikari
7	Nepal Sarbahara Communist Party (Maaobadi)	Bhawana (Bidrohi)
8	Samyukta Rastrabaadi Morcha Nepal	Meghraj Gyawali
9	Nepal Communist Maobadi Kendra	Bharat Dahal
10	Berojgar Yuwa Sangh	Chandra Bahadur Thapa
11	Nepal Communist Party Rastriya Yuwa Morcha	Lekhak Rai
12	Mongol Revenge Group	Formed by a group of ex-combatants
13	Rastriya Madhesi Mukti Morcha	Jaya Krishna Goite
14	Jana Tantrik Terai Mukti Morcha	Nagendra Paswan (Jwalasingh)
15	Magarhang Swayetta Rajya Parishad	Janaklal Thapa
16	Tharu Sena	Laxman Tharu

The Maoist Splinters

In the past few years, at least fifteen groups have formed as breakaway factions of the CPNM (see Table 9.1). These fringe Maoist parties cannot be ignored when it comes to the possibility of the remobilisation of ex-combatants in political and criminal activities.

In 2009, Matrika Yadav, who was the central committee member of the CPNM and also held a position as minister in the Maoist-led government in 2008, split from the mother party. Yadav resisted the CPNM-led government's decision to return lands seized during the war to the original owners. He alleged that the CPNM's decision to sign the peace agreement was a historical betrayal and a total loss of the party's revolutionary rigour.[30] Contending that the CPNM had lost the revolutionary

---

[30] Interview with a politician, Dhangadi, December 2011.

rigour, direction and orientation that was instrumental in uniting public support during the insurgency, Yadav formed a new Maoist party called the true Maoist party. Unemployed and frustrated ex-combatants have been the targets of this party: for instance, during the fieldwork between September and December 2011, several interviewees mentioned that a significant number of VMLRs from eastern, central and western Terai had joined this group of radical Maoists. These moves have been criticised for being associated with potentially violent and disruptive political activities, particularly the involvement of its cadres in frequent land grabbing and collection of forced taxes from businesses in the Terai region (UN, 2011, p. 3).[31]

Similarly, a disgruntled former Maoist leader, Mani Thapa, quit the CPNM and has established another Maoist party, the Communist Revolutionary Party (CRP). The CRP holds a radical Maoist philosophy and seeks to gain publicity at the expense of defaming the CPNM. The CRP has constantly threatened to initiate another revolution, what it calls Armed *Jana Andolan III*. However, given the criminal orientation of its few members and cadres, many believe that the CRP does not hold any significance in the current political arena.[32] Yet, it was reported that some ex-combatants have allegedly joined this party and its youth wing, the National Red-Guard Army. Despite this information, no frequent activities of the army have been reported in the recent past. If ex-combatants from any category choose to join this group, it is more likely to be the ex-combatants who can be identified as being in the opportunistic informal group.

Apart from the Thapa and Yadav-led Maoist groups, other splinter groups are considered less significant in national and local politics, as many of them are "opportunistic political groups".[33] While several of these groups identify themselves as a political party or a politically motivated group, some of them have criminal orientations. For instance, the Mongol Revenge group was reported to carry out violent and disruptive activities in Rukkum and Rolpa districts in 2008–2009.[34] Other groups such as those led by Jai Krishna Goite and Nagendra Paswan, are

---

[31] Also see http://www.ekantipur.com/2009/12/10/capital/matrika-led-maoists-capture-forest-in-kapilvastu/304251.html.
[32] Interview with a journalist, Kohalpur, 2013.
[33] Interview with a journalist, Kathmandu, 2013.
[34] Interview with a lawyer, Ghorahi, 2013.

classified as armed underground groups, which have been carrying out armed insurgencies in the Terai region. Berojgar Yuwa Sangh has mobilised several ex-combatants in carrying out disruptive activities.[35] Due to dispersed settlements of ex-combatants, it is difficult to acquire nationwide information on ex-combatants' involvement in the Maoist splinter groups. However, a significant number of respondents from the Dang and Banke districts reported that since the Maoist splinter groups have different kinds of connections with ex-combatants, it is likely over time that these groups will engage with some ambitious and informal groups of ex-combatants in carrying out their political activities.

REMOBILISATION OR POLITICAL REINTEGRATION?

Based on the responses of ex-combatants during interviews, it appears that it could be difficult to distinguish between political remobilisation and political participation. In the DDR literature, ex-combatants' political participation is under-explored. Of the few studies available, Porto, Parsons, and Alden (2007) have argued that ex-combatants' political reintegration into society is an important indicator of successful reintegration. Political reintegration here refers to ex-combatants' rights and freedom of choice to participate in civic and political institutions, including but not limited to voting, becoming a member of a political party and being able to have uninterrupted access to benefits from the state's formal and informal institutions. In their studies of reintegration in Angola, Porto et al. (2007, pp. 71–75) have explored "election and voting", "knowledge of political parties" and "political participation and party activism" as elements of political reintegration.

Kingma (1999) asserts that in the long run, democratisation is essential for better reintegration outcomes. Democratisation in post-conflict society also means that ex-combatants and rebel leaders are turned into political actors, which is similar to the case of the Maoists in Nepal. In this, context, one line of thinking asserts that ex-combatants' participation in any form of Maoist party activism and political activities could be related to their political reintegration rather than remobilisation. This message was repeatedly echoed in the interviews with politically active ex-combatants.

---

[35] Interviews, Dang, Nepalgunj and Kathmandu, 2013.

Since the initiation of the peace process, a few ex-combatants and their commanders have assumed active political roles and public positions. For example, the vice commander of the PLA, Barsa Man Pun (Ananta), was elected as a CA member, and later became Minister in the Peace and Reconstruction Ministry and Ministry of Finance. Puspa Kamal Dahal, who is the head of the CPNM and someone who became the Prime Minister in 2008, was also the supreme commander of the PLA until he was elected a CA member. Former head of the PLA is elected as the Vice President of the country for two consecutive terms since 2015. This further suggests that political reintegration of ex-combatants is another important dimension of enquiry that is necessary in order to observe long-term effects of democratisation and peacebuilding in Nepal. Political reintegration, as another dimension of analysis, will be further helpful in making a clear distinction between remobilisation of ex-combatants and their rights and willingness to participate in politics.

CURRENT AND FUTURE IMPLICATIONS FOR INSECURITY AND VIOLENCE

Drawing on discussions presented above, ex-combatant-led insecurity and violence can be further comprehended at two levels: micro and macro.

Micro-level Implications of Insecurity and Violence

At the micro level, two types of issues are observed. Firstly, ex-combatant-led security issues relate to petty crimes and political violence. In the last few years, ex-combatant-led criminal cases have increased exponentially. The nature of crime is diverse, ranging from theft, burglary and forced donations to small arms problems and homicide.

There is a trend of ex-combatants' involvement in crime, particularly in urban areas. Crime and violence from remote areas often go unreported—therefore an urban-centric trend of violence appears to have emerged. As a significantly large number of ex-combatants are concentrated in urban and semi-urban areas, ex-combatant-led violence is more likely to concentrate in those areas.

In a number of cases, small groups of people, including ex-combatants and non-combatant youth, are involved in crime. This suggests that these small groups are opportunistic, akin to the (in)formal interest group discussed above; they have formed networks between combatants and non-combatant youth. It is quite likely that unemployed ex-combatants are mobilised by organised criminal groups. This can be substantiated by the report of Basnet (2013), which reveals that there are more than two dozen criminal groups active in the Kathmandu valley and almost all of these groups have engaged one or more ex-combatants. A similar trend of ex-combatants being involved in forced donations, robbery, cross border trade and manipulation of the government tender system were reported in the fieldwork districts. This means that the prevalence of criminal activities will have to be further explored in order to find out the trend of ex-combatant' involvement in petty crime, as well as organised crime.

Economic and material incentives are reported to be the pertinent causes for ex-combatants (with criminal and opportunistic orientations) to involve themselves in crime. Similarly, peer pressure and shared interests with fellow combatants were also reported as major factors. To a certain extent, the social and cultural reasons for violence can help explain some aspects of this nature of crime. However, the behaviour and attitudes of some ex-combatants towards violence has obviously not changed, even after they have relinquished active participation in the war. This is where an organised reintegration programme could contribute by helping ex-combatants change behaviours and attitudes away from violence orientation through psychosocial and economic support mechanisms.

Networks between ex-combatants were explored, and these appear to have played a facilitating factor in getting them involved in political violence and criminal violence. This is particularly the case with ex-combatants who tended to form (in)formal interest groups.

Ex-combatants, especially those who exhibit characteristics of being associated with (in)formal interest groups, along with politically active ex-combatants, are involved in inter-group feuds, threatening confrontations and direct violence. Mobilised by the CPNM and the CPN-M as muscle power, these two categories of ex-combatants are at the forefront of confrontations with other political groups. According to a civil society activist interviewed in Chitwan in January 2011, clashes between the YCL and the YF, which have increased in recent times, is an example of political violence in which ex-combatants are also involved. According to an interviewee, there is a considerable degree of solidarity between members of the YCL and ex-combatants, and they treat each other as members of a fraternal force.[36] Such a fraternal relationship is to a certain extent encouraged by the CPNM to consolidate force on the ground. But, ironically such force is also a source of street violence, as other political parties, especially the CPNUML and the NC have encouraged their youth groups to retaliate against the YCL. Confrontation between CPNM and CPN-M cadres in Chitwan in June 2012 is just one of many examples of such politically motivated violence. These are examples of violent interaction between Maoist factions.

Because of poor management of ex-combatants, micro-level security and violence has some negative implications, although having stated this, a CPNM leader who was interviewed suggested that ex-combatants should not be demonised for the prevalence of such violence, because it is a fundamental feature of every post-conflict society. The interviewee is partly correct, because not all ex-combatants have tended to get themselves involved in violence, especially the economically and socially engaged ones who have taken a different path in conducting their postwar lives more peacefully by pursuing a livelihood or small business enterprise. Nonetheless, given the increasing trend of reported cases of crimes and violence involving the participation of ex-combatants and a growing tendency for their remobilisation into various Maoist factions, these conditions suggest that perhaps the lack of a well-managed reintegration programme is likely to have caused an increase in micro-level insecurity, which may continue into the future.

The disarmament process in the past was incomplete. Many respondents pointed out that many weapons were never surrendered; these same weapons are now being seen in use in different areas, especially in remote areas. An interviewee in Dang mentioned and blamed incomplete disarmament for the continuous circulation of small arms and light weapons (SALW), not only in urban areas, but also in rural parts of the country. It was explored in the fieldwork that there is some sort of relationships between circulation of SALW and incomplete disarmament. However, this dynamic will require further investigations in the field.

Security of Ex-combatants Themselves

When talking about micro-security issues, the literature mostly focuses on insecurity and violence produced by ex-combatants. In contrast, the

---

[36] Interview with a sociologist, Kathmandu, 2013.

other side of the coin was also interesting in that there are equally potential security risks for ex-combatants in communities. Partly because of their involvement in violence in the past, some ex-combatants are more vulnerable to security risks than others. A lawyer interviewed in Ghorahi, Dang (February 2013), mentioned that some ex-combatants have personal issues with people in the villages of their origin. Such issues are often linked to atrocities that took place during the war in which ex-combatants may be actually or perceived to be implicated. He further said that it is partly because of this perceived security risk that some ex-combatants were not willing to return to their communities. Other similar assertions were found during the fieldwork, suggesting that the security of ex-combatants could be another issue at the micro level, which requires further investigation.

Macro Insecurity and Potential for a New Insurgency

Regarding the macro-insecurity issue, two seemingly different but inherently interlinked questions appear in the forefront: Is another insurgency possible? And will ex-combatants re-engage in another insurgency? The framework discussed in this study can be helpful for a brief discussion of this topic.

If the discussion begins with asking whether ex-combatants will take up arms again in Nepal, perhaps the most convincing answer would be "it depends" on several factors. Given that ex-combatants may fit into one of the three categories discussed above, all have a degree of war fatigue and a sense of victimisation and a feeling of being deceived at the end of the war, hence it is less likely that they will be ready to fight another large-scale armed insurgency, at least not in the immediate future. If any of the categories of ex-combatants defy the idea of a new revolution, it is undoubtedly the socially and economically engaged group who are most likely to steer way from such actions. By nature, the (in)formal interest groups are opportunistic; they may be likely to engage in any form of disruptive behaviour, as long as it produces material and non-material incentives but waging another armed insurgency seems most likely to be beyond their interests.

The politically active groups of ex-combatants are divided. Those who are supportive of the CPNM's new line of political thinking on democratic centralism believe that a revolution can be completed through grabbing power via an election process. It was this tactical war psyche that partly drove the CPNM to the peace process in 2006. Overwhelmed by the victory in the 2008 CA election, those Maoist supporters and cadres who are convinced of the idea of democratic centralism are now unwilling to risk taking part in another insurgency. However, this is true only as long as holding onto power is possible through other means, including opportunities relating to participating in mainstream politics.

By contrast, some politically active ex-combatants who support the radical agenda of the CPN-M and the Biplav-led faction of CPN-M think that domestic conditions are favourable while external conditions are unfavourable for a revolution. The domestic conditions are contingent on vulnerability conditions such as endemic socio-economic inequalities: the exclusion, marginalisation and exploitation of the poor, oppressed castes, ethnic groups and women; and the impoverishment and deprivation of ex-combatants and Maoist supporters. At times, these conditions may provoke people sufficiently to agitate against the state. This is because the peace process had its limitations to win the hearts and minds of people through the delivery of a peace dividend. In other words, despite some positive efforts made such as promulgation of new Constitution and ensuring social and political inclusion in the new political discourse, the peace process has not yet sufficiently addressed the root causes of armed conflict in Nepal, while a sense of victimisation has sparked tensions between the state and society. Yet, whether people are ready to take up guns again to fight a revolution is questionable because of existing frustrations and fatigue amongst ex-combatants who were fighting in the PLA for the Maoist cause.

In the meantime, the divisions among the mobilisers of the past insurgency have deepened, which has weakened the position of both Maoist groups as potential re-recruiters of ex-combatants. Recently, there have been some signs of tactical alliances forming among the CPN-M, CPN (Matrika Group) and the CRP, which indicate a more robust polarisation in radical left politics.[37] However, whether or not such an alliance endures is difficult to predict. If this polarisation is sustained though, it can sufficiently destabilise, if not revolutionise, Nepali society. The ex-combatants who have suffered from an identity trap and socio-economic vulnerability can be coerced into participating for the purposes of confrontation politics. However, much on this critical issue will depend on the roles of mobilisers, the effectiveness of their mobilising instruments and the extent to which the ex-combatants experience crisis and vulnerability situations.

---

[37] See http://www.myrepblica.com/portal/index.php?action=news_details&news_id=50249.

Conclusions

This chapter has explored the dynamics of ex-combatant-led micro and macro implications of insecurity and violence. It has used an analytical framework that suggests examining the patterns of remobilisation and micro and macro-insecurity implications in the light of different categories of ex-combatants, their remobilisation vulnerability conditions and the positions of and access to remobilising actors.

It has maintained that the Maoist ex-combatants constitute heterogeneous groups consisting of three distinct social categories—the socially and economically engaged group, (in)formal interest groups and politically active ex-combatants. Though all three categories share a minimum level of war fatigue, the (in)formal interest groups and politically active ex-combatants appear to be key insecurity actors. This chapter has also shown that the peace process failed to address social and economic inequalities that coexist with the poor security situation, proliferation of criminal groups, and militarisation of youth and ex-combatants', all of whom are having difficulties in adjusting to post-war society in Nepal. These are the conditions that increase their remobilisation vulnerability and it has already led some ex-combatants to engage in criminal and violent activities. Having highlighted various types of micro and macro-insecurity implications, this chapter has concluded that ex-combatant-led insecurity and violence are steadily increasing at the micro level while the macro-level threats can, for some time, be limited to confrontational and disruptive political actions rather than another full-scale insurgency.

References

ADB. (2013). *Asia development outlook 2013: Nepal*. Retrieved from https://www.adb.org/sites/default/files/publication/30205/ado2013-nepal.pdf.

Annan, J., & Cutter, A. (2009). *Critical issues and lessons in social reintegration: Balancing justice. Psychological wellbeing and community reconciliation*. Retrieved from http://cartagenaddr.org/literature_press/ART_21.pdf.

Babo-Soares, D. (2012). Conflict and violence in post-independence East Timor. In A. Suhrke & M. Berdal (Eds.), *The peace in between: Post-war violence and peacebuilding* (pp. 211–226). London and New York: Routledge.

Basnet, M. (2013). Aparad Ma Purba Ladaku (ex-combatants in crime). *Nepal National Weekly*, p. 561. http://www.ekantipur.com/nepal/article/?id=5828.

Berdal, M. (2012). Reflections on post-war violence and peacebuilding. In A. Suhrke & M. Berdal (Eds.), *The peace in between: Post-war violence and peacebuilding* (pp. 309–326). London and New York: Routledge.

Bourgois, P. (2001). The power of violence in war and peace: Post-cold War lessons from El Salvador. *Ethnography*, 2(1), 5–34. https://doi.org/10.1177/14661380122230803.

Braungart, R. G., & Braungart, M. M. (1990). Youth movement in the 1980s: A global perspective. *International Sociology*, 5(2), 157–181. https://doi.org/10.1177/026858090005002004.

Burnham, G., Lafta, R., Doocy, S., & Roberts, L. (2006). Mortality after the 2003 invasion of Iraq: A cross-sectional cluster sample survey. *The Lancet*, 367(October), 1421–1428. https://doi.org/10.1016/S0140-6736(06)69491-9.

Call, C. T. (2007). The mugging of a success story: Justice and security sector reform in El Salvador. In C. T. Call (Ed.), *Constructing justice and security after war* (pp. 29–67). Washington, DC: The United States Institute of Peace (USIP).

Carter Centre. (2011). *Political party youth wings in Nepal*. Atlanta/Kathmandu. Retrieved from https://www.cartercenter.org/resources/pdfs/news/peace_publications/democracy/nepal-political-party-youth-wings-022811-en.pdf.

CBS. (2011). *The third Nepal living standard survey 2010/11* (Statistical Report Volume II). Kathmandu: Central Bureau of Statistics (CBS).

Colletta, N. J., Kostner, M., & Wiederhofer, I. (1996). *Case studies in war-to-peace transition: The demobilization and reintegration of ex-combatants in Ethiopia, Namibia, and Uganda*. Washington, DC: World Bank.

Collier, P. (1994). Demobilization and insecurity: A study in the economics of the transition from war to peace. *Journal of International Development*, 6(3), 343–351. https://doi.org/10.1002/jid.3380060308.

Curle, A. (1999). *To tame the hydra: Undermining the culture of violence*. Charlbury: John Carpenter.

Ebo, A. (2005). Combating small arms proliferation and misuse after conflict. In A. Bryden & H. Hanggi (Eds.), *Security governance in post-conflict peacebuilding* (pp. 137–158). Geneva: Geneva Centre for the Democratic Control of Armed Forces (DCAF).

Fajnzylber, P., Lederman, D., & Loayza, N. (2002). What causes crime and violence. *European Economic Review*, 46(7), 1323–1357. http://dx.doi.org/10.1016/S0014-2921(01)00096-4.

Galtung, J. (1969). Violence, peace and peace research. *Journal of Peace Research*, 6(3), 167–191.

Galtung, J. (1990). Cultural violence. *Journal of Peace Research*, 27(3), 291–305.

Geyer, M. (1989). The militerization of Europe, 1914–1945. In J. Gillis (Ed.), *The militarization of the western world* (pp. 65–102). New Brunswick, NJ: Rutgers University Press.

Goldstone, J. A. (1991). *Revolution and rebellion in the early modern world*. Berkeley: University of California Press.

Goldstone, J. A. (2002). Population and security: How demographic change can lead to violent conflict. *Journal of International Affairs, 56*(1), 3–21.

Graham, G. (2007). People's war? Self-interest, coercion and ideology in Nepal's Maoist insurgency. *Small Wars & Insurgencies, 18*(2), 231–248. https://doi.org/10.1080/09592310701400853.

Hamber, B. (1999). Have no doubt it is fear in the land: An exploration of continuing cycles of violence in South Africa. *South African Journal of Child and Adolescent Mental Health, 12*(1), 5–18. https://doi.org/10.1080/16826108.2000.9632364.

Hanggi, H. (2005). Approaching peacebuilding from a security governance perspective. In A. Bryden & H. Hanggi (Eds.), *Security governance in post-conflict peacebuilding* (pp. 3–19). New Brunswick and London: Transaction Publication.

Hughes, C., & Pupavac, V. (2005). Framing post-conflict societies: International pathologisation of Cambodia and the post-Yugoslav states. *Third World Quarterly, 26*(6), 873–889. https://doi.org/10.1080/01436590500089232.

IMF. (2012). *World economy outlook: Growth resuming, dangers remain.* Washington, DC. Retrieved from https://www.imf.org/external/pubs/ft/weo/2012/01/pdf/text.pdf.

Katzenstein, P. (Ed.). (1996). *The culture of national security: Norms and identity in world politics.* New York: Columbia University Press.

Kingma, K. (1997). *Post-war demobilization and the reintegration of ex-combatants into civilian life.* Paper presented at the USAID Conference on Promoting Democracy, Human Rights and Reintegration in Post-conflict Societies, October 30–31, Bonn International Center for Conversion (BICC). Retrieved from http://pdf.usaid.gov/pdf_docs/PNACD095.pdf.

Kingma, K. (1999). *Post-war demobilisation, reintegration and peacebuilding.* Paper presented at the International Conference and Expert-Group Meeting on 'The contribution of disarmament and conversion to conflict prevention and its relevance for development cooperation', Bonn.

Kingma, K., & Muggah, R. (2009). *Critical issues in DDR: Context, indicators, targeting, and challenges.* Cartagena: Center for International Disarmament Demobilization and Reintegration.

Knight, M. (2008). Expanding the DDR model: Politics and organizations. *Journal of Security Sector Management, 6*(1), 1–19.

Knight, M., & Özerdem, A. (2004). Guns, camps and cash: Disarmament, demobilization and reinsertion of former combatants in transitions from war to peace. *Journal of Peace Research, 41*(4), 499–516. https://doi.org/10.1177/0022343304044479.

Lawler, S. (2008). *Identity: Sociological perspectives.* Cambridge: Cambridge Polity Press.

Maringira, G., & Brankovic, J. (2013). *The persistance of military identities among ex-combatants in South Africa*. Centre for the Study of Violence and Reconciliation and University of Western Cape.

Matthew, L. R., Bankston, W. B., Hayes, T. C., & Thomas, S. A. (2007). Revisiting the southern culture of violence. *The Sociological Quarterly, 48*(2), 253–275. https://doi.org/10.1111/j.1533-8525.2007.00078.x.

MoHP. (2011). *Nepal population report 2011*. Kathmandu.

Moser, C., & McIlwaine, C. (1999). Participatory urban appraisal and its application for research on violence. *Environment & Urbanization, 11*(2), 203–226. https://doi.org/10.1177/095624789901100217.

Muggah, R. (2005). No magic bullet: A critical perspective on disarmament, demobilization and reintegration (DDR) and weapons reduction in post-conflict contexts. *The Round Table: The Commonwealth Journal of International Affairs, 94*(379), 239–252. https://doi.org/10.1080/00358530500082684.

Muggah, R. (2010). Innovations in disarmament, demobilization and reintegration policy and research: Reflections on the last decade (NUPI Working Paper 774). Norwegian Institute of International Affairs. Retrieved from http://english.nupi.no/content/download/13642/128894/version/6/file/WP-774-Muggah.pdf.

Nilsson, A. (2008). *Dangerous liaisons: Why ex-combatants return to violence. Cases from Republic of Congo and Sierra Leone* (Doctoral Degree). Uppsala University, Uppasala, Sweden.

Porto, J. G., Parsons, I., & Alden, C. (2007). *From soldiers to citizens: The social, economic and political reintegration of UNITA ex-combatants* (ISS Monograph Series No. 130). Pretoria: Institute for Security Studies.

Pun, K. (2012, April 24). Baidya faction revives People's Volunteers Bureau. *Republica*. Retrieved from http://www.myrepublica.com/portal/index.php?action=news_details&news_id=34269.

Rupesinghe, K., & Marcial, R. C. (1994). *The culture of violence*. Tokyo: United Nations University Press.

Shah, A., & Pettigrew, J. (2009). Windows into a revolution: Ethnographies of Maoism in South Asia. *Dialectical Anthropology, 33*(3/4), 225–251. https://doi.org/10.1007/s10624-009-9142-5.

Spear, J. (2002). Disarmament and demobilization. In S. J. Stedman, D. Rothchild, & E. M. Cousens (Eds.), *Ending civil wars: The implementation of peace agreements*. Boulder and London: Lynne Rienner.

Steenkamp, C. (2005). The legacy of war: Conceptualizing a 'culture of violence' to explain violence after peace accords. *The Round Table: The Commonwealth Journal of International Affairs, 94*(379), 253–267. https://doi.org/10.1080/00358530500082775.

Subedi, D. B. (2012a). Economic dimension of peacebuilding: Insights into post-conflict economic recovery and development in

Nepal. *South Asia Economic Journal, 13*(2), 313–332. https://doi.org/10.1177/1391561412459387.

Subedi, D. B. (2012b). Spaces for private sector in post-conflict economic recovery in Nepal. *Readings on Governance and Development, XIV*(May), 90–109.

Subedi, D. B. (2013). From civilian to combatant: Armed recruitment and participation in the Maoists' conflict in Nepal. *Contemporary South Asia, 21*(4), 429–443. https://doi.org/10.1080/09584935.2013.856868.

Subedi, D. B. (2014). Ex-combatants, security and post-conflict violence: Unpacking the experience from Nepal. *Millennial Asia: An International Journal of Asian Studies, 5*(1), 41–65. https://doi.org/10.1177/0976399613518857.

Suhrke, A. (2012). The peace in between. In A. Suhrke & M. Berdal (Eds.), *The peace in between: Post-war violence and peacebuilding* (pp. 1–24). London and New York: Routledge.

Suhrke, A., & Berdal, M. (Eds.). (2012). *The peace in between.* In *Post-war violence and peacebuilding.* London and New York: Routledge.

Themnér, A. (2011). *Political violence in post-conflict societies: Remarginalisation, remobilisers and relationships.* London: Routledge.

Torres, G. (2008). Imagining social justice amidst Guatemala's post-conflict violence. *Studies in Social Justice, 2*(1), 1–11.

UN. (2011). *Myths and realities of land capture: Some stories from the Eastern districts.* Kathmandu.

UNDP. (2007). *Human development report data 2007/2008.* Retrieved from http://hdr.undp.org/sites/default/files/reports/268/hdr_20072008_en_complete.pdf.

UNDP. (2013). *Summary human development report 2013. The rise of the south: Human progress in a diverse world.* New York.

UNIDIR. (1999). *The management of arms in conflict resolution process.* Geneva: United Nations Institute for Disarmament Research.

Upreti, B. R. (2010). Reconstruction and development in post-conflict Nepal. In B. R. Upreti, S. R. Sharma, K. N. Pyakuryal, & S. Ghimire (Eds.), *The remake of a state: Post-conflict challenges and state building in Nepal* (pp. 129–150). Kathmandu: NCCR North-South and Kathmandu University.

Urdal, H. (2004). *The devil in the demographics: The effect of youth bulges on domestic armed conflict, 1950–2000: Conflict prevention & reconstruction* (Paper No. 14). Washington, DC: World Bank. http://www.eldis.org/vfile/upload/1/document/0708/DOC14714.pdf.

Urdal, H. (2006). A clash of generations? Youth bulges and political violence. *International Studies Quarterly, 50*(3), 607–629. https://doi.org/10.1111/j.1468-2478.2006.00416.x.

Wendt, A. (1992). Anarchy is what states make of it: The social construction of power politics. *International Organization, 46*(2), 391–426.

Winton, A. (2004). Urban violence: A guide to the literature. *Environment and Urbanization, 16*(2), 165–184.

CHAPTER 10

Conclusions: What We Learn from Nepal?

Nepal's transition from armed conflict to peace has been deeply complicated and fragile. Since the signing of the Comprehensive Peace Agreement (CPA), the peace process can be considered still incomplete, and the country is in a "grey zone", characterised by neither armed conflict nor peace. The peace process has made a considerable progress: of the major priorities stipulated in the CPA, constitution writing and state restructuring have completed, and country has for the first time in 20 years, held election of local bodies and the Provencial and Federal parliaments under a federal system. There is much hope and optimism about the future. However, at the same time, critical elements of the peace process, most importantly, transitional justice and reconciliation process, which is necessary to deal with war-time crimes, violence and violation of human rights has lingered to an extent that it has made conflict victims waiting for justice deeply frustrated (Subedi, 2014). Subedi and Jenkins (2018) argue that although reintegration of ex-combatants and post-conflict reconciliation could have mutually reinforcing elements, the lack of justice and reconciliation has enormous negative impact on the way the ex-combatants have experienced community acceptance in the process of their social reintegration.

Similarly, management of the Maoist ex-combatants has been arguably completed: there are no more cantonments of ex-combatants, the People's Liberation Army (PLA) is officially dissolved, and ex-combatants have now returned to the communities of their choice, although many of them are struggling to reintegrate into society on their own.

The decade-long Maoist insurgency has had profound social and economic effects on Nepalese society. War has both integrative and disintegrative functions, particularly in the life of ex-combatants and their families (Hazan, 2007). In Nepal, the disintegrative function of the war saw the PLA fighters detached from normal life, livelihood activities, although it must be noted that most of the combatants had maintained regular contacts with their family.

In contrast, an effect of an integrative function of war was that it created an environment in which the civilians-turned-combatants became a member of the war system. In other words, the combatants were integrated into the war system. The integrative function of war must, therefore, be seen in negative terms and it was detrimental to the society in the long run because the war system threatened social, economic and political order and stability of a society—ex-combatants lost education, conflict victims experienced economic and social losses, families were disintegrated and social organisations collapsed in remote villages that experienced political and organised violence.

In this scenario, both ideally and practically, peacebuilding in Nepal not only needed to redesign national and local political institutions and mechanisms as part of what is known as statebuilding, but it should also inherently need to redress and reverse the disintegrative function of the war system. That means, change and transformation are to happen both at local and national levels rather than changes occurring only at economic and political spheres at the national level (Newman, Paris, & Richmond, 2009; Richmond, 2009).

One such areas where local level change and transformation could be seen is the reintegration of ex-combatants. However, although combatants occupied the centre-stage in the agendas of the peace negotiations, the dominant political view toward the ex-combatants embraced a realist perception that categorised ex-combatants as a "spoiler" of peace rather than seeing them as a subject of peacebuilding. As a result, although there was no disagreement regarding the need for management of the Maoist ex-combatants, there was also no agreement in place as to how this difficult process could be accomplished. By the time management of Maoists arms and armies was declared complete in 2012, parties to the peace process including the CPNM appeared to have dealt with ex-combatants as a "minimum compliance" needed to complete the peace process. The Disarmament, Demobilisation and Reintegration (DDR) dilemma that lasted for nearly five years when the combatants were confined in the cantonments resulted in a flawed policy characterised by a minimalist and short-short-sighted notion of seeing DDR as an instrument of short-term stabalisation. Key political actors viewed DDR as an element of peace agreement implementation rather than seeing DDR as a means to achieve social change in the post-conflict recovery and peacebuilding process. This minimalist approach taken to deal with ex-combatants was narrowly conceived and fundamentally flawed.

The flawed policies adopted can be seen in many stages. One example is that the combatant verification process, conducted by the United Mission in Nepal (UNMIN) in 2007, classified the PLA combatants into "unverified" and "verified" categories. Discrepancies existed in formulating the policy to deal with these two categories of ex-combatants, as the government developed four different sets of policy responses. The unverified ex-combatants, or those also known as Verified Minor and Late Recruits (VMLRs), were provided with formal rehabilitation support, whereas about 80% of the verified ex-combatants retired with a cash package, but without going through any reintegration programme. In addition, 1400 (nearly 8%) of the total ex-combatant population joined the Nepal Army on the basis of an agreement stipulated in the CPA. Regardless of different policy options adopted, the faulty combatant verification process, which can be partly blamed to UNMIN's verification process and partly CPNM's intention to exclude its real combatants out of the DDR process, resulted in the DDR programme dealing with fake ex-combatants while real ex-combatants were deprived of much needed reintegration support.

Although the DDR process was home-grown with limited international engagement, the so-called home-grown processes adopted to reintegrate ex-combatants have also embraced elements of liberal peacebuilding practice. The entire mechanism and structure of the peace process was top-down and state-centric with emphasis given on diffusing the structure of the war through a cash-based approach rather than facilitating a transformatory process of reintegration. The need for DDR was felt to institutionalise democratic system at the top at the cost of the difficulties faced by ex-combatants to reintegrate in communities and ex-combatants-led violence. The lack of community level engagement, and the extremely minimum space provided to the civil society in the peace process further resulted in the lack of local ownership in the DDR process.

It is notable here that in any post-conflict situation, the efforts made to reintegrate ex-combatants eventually aim to turn combatants back into the identity of civilians. Therefore, the heterogeneous community of ex-combatants must be placed at the centre of a DDR process in peacebuilding that aims to induce transformatory changes in post-conflict communities.

Is it possible to think of any measures that help ex-combatants return to civilian life without considering the factors that have driven their participation in the war in the past? This important question that is often overlooked in designing DDR programmes is dealt with in this volume in Chapter 2, which explores how vertical and horizontal inequalities emanating from regional disparities in development, bad governance and the political economy of caste and ethnic marginalisation gave rise to the Maoist insurgency. These conditions have created "structural vulnerability", which provided the Maoists with favourable mobilising conditions in which they applied the tools and techniques of radicalisation and indoctrination to recruit young but unemployed and disenfranchised rural youth as combatants. Furthermore, the Maoists' coercion and the state's repression pushed many into the insurgency, both voluntarily and involuntarily. This very dynamic of war participation suggests that peacebuilding in Nepal must deal with conditions of structural vulnerability in order to reduce opportunities for political extremism that may have the potential to remobilise people into violence and insurgency in future.

The highly politicised context of DDR had spill-over effects on the rehabilitation programme that was implemented and targeted the VMLR ex-combatants. The rehabilitation programme is shown to have taken an extremely narrow "ex-combatant focused" approach that brought ex-combatants "back to work" rather than what it should have been addressing that is the issue of getting them "back to community". Since no significant efforts were made to rehabilitate ex-combatants socially, there have been limitations in fostering of non-violent relationships between ex-combatants, their families and communities. This leads to the question: can a "back to work" approach successfully help reintegrate ex-combatants? The results presented in this volume are mixed, but also discouraging. Some ex-combatants who were able to receive support from their families and relatives, as well as from the war-family, are able to earn a living, and experienced fewer problems in terms of how they experienced their rehabilitation. But overall, this volume demonstrates that even the success of a "minimalist rehabilitation" approach depends on the macro conditions of the post-conflict economy, effective local and national ownership of the programme and social and the micro factors such as the personal circumstances of ex-combatants themselves. It is also argued that a successful reintegration programme cannot be effectively accomplished in isolation from a wider peacebuilding and recovery programme.

An important theme dealt with in the volume is ex-combatants' livelihood security as a marker of their economic reintegration. Without analysing livelihood capitals such as human capital, physical capital, social capital and financial capital and how ex-combatants are able to foster and apply them in generating livelihood, reintegration of ex-combatants cannot be simply comprehended. However, it must also be recognised that from a broader perspective, economic reintegration must be conceptualised taking into account the causes of conflict and the political and economic conditions affecting peace. According to the views of ex-combatants themselves, livelihood security is a bottom-line indicator of economic reintegration. Focusing on livelihood can shed further light on what individual-level changes have been induced in the lives of individual ex-combatants and whether or how such changes reduce the possibilities of ex-combatants being involved in crime and violence.

The relationship between social reintegration and social capital is another thematic issue that this volume brings forth while analysing social reintegration of ex-combatants. Exploring informal processes that the ex-combatants used and adopted to reintegrate themselves into society, and further investigating facilitating and constraining factors at both the individual and societal levels, it was found that "community acceptance" and "community avoidance" are two major themes that can have negative implications for social relationships, networks and trust between ex-combatants and the community. From a post-conflict peacebuilding perspective, these findings encourage us to think about how to bring about changes in relationships between ex-combatants and the community. This volume demonstrates how social capital is important for a peaceful society to emerge after an armed conflict. A fully implemented reintegration policy that could address social and psychosocial needs and concerns of ex-combatants, but also address the needs of conflict victims, could have significantly increased community harmony. However, as the management of ex-combatants has missed such an opportunity, an overwhelming number of ex-combatants still face social stigma, while, the grievances associated with other conflict-affected groups have intermittently resulted in backlashes. The argument in Chapter 8 is that social reintegration of ex-combatants would have achieved better results had it been organised in tandem with a post-conflict reconciliation programme.

An analysis of the immediate consequences of economic and social reintegration in post-conflict society, using violence as an indicator in chapter 9, reveals that critical concerns are mounting about ex-combatants reappearing as actors wielding direct violence. This happens either when they voluntarily get involved in crime and political violence, or are remobilised into joining extremist, radical and criminal outfits. Not all ex-combatants are likely to be violent, as some have taken a different direction in their lives and become socially and economically engaged; therefore, they are more likely to gradually return to peaceful civilian life, having taken pro-active steps to enter main-stream society. Yet, this volume found other categories of ex-combatants who have increasingly engaged in petty crime and low-level violence in the community. However, a full-scale insurgency involving ex-combatants seems less likely at present.

Major Conclusions and Lessons to Be Learnt from the Nepali DDR Process

There are several major conclusions and lessons learned to be drawn from DDR in Nepal. Firstly, the war to peace transition in Nepal has produced a typical political and economic environment in which political views are very strongly influenced by economic interests. Thus, for example, some PLA commanders as well Maoists leaders favoured cash payments under the DDR as they could readily be tithed.

Peacebuilding requires changing perceptions, attitudes, behaviour and relationships. The decision to release ex-combatants without accompanying reintegration support is a testimony to how the typical political constraints of the peace process in Nepal set a narrow scope for DDR. The scope for a DDR programme was politically negotiated whilst limited attention was given to peacebuilding needs of the war-torn country.

To put it differently, management of Maoist ex-combatants was seen as a political process rather than social and economic process. As a result, the Maoists used it as their nominal commitment to the peace process and in fact as a chip for power-bargain in the national politics. The government and major political parties (other than Maoists) on the other hand, aimed at diffusing the structure of PLA as a potential threat to consolidation of democracy and peace. The cash-based scheme introduced to reintegrate ex-combatants was an outcome of the convergence of tactical and strategic interests of the key actors involved at the centre. As a result, the unconventional DDR programme in Nepal was used to pacify ex-combatants and de-politicise DDR; rather than what DDR should have been a vehicle for social, economic and political change and transformation at the community level. This does not mean that DDR should have been led by external actors; indeed, Nepal could have developed its own model of reintegration which would link reintegration of ex-combatants with post-conflict economic development, ideally led by national and local actors.

Secondly, this study has found that the modality of reintegration can depend on circumstance where it operates. For instance, the use of cash to reintegrate ex-combatants reflects a typical approach decided upon at the political level, but not taking into account the actual needs and aspirations of ex-combatants on the ground. Turning ex-combatants into passive participants in a process of reintegration can be much easier to accomplish than engaging them as change actors in peacebuilding. Despite the operational convenience of the distribution of cash to individual ex-combatants, this study concludes that if a cash-based approach is adopted to reintegrate ex-combatants, it cannot be taken as a general rule that ex-combatants will misuse the cash given to them. However, it is still necessary to explore how far the cash paid to ex-combatants can address their economic vulnerability, the same vulnerability that supposedly had pushed them into a war against the state in the first place, rather than just looking into the use or misuse of cash. The conclusion is straight forward: cash can be attractive to ex-combatants, but it cannot reintegrate them; using cash in lieu of a well-organised reintegration programme does not meet the needs of effective peacebuilding in a post-conflict society.

Thirdly, social reintegration can be more complex than economic reintegration, mainly because it involves several aspects of rebuilding relationships. A war-torn society such as Nepal is essentially fragmented and polarised in political, ethnic, caste and religious terms. In such an environment, social reintegration of ex-combatants should be an early focus of post-conflict peacebuilding. The fact that ex-combatants are not well accepted in communities and the reality that the ex-combatants themselves avoided the community, suggest the existence of unresolved undercurrents of animosity, hostility and adversarial feelings, which are very much present in post-war Nepali society. Many people were killed or had their lives ruined during the war. This cannot be fixed just through the release of ex-combatants from the cantonments where they were being held, and ticking a box confirming that this act alone is a means of progressing the peace process. Rebuilding social relationships requires a commitment from ex-combatants, community members, the rebel organisation, the war mobilisers, civil society and, indeed, the government. In other words, creating a congenial environment for ex-combatants to return to the community and lead a peaceful civilian life requires the commitments and collaborations of many and varied groups and individuals. Of course, some ex-combatants can respond quickly and effectively while others may have some limitations because of their personal circumstances and experiences during the war. In this situation, social reintegration is about empowering and encouraging victims and perpetrators so that they recover from the social and personal wounds of the war and move toward a shared future. In the case of Nepal, this study has suggested that this cannot be fully achieved unless the people start post-conflict reconciliation, because ex-combatants are seen to be experiencing difficulties in social adjustment in their communities. Here, a symbiotic relationship between reconciliation and social reintegration is highly visible, although unfortunately peacebuilding in Nepal has missed the opportunity to realise the importance of this difficult step in rebuilding a peaceful society after a war.

The way ex-combatants experienced their social and economic reintegration amply suggests that not all ex-combatants reintegrate in the same manner and this is more so when DDR programme replaces reintegration programme with a cash-based option. A key conclusion that can be drawn from this volume suggests that ex-combatants capacity and ability to reintegrate depends on the extent to which they are able to forge social capital in the communities they return to.

Fourthly, it is demonstrable that that some ex-combatants reintegrated, both socially and economically, much better than others, even if there was no formal reintegration programme. This suggests that reintegration can be significantly determined by individual ex-combatants' personal and social backgrounds, and capacity and ability to build relationships with the people in the community where they return. This conclusion, however, does not and should not rule out the need for a comprehensive reintegration programme because there are certainly a large number of ex-combatants who have difficulties in their reintegration and who, therefore, require assistance and support. Individual ex-combatant's war-time conduct and behaviour can be another decisive factor. Similarly, in the context of Nepal, it can be concluded that the role of the "war family" is not always negative and detrimental. For some ex-combatants, the war family provided emotional and psychosocial support, a sense of security, and social capital. This insight further encourages us to find creative ways to engage the war family, in addition to the biological families of ex-combatants, in post-conflict reintegration programmes. In a similar vein, it is also concluded that not all ex-combatants are a source of insecurity and violence; generalising ex-combatants as a threat to security can be simplistic and misleading. This conclusion suggests considering ex-combatants as a constituency of heterogeneous actors thus the need for responding to and engaging with ex-combatants based on individual needs, interests, and personal, social and violence profiles.

Finally, a minimalist goal for peacebuilding could be addressing direct violence caused by war; stopping the violence and ending the war would superficially achieve this. This is what Galtung (1990, 1996) calls "negative peace". However, a maximalist goal of peacebuilding should be to work towards addressing and removing inequalities and injustices that drive violent and extremist behaviour, and promoting collective actions that are taken to bring about equalisation and end structural and cultural forms of violence. This is the ideal of "positive peace". This study has concluded that management of ex-combatants has not adequately contributed even to stopping direct violence, let alone addressing structural and cultural inequalities, as there are increasing numbers of cases of ex-combatant involvement in petty crime and violence at the micro level. The argument here is that much remains to be done in addressing structural inequalities and root causes of conflict in Nepal. In other words, peacebuilding through reintegration of ex-combatants involved a top-down process with limited scope for emancipatory goal of the idea of transformatory peacebuilding discussed in Chapter 1. The way the management of ex-combatants ended has further deepened the grievances of ex-combatants. A group of ex-combatants have a feeling of being deceived by the government, but also by the CPNM. This means that despite a huge amount of resources invested in dismantling the war structure, this has only ended up producing "winners" and "losers". Spoiler behaviour among ex-combatants is on the rise in a situation where potential remobilisers are well placed to tap into and manipulate the grievances of frustrated, disillusioned and angry ex-combatants. Consequently, post-conflict Nepal is still grappling with the challenges of maintaining "negative peace". DDR, therefore, should have been conceived and implemented as an element of post-conflict recovery and peacebuilding, so that it could be utilised as a means of addressing the socio-economic concerns of ex-combatants, and fostering social capital during the post-conflict period. In other words, for peace and long-term stability, peacebuilding in Nepal should have moved beyond taking a liberal peace approach and instead embraced transformatory idea of peacebuilding in which the resources invested to release combatants from cantonments could be tied to foster local development in which ex-combatants could be engaged. Unfortunately, in the current situation, DDR of the PLA ex-combatants has left fissures that can develop into pitfalls or even craters, all of which have potential to produce negative consequences for peace in the future.

Recommendations for Future Research

There are several thematic clusters, which deserve further research. Firstly, army integration was a central agenda item with respect to the management of Maoist ex-combatants. Yet, in order to keep the research focused on economic and social aspects of reintegration, this issue is not included in this volume. This issue is worthy of a separate research project, particularly from a security sector reform (SSR) and state-building viewpoint. Secondly, the mutually reinforcing nature of reintegration and reconciliation was briefly discussed in Chapter 8. A further study concentrating on reconciliation, but concurrently taking into account potential effects and implications of the social and economic reintegration of ex-combatants, could be more helpful in understanding peacebuilding in Nepal.

Similarly, there was no scope in the research on which this volume is based to focus on direct and indirect external support for the management of ex-combatants. There is a need to explore whether there was any external influence in the way in which an "unconventional" DDR eventually emerged in Nepal.

A longitudinal study of rehabilitation and reintegration with particular emphasis on gender analysis could be another area of future inquiry. This recommendation is made taking into account of the fact that the community of ex-combatants is heterogeneous constituted by both men and women. Although gender needs of ex-combatants have been highlighted briefly in this volume, in future, another study exclusively focusing on how gender realities affected the needs and expectations of ex-combatants from reintegration could be a subject of a separate inquiry. Finally, since Nepal has now promulgated a new Consitution that has ensured provisions for social and political inclusion, and promoted a vision of social and economic transformation under the Federal Democratic system. With this historical change in place, it might be worth investigating what ex-combatants would think about the vision of transformation that has been institutionalised in recent years since they were released from the cantonments. It might also be relevant to explore whether their perceptions towards the outcome of the peace process have changed and if the new political changes in the country have any effects on the ex-combatants', experience of their social and economic reintegration. Perhaps, it would also be a useful idea to examine if the recent outcome of the peace process has had any significant effects, either positive or negative, in peacebuilding with its emancipatory and transformatory aspirations.

References

Galtung, J. (1990). Cultural violence. *Journal of Peace Research, 27*(3), 291–305.
Galtung, J. (1996). *Peace by peaceful means: Peace, conflict, development and civilisation*. Oslo and London: International Peace Research, Oslo and Sage.
Hazan, J. (2007). *Social integration of ex-combatants after civil war*. Retrieved from http://www.un.org/esa/socdev/sib/egm/paper/JenniferHazen.pdf.
Newman, E., Paris, R., & Richmond, O. P. (2009). Introduction. In E. Newman, R. Paris, & O. P. Richmond (Eds.), *New perspectives on liberal peacebuilding* (pp. 3–25). Tokyo, New York and Paris: United Nations University Press.
Richmond, O. P. (2009). Beyond liberal peace? Responses to "Backsliding". In E. Newman, R. Paris, & O. P. Richards (Eds.), *New perspectives on liberal peacebuilding* (pp. 54–77). Tokyo, New York and Paris: United Nations University Press.
Subedi, D. B. (2014, April 2). Instrument of peace: Truth and Reconciliation Comission (TRC) in Nepal. *Republica*. Retrieved from http://www.myrepublica.com/portal/index.php?action=news_details&news_id=72004.
Subedi, D. B., & Jenkins, B. (2018). The Nexus between reintegration of ex-combatants and reconciliation in Nepal: A social capital approach. In B. Jenkins, D. B. Subedi, & K. Jenkins (Eds.), *Reconciliation in conflict-affected communities: Practices and insights from the Asia-Pacific* (pp. 41–56). Singapore: Springer.

Index

A
Agreement on Monitoring of the Management of Arms and Armies, 7
Amnesty International, 62, 76
Armed conflict, 1–3, 8, 11, 15, 16, 21, 23, 25, 26, 28, 30, 44–47, 49, 51–54, 59–63, 65, 66, 71, 72, 75, 76, 96, 130, 131, 133, 136, 164, 184, 202, 209, 210, 217, 226, 228, 241, 244, 248, 257, 263, 267
Armed recruitment, 43, 44, 61, 65
Army integration, 4, 81–85, 88, 101, 103, 112–114, 124, 125, 188, 272
Army Integration Special Committee, 79, 82, 86, 169, 189
Auxiliary Nurse Midwife, 134

B
Banke, 5, 7, 170, 179, 180, 182, 185, 189, 214, 230–234, 238, 252
Bhattarai, Babu Ram, 150

Blood money, 189

C
Cantonments, 2, 6, 77, 78, 80–82, 85, 88, 101, 109–115, 117–125, 131, 132, 135–137, 148, 149, 152, 156, 166, 171, 173, 175, 181, 187, 189, 193, 194, 199, 206, 207, 212, 233, 263, 264, 269
CAR, 28
Cash-based scheme, 3, 4, 189, 193, 268
Caste-based discriminations, 51, 178
CDO, 146
Ceasefire, 28, 74, 75, 78, 181
Ceasefire agreement, 6
Chief of the Army Staff, 101
Children Associated with Armed Forces and Groups (CAFAG), 28, 147
Child rights, 132, 133
Child soldiers, 28, 80, 111, 131–133, 159

Chisapani (Kailali), 189
Chitwan, 5, 7, 55, 111, 126, 132, 170–172, 180–182, 185, 187, 189, 205, 207, 212, 230–235, 243, 246, 254, 255
Chulachuli (Ilam), 121, 189
Civil society, 7, 16, 23, 26, 53, 58, 60, 62, 75, 76, 85–87, 112, 119, 122–124, 139, 144, 145, 147, 175, 179, 181, 187, 204, 206, 207, 211, 213, 214, 244, 254, 265, 269
civil society organisations, 16, 53, 147, 181, 213
Code of conduct, 74, 78
Combatant-army integration, 4, 84, 100, 101
Commission for Investigation of Abuse of Authority (CIAA), 123
Communist Party of Nepal Marxist and Leninist, 7, 45, 62, 75, 81, 97–100, 109, 112, 113, 122, 135–137, 209, 213, 255
Community, 1, 4, 5, 10, 13, 14, 17–20, 22–27, 29, 30, 45, 54, 63, 66, 103, 124, 129, 130, 134, 139, 141, 147, 158, 164, 168, 170, 172, 183, 189, 191, 199–209, 211–213, 215–219, 228–230, 234, 235, 242, 243, 245, 246, 263, 265–270, 272
Community development, 19, 20
Comprehensive Peace Agreement, 1, 7, 72, 73, 76, 78, 87, 131, 263
Conflict, 1, 3, 6, 8–23, 25–31, 43, 44, 46–48, 51, 60, 72–74, 76, 77, 80, 84, 86, 88, 93, 94, 101, 104, 118, 130–132, 140–142, 144, 145, 147, 163, 167, 174, 176–178, 183, 184, 190, 191, 193, 194, 199–201, 209–211, 213–215, 217, 219, 223–229, 236, 237, 241, 244, 263–264, 267, 271
Conflict transformation, 11
Constitution assembly, 76, 97, 98, 113, 211, 234, 253
Constitution assembly election, 97–101, 257
Cooperatives, 157, 234
Corruption, 72, 114, 116–123, 167
CTEVT, 146

D

Dahaban (Rolpa), 189
Dahal, Puspa Kamal (Prachanda), 99, 175, 234, 253
Dalits, 49–51, 54, 64, 210, 213, 241
Dang, 5, 7, 55, 74, 119, 170–172, 176, 177, 179, 180, 182, 189, 202, 211, 215, 230–232, 234, 248, 252, 255, 256
Demobilisation, 8, 79, 81, 84, 88, 95, 110, 111, 132, 168, 227
Development, 7, 11, 12, 15, 16, 19–22, 49, 63, 64, 72, 79, 86, 114, 132, 133, 138–141, 143–145, 151, 165–168, 171, 172, 176, 180, 183, 189–191, 193, 208, 213, 216, 228, 240–242, 247, 266
long-term development, 15
Development and reconciliation, 11
Dhangadi, 7, 54–58, 60–62, 99, 102, 111, 112, 132, 139, 140, 144, 148–150, 178, 202, 250
Dictatorship, 75
Disarmament, 2, 8, 15–17, 79, 80, 84, 85, 88, 95, 107–109, 117, 120, 132, 167, 168, 227, 255
blanket disarmament, 80, 88, 107
Disarmament, Demobilisation and Reintegration (DDR), 2, 3, 10, 11, 14–16, 19, 20, 23, 29,

44, 66, 72, 73, 83, 84, 86, 88, 93–95, 100, 101, 103, 104, 107, 110, 115, 116, 126, 129, 135, 145, 163, 167, 200, 227, 252, 265, 268, 271, 272

E
Economic rehabilitation, 140, 141, 144, 148, 157, 219
Education support, 133
Emancipation, 248
Embezzlement of PLA fund, 118
Ex-combatants, 1–8, 10, 11, 14–31, 43, 44, 54–56, 58, 62, 64, 73, 79–88, 93, 95, 96, 99–104, 107–115, 119, 124–126, 129–133, 135–143, 145, 147–159, 163–194, 199–209, 211–213, 215–219, 223, 224, 226–258, 263–272

F
Fake combatants, 110, 111, 113, 120
Family, 4, 7, 23–25, 43, 62, 65, 75, 131, 138, 139, 148, 150, 152, 154–158, 168, 173, 174, 181–183, 187, 199, 202, 204–207, 214, 264, 266
Family support, 157
Far-west, 49, 57, 60, 149, 170, 233, 241
Forced displacement, 72
Freedom, 19, 59, 75, 168, 238, 252

G
Galtung, Johan, 9, 224
Gender, 4, 24, 48, 64, 72, 135, 152, 168, 239, 272
Gender-based discriminations, 72
Gender support, 134, 152
Grass-root mobilisation, 56

H
Hard line faction, 99, 124, 125
Human rights, 11, 29, 56, 62, 76, 77, 86, 111, 130, 131, 202, 203, 213, 214, 263

I
Identity, 1, 3, 4, 15, 22, 26, 29, 43, 47, 59, 60, 80, 114, 129, 139, 144, 159, 172, 183, 184, 188, 191, 203, 204, 208–211, 216, 217, 224, 229, 242–245, 257
Ideology, 30, 45, 47, 48, 52, 53, 56, 58, 59, 138, 153, 182, 183, 199, 203, 225, 232, 237, 241, 246–249
ILO, 21, 22, 50, 132, 141
India, 84, 85, 210, 249
Indigenous rights, 49–51, 53, 54, 64, 98, 210, 213
Individual-combatant focused, 135
Indoctrination, 48, 55, 59, 63–65, 192, 204, 209, 266
Inequalities, 10, 12, 47, 49, 51, 55, 63, 176, 210, 211, 238–241, 257, 258, 266, 271
Informal interest group, 238
INSEC, 214
Institutionalisation, 14
Integrated DDR Standard, 16, 85
Integration, 4, 17, 27, 79, 81, 83, 84, 87, 95, 96, 100, 101, 113, 122, 123, 125, 126, 182, 188
Inter-caste marriage, 25, 152, 158, 178, 207
Inter-ethnic relations, 211
Inter-group relations, 213
Interim constitution, 96, 97, 101, 102
Internally Displaced Person, 12, 214, 217
International community, 8, 132, 136, 176

J

Janajati, 210, 211
Joint Monitoring and Coordination Committee, 78, 79
Justice, 9, 17, 23, 29, 57, 98, 213, 263

K

Kailali, 5, 7, 56, 57, 102, 149, 170, 231
King Birendra, 75
King Gyanendra, 62, 74, 75
Koirala, Girija Prasad, 98

L

Labour migration, 144, 186, 187
Late recruits, 6, 80, 81, 112, 129
Lederach, John Paul, 10
Lenin, 53, 55
Liberal peacebuilding, 12–14, 31, 85, 86, 265
Life skill, 21, 23, 179, 240
Livelihood capitals, 164, 165, 191–193, 267
Livelihood strategy, 185, 186
Local ownership, 12, 17, 85, 87, 145, 147, 159, 265
Local Peace Committee, 147

M

Madesh, 98
Madhesi, 49, 54, 210, 213, 250
Madhsi Janadhikar Forum, 210
Mao, 52, 53, 55
Maoist armed conflict, Maoists, 8, 30, 44, 52, 130, 209, 244
Maoist hinterlands, 61, 131, 202
Maoist party, 54, 102, 108, 113, 142, 184, 205, 211, 212, 235, 247, 251, 252

Marx, Karl, 55
Maximalist, 19, 20, 192, 271
Micro enterprises, 7, 22, 133, 140, 142, 156, 157, 173, 174, 176, 179, 180, 183, 185, 187, 208, 231
Migration, 144, 145, 185–187, 241
Minimalist, 19, 20, 138, 158, 264–266, 271
Ministry of Peace and Reconstruction (MoPR), 114, 122, 136, 147, 170, 177, 214

N

National identity, 159
National struggle committee, 150, 233
Nepal, 1, 2, 4, 5, 7, 15, 17, 21, 25, 28, 43, 45, 48–51, 54–56, 59, 60, 64, 66, 71–73, 75, 77, 81, 82, 84–88, 96, 99, 102, 114, 120–122, 126, 131, 134–136, 142–144, 146, 158, 164, 166, 169–173, 175, 176, 186, 187, 189–191, 193, 194, 199, 200, 202, 209–212, 216–219, 223–225, 232–234, 237, 238, 240–245, 248, 250, 252, 253, 256–258, 263–266, 268–272
Nepal Army, 45, 62, 71, 75, 77–79, 101, 124, 130, 189, 265
Nepali Congress, 7, 45, 61, 73, 76, 81, 84, 135, 190, 211
Nepal Peace Trust Fund, 170
Nonviolence, 237

O

Organisational context, 135
Ownership, 17, 23, 87, 143, 145, 147, 266

INDEX 279

Ozerdem, Alpaslan, 1–3, 15, 17, 23, 24, 73, 93, 108, 116, 140, 168, 169, 223

P

Panchayat system, 71
Peace, 1–6, 8–15, 17–21, 26, 28–31, 43, 53, 55, 66, 72–78, 80, 81, 83, 85–88, 93–104, 107–109, 112, 115, 120–123, 126, 130–132, 135, 146, 147, 163, 164, 170, 190, 192, 193, 199–201, 212–214, 218, 219, 223–226, 228–230, 234, 236–240, 243, 248–250, 253, 256–258, 263–265, 267–269, 271, 272
  negative peace, 9, 10, 271
  positive peace, 9, 10, 13, 225, 271
Peace agreements, peace talks, 73
Peacebuilding, 1, 2, 4, 5, 7, 8, 10–15, 17–19, 21–23, 27, 28, 31, 44, 73, 85, 94, 129, 130, 147, 164, 200, 212, 215, 217, 219, 238, 253, 264–272
  community peacebuilding, 10, 13, 18
  sustainable peacebuilding, 11
Peace negation, 9, 271
People's Liberation Army, 44, 75, 77, 79, 80, 169, 234, 246, 248, 264
People's power, 55
Perpetrators, 25, 28, 29, 141, 213, 215, 216, 225, 226, 229, 270
PLA fund, 117–119, 121, 122, 125
Polarisation, 26, 104, 126, 209, 217, 257
Police post, 44, 45, 73
Post-conflict recovery, 11, 19–21, 133, 159, 164, 191–193, 265, 271
Post-conflict society, 24, 26, 159, 163, 164, 194, 209, 215, 219, 223, 227, 252, 255, 267, 269

Power bargain, 75
Power sharing, 93, 94, 96, 98, 100, 107
Prachanda Path, 53, 58, 205
President, 99, 102
Prime Minister, 73–75, 79, 96, 98, 99, 101, 102, 122, 124, 214, 253

R

Reconciliation, 11, 23, 28–30, 201, 209, 213, 215, 216, 219, 229, 239, 240, 243, 263, 267, 270, 272
  community reconciliation, 216, 243
  horizontal reconciliation, 213
  vertical reconciliation, 49
Reconstruction, 12, 83, 122, 147, 253
Rehabilitation, 6, 7, 31, 79, 81–83, 85, 99–104, 112–115, 122, 123, 126, 129–156, 158, 159, 167, 169, 176, 177, 187–189, 191, 233, 242, 265, 266, 272
  rehabilitation package, 81–83, 112, 115, 129, 132–137, 147, 149–153, 155, 169, 177, 189, 191, 233
Reintegration, 1–5, 7, 8, 12, 15–26, 28, 29, 31, 43, 44, 77, 79, 81, 83–85, 87, 88, 96, 99–104, 110, 114, 115, 117, 126, 129, 130, 132, 134, 135, 138–141, 148, 157, 159, 163–169, 172, 176, 178, 181–183, 185, 186, 188–194, 199–203, 208, 209, 211, 212, 215–219, 224, 227–229, 241, 242, 252–255, 263–270, 272
  political reintegration, 234, 235, 252–253
  social reintegration, 7, 23–26, 31, 139, 188, 191, 194, 199–203,

208, 209, 211, 212, 216–219,
    242, 267, 269, 270
Religion, 239
Remobilisation, 31, 110, 138, 150,
    190, 219, 224, 229, 233, 245,
    250, 252–253, 255, 258
Revolution, 48, 49, 52, 53, 55, 57,
    58, 71, 77, 111, 205, 206, 210,
    237, 247, 248, 251, 256, 257
Revolutionary principles, 53
Richmond, Oliver, 13
Rolpa, 44, 57, 58, 61, 76, 251
Royal massacre, 75
Royal palace, 88

S
Samanti, 203
Samayojan, 83, 103
Security dilemma, 95
Security sector reform, 4, 84, 104, 272
Self-employment, 22, 141, 185, 188
Seven Party Alliance, 78, 84, 123
SIDDR, 16, 19, 21, 23, 141, 142, 145
Small Arms and Light Weapons, 11, 255
Social acceptance, 26, 203
Social capital, 3, 4, 26–28, 31, 130,
    148, 159, 165, 166, 181–183,
    186, 199, 201, 208, 211, 217,
    219, 239, 267, 270, 271
Social cohesion, 20, 199, 217
Social contract, 108, 109, 112, 116, 120, 169
Social harmony, 9, 28, 199, 216
Social inclusion, 72, 77, 98, 210
Social justice, 9, 10, 13, 77, 238, 239
Social relation, 166, 182, 204, 205,
    211, 219, 226, 228, 239, 267, 269

Social stigma, 139, 140, 144, 152,
    172, 178, 188, 200, 202,
    205–207, 217
Social trust, 3, 211
South Asia, 48, 186
Special Committee, 79, 102, 122, 123
Sri Lanka, 14, 225
Statebuilding, 52, 71, 73
Strategic, 44–46, 72, 75, 76, 87,
    94–96, 100, 101, 104, 107, 131,
    201, 245, 268
Structural conditions, 47, 65, 225, 226

T
Tactical, 59, 75, 94, 95, 104, 245,
    256, 257, 268
Technical committee, 79
Terai, 49, 50, 81, 98–100, 144, 210,
    241, 250–252
Timor Leste, 15, 17, 225
Top-down, 12, 189, 265
Transformation, 3, 4, 16, 18, 29, 64,
    77, 114, 144, 158, 189, 207,
    208, 215, 226, 232, 233, 237,
    242, 264, 268
    political transformation, 237
    social transformation, 64, 207
Transformatory peacebuilding, 13, 14
Transitional justice, 11, 29, 201, 209,
    213, 214, 263
Truth and justice, 29
Truth and Reconciliation Commission (TRC)
    the Commission of Inquiry on
        Enforced Disappeared Persons
        (CIEDP), 213

U
Unconventional DDR, 2, 3, 88, 268

UNDP, 18–20, 79, 132, 216, 240
Unemployment, 21, 49, 134, 185, 187, 188, 241, 244
UNICEF, 79, 132, 147, 155, 179
United Madhesi Democratic Front, 81, 98
United Nations, 2, 6–8, 77–79, 83, 85, 129, 132, 146, 167, 179, 216, 240
United Nations Inter-Agency Rehabilitation Programme (UNIRP), 7, 83, 86, 129, 132–140, 142–147, 149, 151–155, 157–159, 178
United Nations Mission in Nepal, 78, 79
United Nations Security Council Resolution, 136
Urban-centric, 253

V
Vaidya, Mohan (Kiran), 250
Verification process, 8, 79, 80, 109, 111, 245, 265
Verified minors and late recruits (VMLRs), 6, 31, 83, 86, 112, 115, 118, 129–141, 143, 144, 146, 148–159, 233, 251, 265
Victim, Victimhood, 6, 10, 20, 25, 26, 28–30, 45, 48, 61, 62, 64, 65, 130, 133, 141, 142, 147, 177, 184, 193, 203, 213–215, 217, 225, 229, 239, 263, 264, 267, 270
Violence, 1, 8–12, 16, 23, 28–31, 43, 48, 52, 60–63, 65, 71, 86, 94, 124, 131, 150, 163, 168, 172, 189, 190, 194, 202, 203, 205, 209, 210, 217, 219, 223–230, 233, 236–239, 242–245, 249, 253–255, 258, 263–268, 271
criminal violence, 190, 254
cultural violence, 9, 224
direct violence, 9, 224, 237, 238, 254, 268, 271
political violence, 61, 209, 225–227, 237, 242, 244, 253, 254, 268
structural violence, 9, 10, 16, 63, 224, 225, 238–239
Vocation training, 146
Voluntary recruitment, 30
Voluntary retirement, 81–83, 121, 212, 240

W
War family, 3, 4, 27, 59, 60, 65, 148, 181–183, 186, 199, 270
War network, 64, 155, 156
Weapon collection, 88, 167
Whole-time (WT), 54, 56, 204

Y
Young Communist League, 111, 120, 150, 234
Youth Force, 60, 255

CPSIA information can be obtained
at www.ICGtesting.com
Printed in the USA
LVOW13*1735110518
576868LV00015B/409/P